THE POWER OF
MAGIC

SECRETS AND MYSTERIES
ANCIENT AND MODERN

THE POWER OF
MAGIC

SECRETS AND MYSTERIES
ANCIENT AND MODERN

DEREK & JULIA
PARKER

SIMON & SCHUSTER
NEW YORK   LONDON   TORONTO   SYDNEY   TOKYO   SINGAPORE

SIMON & SCHUSTER
Simon & Schuster Building
Rockefeller Center
1230 Avenue of the Americas
New York, NY 10020

Edited and designed by Mitchell Beazley Publishers
part of Reed International Books Limited
Michelin House
81 Fulham Road
London SW3 6RB

Executive editor: James Hughes
Art director: Tim Foster
Art editor: Rozelle Bentheim
Production: Sarah Schuman
Index: Hilary Bird

Typesetting by SX Composing Ltd, Rayleigh, Essex
Color separation by Mandarin Offset, Singapore
Produced by Mandarin Offset
Printed and Bound in Hong Kong

10 9 8 7 6 5 4 3 2 1

Library of Congress Cataloging in Publication Data

Parker, Derek.
    The power of magic : ancient secrets and modern mysteries /
Derek and Julia Parker.
        p.   cm.
    Includes bibliographical references and index.
    ISBN 0-671-76921-9
    1. Magic.   I. Parker, Julia.   II. Title.
BF1611.P36   1992
133.4′3—dc20
                                                            92-12175
                                                            CIP

ISBN 0-671-76921-9

Contents

Introduction
The meaning of magic, what it is
– and what it isn't [6]

Introduction

The conventional definition of magic is probably that in the *Oxford English Dictionary*:

> *Magic: the pretended art of influencing the course of events, and of producing marvellous physical phenomena, by processes supposed to owe their efficacy to their power of compelling the intervention of spiritual beings, or of bringing into operation some occult controlling principle of nature.*

But that definition is really no more satisfactory than any other brief definition – chiefly because no two people define magic in the same way.

Many aspects of everyday life in the 20th century would once have been regarded as magical; many apparently magical or occult phenomena which remain mysterious to us, may be explained within the next century, or even sooner. But at present we must include them – and we also deal for instance with the "magical" power of sexuality, which may be explicable in terms of physiology and psychology, but which still compels men and women to great feats of imagination and ecstasy.

Modern magicians have defined magic in various ways, depending on their individual attitudes. Both Eliphas Lévi, the 19th century French writer on the subject, and Aleister Crowley, probably the best-known modern British magician, concentrated on the idea of magic as the method of releasing powers of the mind which we all possess, but on the whole never use: in fact – "will power", for again and again they emphasize the word "will" as the means of "reigning over yourself and others".

For most people, the idea of magic has been devalued in the 20th century: it is now a word which is on the whole used sparingly. For millennia that was certainly not the case, for it was still remembered that the magic road was one of three which men trod on their quest to discover how the world worked. Another led by way of science, of empirical study; the third by way of religion.

Magic, past and present, may have a basis in fact; but often works in disguise. Witches claimed to be able to fly; to many of them it was no doubt self-evident that they did so – they believed that they possessed the physical experience which confirmed it. We now know that the magic ointments they used, the "flying ointments", contained drug elements which in all probability, together with the psychological state into which they had been persuaded, convinced them that they were flying. So – they flew, and knew that they flew. Magic?

There are examples of witches' curses which seem to have worked and in modern times there are examples of aboriginal curses which have sometimes resulted in the death of the accursed. Psychologists will confirm the belief that a curse can be efficacious. Nothing magical about that, maybe. But the grandfather of one of the authors remembered discovering a phial containing urine, hair and nail-clippings, built into the wall of a Cornish cowshed, and recalled that herds kept in that cowshed never prospered. So how did the cows know of the curse? Magic?

The many formulae contrived to present a vision of one's future lover, in dreams, also often seem to work. Psychologists will say that the formulae simply stimulate the unconscious mind to produce a vision of the man or woman whom one has already chosen as a possible partner. And there is some evidence that concentrated attention on such a person can provoke love. Magic?

The word magic also borders on areas of extra-sensory perception (ESP) in which increasing scientific interest is reluctantly being expressed. Can anyone doubt that the Inquisition would have burned Uri Geller, that mercurial figure whose showbusiness activities have sadly diminished the serious effect of his quite remarkable powers, still unexplained by scientific enquiry? But what he appears to be doing – in a direct line from Crowley and Lévi – is using the uncommon strength of his will to produce effects which most of the rest of us cannot achieve.

We may throw a pinch of salt over our shoulder, decline to walk under a ladder – but such superstitions are now regarded as harmless fun, though we continue to observe them! The powers of the earth are still strong, and we are beginning to recognize that they exist. If fairies do not inhabit the deep woods, some spirit still moves us to reverence nature, and be vehement in trying to protect it. The Green Movement is not entirely founded upon the (perfectly accurate) conviction that we may kill off the human race if we do not preserve its environment. It has something to do with recognition of the spirit of the earth itself – in whatever form we believe that to exist.

Magic and religion have always been inextricably fused. As Professor E. M. Butler writes in his *Ritual Magic* (1949): "There would appear to be no religion without some magic at its foundation, and certainly there is no magic in any significance without deep roots in religion." Sir James Frazer (1854-1941), the anthropologist and author of the famous *The Golden Bough* (subtitled *A Study in Magic and Religion*) believed that magic came first, as humans attempted to influence the operations of nature. Religion followed, and was different in that rather than trying to compel unseen forces, it sought to propitiate them – a distinction we would still make.

Conventional Christianity will insist that while the idea of magic grew, perhaps for centuries, in tandem with the idea of a creating and supervising God or gods, the two took disparate and irreconcilable paths at the birth of Christ, and that to link them is at best a discourtesy and at worst a blasphemy. Agnostics or rationalists on the other hand will tend to claim that all religions are related to the idea of magic: that to believe in the efficacy of prayer has something in common with believing in the efficacy of a curative spell.

Where we appear to take the ritual invocations of a Wicca meeting as seriously as the ritual invocations of the Book of Common Prayer, we do so because the people concerned do so. Both parties hold their convictions with the same passion. We take no sides.

Towards the end of the nineteenth century, modern technology began to make magic come true. In 1877, for instance, the voice of Thomas Edison issued from a trumpet attached only to some kind of mechanical contraption, while in 1900 R. A. Fessenden heard the disembodied voice of a friend emerge from something called "a radio". In the seventeenth century, St Joseph of Copertino was apparently able to levitate, soaring sometimes to a height of 40 feet; in the 1880s Otto Lilienthal flew like a bird in his glider, and in 1903 the first powered aeroplane mounted the skies.

Some saints are credited with being able to appear in visions to devout admirers many miles away (Padre Pio is said to have done so in the present century). In 1936 people sitting in their homes in London saw on a screen entertainers singing and dancing in a studio miles away. Other inventions gave the impression of being "magical" when they were first demonstrated: the X-ray, electric light, photography. Many of us find the computer and its feats magical enough, though while we may not understand how they work we accept the fact that others do – that no supernatural agency is involved.

All these things would have seemed genuinely magical in 1600. Magic is only supernatural until it is explained. One distinguished scientist announced in 1901 that it was as impossible that Marconi should succeed in sending a message through the air from England to America, as that man should ever stand on the face of the moon.

In the 1990s we find a graduated structure of magic: at one end are such phenomena as ghosts, which have been experienced by so many people that the odds must be on their being in some sense "real"; at the other, those aspects of magic which are so self-evidently practical that they are beginning to attract the reluctant attention of science. These include such phenomena as what Lilly called "the use of the mosaical rods" – the ability to discover the presence of metal or water beneath the ground by means of rods or pendulums. It is rare now to find anyone who will deny that this can be done though there is still a reluctance to take it seriously.

If dowsing is at that edge of the paranormal which science is beginning, grudgingly, to recognize, there are other areas to which the word "magic" will be more dogmatically and pejoratively applied: distant healing, astral travel, regression, psychokinesis, the aura and Kirlian photography . . . Much of the "evidence" (and never did a word more clearly merit inverted commas!) is largely anecdotal, and often very confused. Apart from this our own emotional and intellectual attitudes cloud even the evidence of our own eyes.

After all excuses have been made, the result of a survey of magic must be a confirmation of that over-quoted remark of Hamlet's – "There are more things in heaven and earth, Horatio, than are dreamed of in your philosophy." Some of the phenomena we deal with are difficult, perhaps impossible to explain away. And it is those that are most fascinating.

Why should particular combinations of numerals appear to follow us about – invading our car numberplates, our house and telephone and credit card numbers? How can it be the case that some people are capable of influencing the course of an illness simply by concentrating their minds on the sufferer? Why should some forms of alternative medicine work so well, when there is no scientific explanation for their effect? How can it be that some remarkably detailed prognostications of future events have been recorded long before they took place?

One day we may know why. Science has been notably shy of pushing towards the extremes of the unconventional, chiefly, it seems, because scientists are shy of being ridiculed. Some, braver than others, have recognized the fact that science is not yet able to explain every aspect of life in the known universe – but the record of the scientific community in general towards the occult and the paranormal is almost entirely shameful, while the activities of such bodies as the Committee for the Scientific Investigation of Claims of the Paranormal (CSICOP) are as emotionally biased as those of the most rabid psychic.

When science shakes off its inhibitions (as one day it surely must) and looks seriously at apparently magical phenomena, it may be that they will be found to be, at least in some sense, "explicable". On the other hand, perhaps not. Magic is a fascinating subject. We have approached it with a degree of scepticism sufficient to upset some believers. What we have found has confirmed us in our approval of J. S. Haldane's celebrated remark that the universe is not only stranger than we think, but stranger than we can think.

There is one more thing to say by way of introduction. We may be accused of ignoring or at least underplaying the dark side of magic. There has been much play in the media in the past decades with the idea of diabolical possession, of witchcraft ritual in which human sacrifice and cannibalism take place. Some evidence for this has certainly from time to time turned up – but it is often explicable. General accusations have been made, but they have nearly always fizzled out in the face of proper investigation, and have turned out to originate in the fevered imagination either of adults or of children.

However, after all that has been said, it is worth remembering that whatever one's belief about the nature of magic, there is quite sufficient evidence to show that its effect on the human psyche can be alarmingly powerful. It is sometimes unfortunately the case that those who feel drawn to the occult in general do so because they feel a strong emotional pull towards the general proposition that unknown forces can be used for human purposes.

Derek and Julia Parker.

PART I
ANCIENT

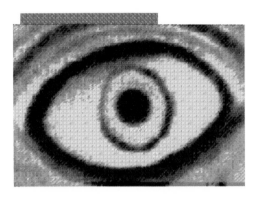

MAGIC

1.

Historical Survey

Although we know nothing of the earliest religious or magical practices, the first hint of either can perhaps be seen in the paintings and carvings of prehistoric humans which survive in caves at Lascaux in France and Altamira in Spain. It seems more than likely that the bison, reindeer, chamois, mammoth and other animals so vividly depicted there were drawn in an attempt to communicate with the spirit of nature which would then guide the animals towards the hunter. If this was early magic, then other phenomena were perhaps signs of early religion: for instance the bear skulls placed carefully in niches in a cave in eastern Switzerland, in such a manner as to suggest ritual worship of some kind: worship perhaps of the Spirit of Bear?

By the Neolithic Age (from about 3500 BC in Europe but as much as 4,000 years earlier in Egypt) man was convinced that unseen forces were everywhere at work and that certain individuals had a special talent for getting in touch with those forces – individuals who were priests, shamans, witch doctors or medicine-men, sometimes the chiefs of tribes, but sometimes just ordinary people with an extraordinary talent.

Already some of the symbols of the traditional witch can be seen (the term indicates witches of both sexes: "wizard" or "warlock" traditionally signifies a male witch). The medicine-man or shaman usually had a staff or wand, and wore robes (sometimes made of skin, sometimes of feathers). As a term, shamanism seems to have originated in North Asia, in Siberia and among the Eskimo; it is also used of

*The first magician was probably a shaman (**right**), or tribal sorcerer, healer and medium, who travelled the spirit world in trance.*

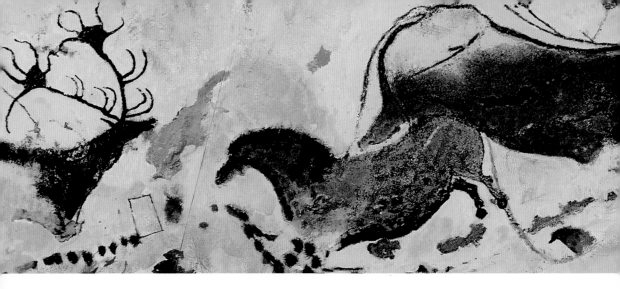

Animal paintings of the Old Stone Age, wrought in the darkest recesses of a cave in Lascaux, France, probably reflect magical activity from 16,000 years ago. By depicting these animals of the hunt, the tribal sorcerers or shamans may have sought to gain power over their spirits.

those men (and sometimes women) who used to be called medicine-men in north America, and are still called witch doctors in Africa. Shamans of the Far North were the priest-magicians of hunter-gathering communities whose nomadic lifestyles may have resembled those of the cave-painting peoples of Lascaux and Altamira.

Shamanism is preoccupied with animism – a term which derives not from animals, but from the word *anima*, the soul. Animists believe that animals, plants and even what we would call "things" have souls or spirits like men and women, and that it is possible to contact them. Not everyone, however, can do this: those who can possess a particular power (known by various names: *mana* in Melanesia, *wakan* to the Sioux Indians, *orenda* to the Iroquois, for instance).

Those who possess this power can enter the spirit worlds through trance, and communicate not only with spirits, but with the gods themselves. They may convey messages from them, and use the power of the spirits to heal mental or physical sickness. The power of the shamans was emphasized by their dress which often indicated the animal "allies" that assisted them in their magical trance journeys. In America great cloaks were made of buffalo hide; in Polynesia tapa-cloth robes were wonderfully embroidered; the medicine-men of Tahiti and Hawaii wore perhaps the most magnificent robes of all, made of the feathers of rare birds. Shamans, medicine-men, witch doctors, all possessed the ability to communicate with the spirits of the dead. Brazilian shamans usually inherited their powers, son from father – though occasionally it would be generally recognized by a community that a person possessed the unusual power which qualified him to be trained to recognize the individual spirit which would possess him and turn him into a great shaman (the most prestigious spirit was that of a jaguar).

SEXUAL MAGIC

Sexual magic existed almost everywhere in the early world: Palaeolithic man was not only preoccupied with the hunt (hence his splendid drawings of animals) but with the continuation of the race – so his artists produced magical figurines whose purpose was to increase fertility. The most famous of these are the prehistoric Venuses of Willendorf and Laussel, which show us prehistoric man's ideal of female beauty – a plumpness still desirable centuries later in Africa, where plump women are believed to be healthy, well-fed and therefore fecund.

It was in India that sexual magic was most markedly developed – sacred prostitu-

tion (for lovemaking was regarded as a sacrament) probably predating the same activity in Greece. The Hindus regarded man's urge to procreate as one of the strongest natural instincts, and therefore a paradigm of the power of the gods. Their homage was to the art of love as well as its procreative aspect; in the magnificent temple carvings at Khajuraho a multitude of sexual attitudes are depicted with such tender beauty that the force of the theory is unforgettably expressed.

Phallic symbols are common in various parts of the world – and so are depictions of men obviously intent on expressing the life force. Predynastic Egyptian ivories and the Cerne Abbas giant in Dorset both display phalluses evidently capable of doing good work, and it must have been believed that they magically endowed men with sexual vigour. In recent times, it was still commonly believed that if an infertile couple copulated while lying on the phallus of the Cerne Abbas giant, pregnancy would certainly result.

MAGICAL SITES

Particular places were significant in early magic or religious practices, and natural sites were enhanced with temples, menhirs, dolmens, rows and circles of giant stones. These can be found not only in Europe, including the British Isles, Spain and Portugal, France, Sweden, Denmark, Germany and the Mediterranean islands (there are specially fine examples in Malta), but also in the Caucasus and the Crimea, in Africa and Asia, Syria and Persia, Korea, Japan, Mexico and Peru. There are many other examples of huge structures around the world – from the monoliths of Tiahuanaco in the Andes to the fascinating giant heads on Easter Island. That they had an origin in magic or in religion is surely impossible to doubt.

It is no use pretending that we can do anything but guess at the nature of those ceremonies that actually once went on at sites like Carnac in France, Externsteine in Germany, or Stonehenge in Britain. But considering the size and importance of these sites, it is not surprising that almost every conjecture about, say, Stonehenge, has involved the supernatural. Our forbears, unable to imagine how such vast stones could have been assembled and set up, assumed that their purpose was magical and that giants and witches were concerned. Geoffrey of Monmouth (d.1155), that charmingly inventive early historian, claimed that the chief mover of the stones was Merlin, wizard to King Arthur; French historians suggested that the giant Gargantua had erected many megaliths in their country.

However sceptical we are, many of us walk around these ancient sites – ravaged though they are by tourism – with an irrational feeling of awe, and the conviction that there is "something strange" about them – a force or perhaps merely the shadow of a force which we cannot deny. Attempts to measure this force have not been entirely unsuccessful; one day, their magic may be explained.

The ancient stone rows of Carnac, Brittany, erected some 4,000 years ago, stand as mute witness to a time when magic and religion were almost synonymous.

THE ROOTS OF WESTERN MAGIC

If a degree of mystery attaches itself to ancient stones, it is not surprising that even more has been attached to the pyramids of Egypt. In the nineteenth century a whole industry was devoted to discovering the magic principles on which they were constructed – the theory being that magic was the only motive strong enough to persuade the men of dynastic Egypt to build such vast structures. Their very measurements are in some quarters still regarded as significant, and it is claimed that small pyramids constructed to the same proportions will preserve fruit which is placed inside them, or persuade razor blades to remain sharp for many months.

Magic and religion in Egypt appear to have been almost indistinguishable. Priests ruled the land, using magic as their chief weapon – while the Pharaoh was said to control both the elements and the River Nile, essential to Egypt's prosperity. Later, the dead were embalmed and buried, the attendant ceremonies designed to ensure that in the next world they would be united with the great Osiris.

Magic also involved the planets, which early man had regarded literally as gods. It was probably in the land between the Euphrates and Tigris rivers, now called Iraq but originally called Accad and Sumer, that the study of astrology was born. Here stood the mighty city of Babylon with its legendary magicians. Even earlier, the Chaldean people of Babylonia were ruled, at the city of Ur, by magician-kings who used their power to control the growth of crops throughout the kingdom. Under them, priests occupied much of their time in divination. Women too attained priestly rank, perhaps as incarnations of the city goddess.

The Chaldeans were probably the first to replace their sky gods with an astrological system of divination, predicated on the belief that the movement of the heavenly bodies influenced human affairs and determined the course of events. Although developed to almost scientific levels under the Greeks, a magical aura continued to cling to the planets both in the ancient West and in other cultures, especially in India and Mexico, where a whole country was organized in an attempt to bring it into conformity with the heavens.

Egypt, however, was generally held to be the starting point for the Western tradition of magic, refined and amplified during the Classical era of Greece and Rome. The central figure of this tradition, Hermes Trismegistus (Thrice-Greatest Hermes), bears the name of a Greek god, but was identified as long ago as 400 BC with Thoth, the Egyptian deity of magic, writing and wisdom. A number of literary works, collectively known as the Hermetica and written in the form of dialogues with Hermes Trismegistus, taught the duality of spirit and matter, and the possibility of salvation through special knowledge.

This concept was developed by the gnostics, a movement that culminated in the

*A magician king of Babylonia approaches Ishtar,
personification of the planet Venus. Mother goddess
and, later, deity of love and voluptuousness, Ishtar's
cult included sacred prostitution.*

second century AD. Gnostics claimed knowledge (*gnosis*) deriving from ancient Greek mystery cults such as the Eleusinian Mysteries, and systems like the Jewish Caballah, that would lead the knower to salvation.

Simon Magus, sometimes said to be the father of gnosticism, was a magician (mentioned in the New Testament) who attempted to buy sacramental powers from St Peter, and when rebuked by the latter, spitefully imitated Christ by ascending into the air. The apostles, however, cast a spell which resulted in his crashing to earth and injuring himself. He then announced that he would be buried, and rise on the third day. His disciples buried him, but (according to St Hippolytus, our authority for these stories) he never reappeared.

Gnosticism pre-dated Christianity, and in one form or another was common during the first two centuries after Christ and from time to time has reappeared in various forms ever since. The gnostics' interest in magic was sometimes minimal, though they frequently believed that angels walked the earth, and trusted in numerology, sigils, and the like. Perhaps the most prominent magician among them was Marcus, a second century gnostic who believed that the whole truth about life and death was to be found in the Greek alphabet (Jesus, after all, had been called the Alpha and Omega).

Since some gnostics believed that the world had been created by an evil force, devil-worship or something like it was not uncommon with them. Mani, the founder of Manichaeism (who first announced his creed in 241, at the Persian court) believed that only particles of goodness existed in wicked humans, and that Jesus had been sent to rescue them. He encouraged the development of a magical cult – as did his followers, one of whom (a Christian bishop called Priscillian) was put to death in 385 for practising it.

Gnostic sects continue to exist today – in Mesopotamia, Kurdistan, Armenia and the Caucasus, for instance, the Yezidis worship in sacred caves, keep sacred snakes and images of Satan (*Melek Taos*, the Peacock Angel).

THE MIDDLE-EASTERN TRADITION

Almost as soon as there was a Western tradition of magic (due to the Romans who spread the Classical view) it was submerged under waves of barbarian invaders. Serious magic became the province of the Middle East. Magic pervaded the civilization of Islam – much of it predating Muhammad (c.570-632). A reading of the *Thousand and One Nights* shows the kind of magic in which everyone seems more or less to have believed. The *Djinni* were recognizable counterparts of Western angels: creatures of light, capable of flying and chiefly invisible.

We cannot of course mention every formula by which man has attempted to "compel the intervention of spiritual beings". However, it is certainly necessary to mention the Caballah (or Kabalah, or Qabbalah) of the Jews, which is seen at work in Spain and Provence in the twelfth and thirteenth centuries, and involved mysticism – supposedly texts – from a much earlier period, certainly pre-Christian (legend asserts that God whispered the secret lore of the Caballah to Moses on Mount Sinai).

The movement of which the Caballah itself (a giant encyclopaedia of occult knowledge) was the hinge, seems to have derived from the Merkavah or Chariot religion – the original chariot being that in which Elijah ascended to heaven, which was a symbol for man's spiritual ascent to the highest realms of experience. The Caballists were particularly interested in techniques of meditation and ecstasy, which have certain affinities with magic, and their writings (most of which were kept secret until comparatively recent times) enshrine the widest selection of occult principles. The two most important Caballist books were probably the *Sefer Yetzirah*, or *Book of Creation* (written perhaps in the third century AD) and the *Zohar*, or *Book of Splendour* written in the late thirteenth century.

The Caballists believed in Correspondence – that the universe is one whole, and that therefore an influence exerted on one thing can, indeed must, affect others. It was proper to attempt to understand the secret laws which governed the known world – though in the final analysis God, by His very nature, was unknowable, and mystery would always win in the end.

In order to make use of the Caballah to aid him in an ambition, hurt an enemy or accomplish any particular aim, the student worked within a circle drawn to keep out evil spirits. He must pass through ten sefiroth, or forces controlling the universe. This was a complex matter, for 22 Paths of Wisdom connect each sefira to the next as one mounts the Tree of Life (the theory has much in common with the modern idea of astral travel which itself connects with shamanic flight). The journey might involve meetings with both evil and good forces – travelling the Path of Saturn (the 22nd, leading from Malkhuth or earth to Yesod, the gate to another world) one might encounter either the Saturnian guardian crocodile or a beautiful naked girl, wreathed with flowers – a more reassuring figure. At the climax of this occult journey, the traveller was inhabited by the spirit of a god or goddess, who visualized the aim he wished to accomplish, and then had to make his way back through the sefiroth to reality, where he found his request granted.

MAGIC AND CHRISTIANITY

Islam kept alchemy, astrology and other traditions alive while early Christendom tore itself up over outlawing magic. For the coming of Christianity confused the magical scene more than a little. One of the main characteristics of Christ was, of

course, his supernatural power – the power to walk on water, cure the sick, cast out demons, raise the dead: a power that was certainly regarded at the time as magical. At the same time, there were many magicians who claimed similar powers, such as Simon Magus, who is mentioned in the New Testament as having "swept the Samarians off their feet with his magical arts". As we have seen, anecdotes credit him with the power to levitate and to remain alive while buried underground (both acts reproduced by Indian yogis in modern times). He seems to have been interested in sexual magic, for he is said to have used semen and menstrual blood for magical purposes; his followers were believed to have used spells.

The Christian religion had a hard row to hoe when it came to arguing that it was not merely another organization based on magic. Jesus himself was in his lifetime accused of diabolism ("It is only by Beelzebub, prince of devils, that this man drives the devils out," the Pharisees cried.)

As Christendom strengthened its hold, in order to convert barbarians it adopted their magics as miracles. Christianity also lacked any real access to the Classical tradition. All that could really be accomplished was "academic magic" – study of fragments and of barbarian magic (which was discredited anyway). From these fragments came the modern view of magic: Merlin, Bacon, court magicians, flying machines, flashes and spells . . . But if converted magicians were easily persuaded to burn their magical books, there were other difficulties – it was hard for instance to persuade some people that there was a great deal of difference between a piece of a dead saint's tibia, revered as a relic, and any other object used as an amulet and credited with magical powers.

Meanwhile, in Western Europe magic had long been at work. We know little about the druids, the magician-priests of the ancient Celtic peoples, and most of

Spiritual ascent to the highest plane is implicit in the mystic Cabbalah.

that knowledge derives from Roman sources. But it seems likely that they were nature-worshippers, and there is evidence of animal sacrifice and, perhaps, human sacrifice as well. Their religious ceremonies usually took place in the open air, in groves of trees (where mistletoe-bearing oaks were especially venerated), beside lakes, and at the sources of rivers. Druids included women as well as men in their number, and their societies transcended tribal divisions. One of their greatest centres was at a site where Chartres cathedral stands today. Here they met once a year to mediate between individuals and tribes. They may have used earlier sites, too, such as Stonehenge, to judge from the legendary connection between Merlin and the moving of the stones. For Merlin himself was almost certainly a druid, and the Arthurian legends are full of magic – the magic sword Excalibur as well as a number of enchantresses (witches?) such as Morgan la Fay, not to mention the great magician himself. Druids believed in the immortality of the soul and the existence of a world beyond death. With the coming of Christianity, many of their deities lingered on as the "Divine Peoples" of Celtic myth, inhabiting fairy mounds still recognized in the countryside of Ireland. It seems likely that some continue to be reverenced to this day by modern "Pagans" and devotees of Wicca.

German and Norse beliefs have also survived the onslaught of Christianity by taking on a magical and folkloric form. Thus the great god Odin, deity of battle and death, can still be seen in the magical rock forms of Externsteine in Germany, and Wagner's operas offer a potent brew from pagan ingredients.

THE MIDDLE AGES

The last great synthesizing period, from which modern occultism emerged, owes much to the Crusades when suddenly Classical magic, Arabian occultism and the Caballah became available for study. During this period universities were founded, and both alchemy (the precursor of chemistry) and astrology (the brother of astronomy) were popular subjects.

St Thomas Aquinas (1225-74) argued that miracles had nothing to do with what people meant when they spoke of "magic" – magic was diabolical, and Christians should not use it, though they could study it for the purpose of showing how evil it was. But in some areas, at least, Islam had no such reservations – a Moslem was allowed to raise the dead and cure disease or impotence (if he was capable of it, of course); he could also wear an amulet as a protection against witchcraft. Both Christians and Moslems thoroughly believed in witchcraft, and had no doubt that it could be practised against them.

Alchemy and astrology had been practised from ancient times; alchemy certainly had an element of magic about it – astrology much less, for though the planets were originally believed to be gods, the theory soon developed that the relationship between the heavens and the earth was causal or symbolic, but not magical.

A large number of medieval and Renaissance European scholar-magicians,

Demons threaten seafarers with fearful storms, according to a 13th century illuminated manuscript.

*Macrocosmic man, set among the four elements and the winds (**above**), expresses a vision of the medieval German abbess and mystic, Hildegard of Bingen (see enlargement, **bottom right**). Known as the "Sybil of the Rhine", Hildegard's mystical visions began in childhood.*

including Paracelsus and Cornelius Agrippa, worked in and around the area of alchemy, though they also often had a general interest in magic. Several of them, unexpectedly perhaps, held high office in the church – both St Albertus Magnus (1200-80) and his pupil St Thomas Aquinas believed alchemy to be a respectable preoccupation, which made it possible, indeed desirable, for other Christian scholars to interest themselves in the science.

Roger Bacon (1214-94), an early scientist, was popularly supposed to be a black magician because of his preoccupation not only with alchemy but with magic in general. Arnold of Villanoca (1235-1313) believed in transmutation, and wrote a treatise comparing the process of refining base materials into precious ones with the life, death and resurrection of Christ; Vincent of Beauvais (c.1190-1264) wrote a remarkably complete encyclopedia, much of which dealt with magical matters.

We deal with alchemy in detail in Chapter Eight; its literature is vast and its practice was wide – from ancient Egypt to Taoist China, from Persia to Western Europe. There was a strong connection with Rosicrucianism, or the Fellowship of the Rosy Cross. The rose was a symbol of secrecy, and the Rosicrucians certainly went to great lengths to keep their activities secret; even now, the history of the movement is imperfectly known. "Modern" Rosicrucianism was founded in the 17th century by the German Christian Rosenkreutz, a student of the occult who travelled to the East and spent some years in Arabia, Egypt and Morocco, where he claimed to have learned to raise and converse with spirits.

In Germany, he collected together a small group of men who conversed in their own invented language, and worked with the sick. Over a century after Rosenkreutz's death, his tomb was opened, and in it – where a lamp still burned – was found a library of occult works.

The Rosicrucian movement persisted, and was revived in England in the late nineteenth century as the Order of the Golden Dawn, the

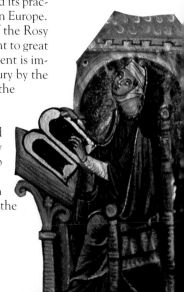

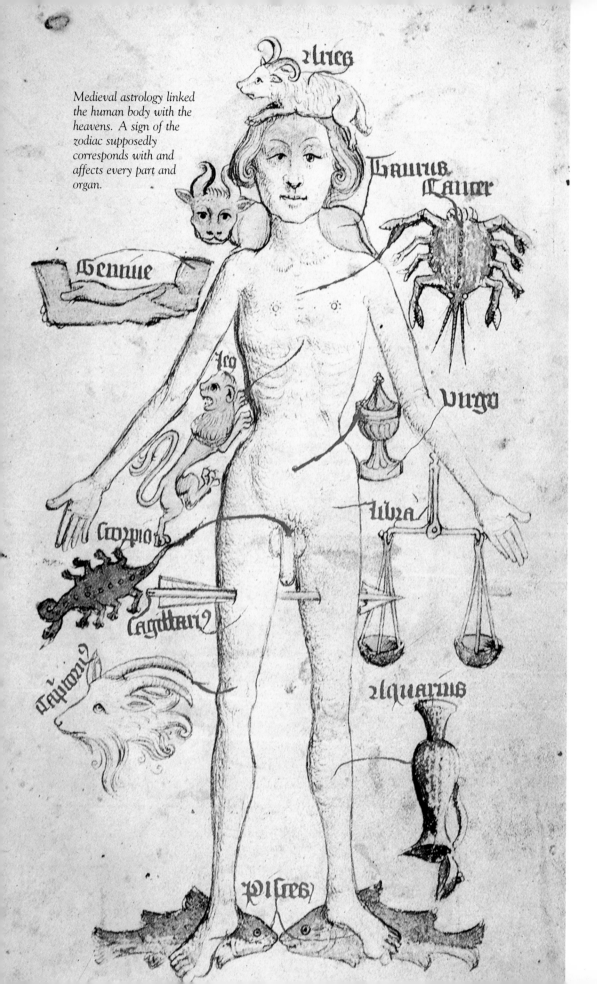

Medieval astrology linked the human body with the heavens. A sign of the zodiac supposedly corresponds with and affects every part and organ.

officers of which were supposed to have magical powers (including the ability to kill rogue members by putting the evil eye on them). Aleister Crowley was an enthusiastic member of the organization, and set up a group in a Temple near Loch Ness, where he practised magic rituals. A number of prominent men and women associated themselves with the sect, including perhaps the greatest poet of his time, W. B. Yeats (1865-1939) – whose friendly relationship with Crowley was abruptly broken off when the latter came to believe that Yeats was using the magic he had acquired to cast a spell on him and his then mistress.

Celebrated black magicians are recorded in history – men such as Abra-Melin, or Abraham the Jew, who performed a number of impressive magical acts in the fifteenth century, conjuring 2,000 horsemen out of air to help his patron Frederick, Elector of Saxony, and magically releasing the anti-pope John XXII from prison. An early manuscript lists his familiars, including Lucifer, Leviathan, Satan, Belial and a number of lesser helpers including Asmodeus and Beelzebub.

HIDDEN MAGIC

By the fifteenth century practice of magic had become sophisticated, broadly based and readily available. Like all trades facing reduction in numbers magicians instituted controls on the availability of knowledge. This cult of secrecy led to the emergence of magical texts, or *grimoires* (which will be discussed more fully elsewhere). These medieval books of magical spells (the most famous is perhaps *The Key of Solomon*), were regarded as extremely dangerous if used by the inexperienced. Such books as the *Goetia* and *The Grimoire of Honorius* were believed to contain powerful coded instructions for contacting the strongest black powers of the supernatural world.

During the past century attempts have been made to work with the *grimoires* – notably by Aleister Crowley , who described himself as the Great Beast, "the wickedest man alive", and who spent most of his adult life exploring the occult throughout the world, but most particularly at the Abbey of Thelema near Cefalu in Sicily, where his activities with a group of male and female acolytes strongly suggest that perverse sexuality was at least as strong an interest as witchcraft.

Some serious students of the occult can really be called scientists, for they were interested first and foremost in how things worked; and if this meant indulging in the somewhat dangerous pastime of raising spirits in order to question them about the matter, well, so be it.

Some popes, though interested in such matters as astrology, took a stand against the alchemical theory – Popes John XXII and Innocent VI, for instance; but this did not prevent scientists and scholars experimenting and theorising. Apart from the more famous among them – Paracelsus and Cornelius Agrippa – a Scot called Alexander Seton (d.1603) travelled through Europe demonstrating alchemical experiments (despite enduring arrest and torture he refused to explain his method). Though some of the most prominent scholars of the seventeenth century, such as Robert Fludd, the prominent Rosicrucian, chemist and healer, had only an academic interest in alchemy or magic, others experimented in both. A. Kircher (1601-80) tried transmutation and considered it impossible, but did believe in spontaneous generation, and wrote widely on numismatics.

RELIGION AND WITCHCRAFT

Meanwhile, the belief that magic was a natural and usable aspect of creation remained strong among the general public, and even among the clergy. The latter had difficulty in giving a rational explanation of the ravages of the plagues which swept the continent of Europe, especially the so-called Black Death of the fourteenth century. The idea that it was a punishment for sin was not a very sympathetic one – yet what other reason could an ostensibly loving God have for visiting such horrors upon His people? There seemed no answer: preachers simply confessed their ignorance as to "whence [the plague] cometh, whereof it ariseth and wherefore it is sent . . .". They did not contest the popular supposition that magic of some kind was involved – nor indeed, therefore, that magical protection might be invoked. So, since the medical profession was as ignorant on the subject as the clergy, people relied on amulets and such preventive medicines as powder of dried toad, alcohol and arsenic. Some made pilgrimages to important shrines such as Walsingham or Canterbury in England, St James of Compostela in Spain, or even to Jerusalem. Many died travelling, or while they were there.

The popular attitude to the saints was quite similar to that of the Greeks and Romans to their gods:

> We worship saints for fear, lest they should be
> displeased and angry with us, and plague or hurt us;
> as who is not afraid of St Laurence? Who dare deny
> St Anthony a fleece of wool for fear of his terrible
> fire, or lest he send the pox among our sheep?

The man who thus placed St Anthony on the level of a witch was William Tyndale (1494-1536), the celebrated translator of the Bible.

Liturgical books in the late Middle Ages contained what were really spells – such as rituals for the blessing of houses and ships, or cattle and crops. There were spells for driving away storms and making sterile cattle and wives fertile. There were prayers for blessing church bells so that evil spirits could not inhabit them and ring them all night, to the disturbance and possibly the danger of the community.

All these were indistinguishable from the spells of harmless witches, but were recited by priests equipped with cross and holy water. The Devil had his hand in the misfortunes of man, and must be driven out; it was natural that the church should offer the means to do it. Holy water, in particular, was very efficacious, though some said its virtue was in direct proportion to the holiness of the priest using it.

Sometimes this confusion between magic and religion could present the priesthood with difficulties. A certain Widow Wiseman, accused of witchcraft, threw holy water at her accuser, Topcliffe, whose horse promptly dashed him to the ground. Clearly the woman was a witch, yet it was holy water she had used. It was pointed out that the division between religion and magic could become simply too thin to discern. Even the Host itself was profaned by being used for mundane purposes. Ordinary worshippers, seeing it treated with such care and reverence, thought of it as the ultimate magic charm and, carefully refraining from swallowing it at Communion, carried it away to use as a love charm, to make them invisible so that they could successfully thieve, or to cure swine fever or encourage bees to make honey.

Protestants, at the Reformation, organized a strong backlash against all this, viewing such superstitions as the natural properties of Roman Catholicism. Writers like the English political philosopher Thomas Hobbes (1588-1697) inveighed against "conjuration", by which he meant not only witchcraft but such ceremonies as the Roman Mass. Puritans went even further – the Lollards described Confirmation as

> plain sorcery, devilry, witchcraft, juggling,
> legerdemain and all that naught is. The Bishop
> mumbleth a few Latin words over the child, charmeth
> him, crosseth him, smeareth him with stinking popish
> oil, and tieth a linen band about the child's neck, and
> sendeth him home.

The Reformation did not succeed in divorcing magic and religion, however; white witches still used prayers as spells to cure people of minor illnesses, and lay people recited charms which were often a mumbo-jumbo mixture of prayer and superstitious abracadabra. Even men and women of considerable intelligence continued to confuse the two. Sir Thomas Middleton (c.1560-1631), the Puritan banker, ordered sigils to be made for him and consecrated at the astrologically proper moment but would recite a prayer as he put them on. The archbishop of St Andrews in Scotland consulted a "cunning woman" in 1579 – though another clergyman was relieved of his living in the same year because he had recourse to similar advice.

This mixture of reactions went on for the next 200 years at least, both in Europe and the British Isles. In 1606 the Rev. John Bell was reported to the Royal College of Physicians for treating fevers by written charms; in 1637 the Vicar of Fleckney made charms to cure toothache; Daniel Defoe (1660-1731) knew a baptist preacher who cured the ague with a spell and a charm; as recently as 1804 the Vicar of Alfpuddle in Dorset, believing his child to be bewitched, cured him by similar means.

Despite the witch craze (see Chapter Five), rural Europe remained full of the idea of witchcraft through the sixteenth and seventeenth centuries. Most witches, whether real or imagined, took little part in group activity – there is not much evidence of regular meetings of covens or Wiccas. Witches were often individual outsiders, sometimes crazed, who lived alone with a chip on their shoulder, alienated from humanity in general and their local community. Many such witches were resented by their contemporaries because they were "different" – they were seen as either mentally or emotionally disturbed, or simply determined to keep a hold of their independence and continue their own way of life.

Saint Zeno expels a demon from a bewitched woman, as portrayed on the bronze doorway of his 12th century church in Verona, Italy.

Witchcraft and Witch-hunts

The history of witchcraft is sometimes confused with the history of black magic, which is in fact another matter. The Left-Handed Path, as it is sometimes called, has always been condemned by the Christian church, for which there is in fact no such thing as "white magic". By the seventeenth century although some cities were becoming large enough for witches to vanish within the community, the average town remained relatively small – everyone knew everybody's business and took a keen interest in it, to the extent of unhesitatingly interfering should there seem to be good reason. Thus when in 1661 Andrew Camp suspected Goodwife Bailey of having bewitched his children, he immediately broke into her house, beat her and knelt on top of her, and was then joined by his wife, who clawed at her eyes and called her a damned witch (if you drew blood from a witch, you went some way towards denying her access to her power).

Cruelty at this level of society was often almost as dreadful as the official cruelty of witch-finders. In an entry for his diary of March 1680, Oliver Heywood of Wakefield records hearing a commotion in the street, and finding his fellow townspeople harrying a supposed witch:

> They abused her body in a prodigious manner,
> whipping her fearfully, carrying her into a dark place
> like an entry, or dungeon, where they lay their dung.
> There she lay all night. In the morning her body rose
> in blebs [blisters], miserable sore. Oh, horrid cruelty.

Between the hysteria of the witch-finders and simple disregard, there was an area of life in which witchcraft was taken rather seriously by intelligent people. This was particularly the case when misfortune or illness could not be explained in any other way than by malicious magic. Illness or death from apoplexy, cancer, tuberculosis were frequently supposed to be the result of curses, for nothing was known of them, medically, and there seemed no other explanation. In one case, in 1623, even the Royal College of Physicians was inclined to believe that "there may be [witchcraft], by the strangeness of the sick man's infirmities", while Justices of the Peace were invited to believe that "when a healthful body shall be suddenly taken . . . without probable reason or natural cause appearing", witchcraft was to be suspected. Inexplicable illness in animals was even more readily explained by the belief that they had been bewitched.

Even those authors who have made exhaustive studies of the subject – Keith Thomas, for instance, in his admirable *Religion and the Decline of Magic* (1971) – find it impossible to explain why, in the late seventeenth century, belief in witchcraft began steeply to decline, both at the level of senior clerics and in ordinary people (who nevertheless still clung to the idea of charms and spells, and continued to believe in "luck"). It was not the result, it seems, of the church's teachings – on the contrary, many people who regularly attended church as a social duty remained sadly ignorant of religion. As late as 1870, the Rev. Francis Kilvert recorded in his journal that he gave Communion to two parishioners, one of whom on receiving the Host touched his forelock and said, "Here's your good health, sir," while the other at least drank the health of the Lord Jesus Christ. Such simple countrymen knew much more about country superstitions, charms and spells than about theology.

Among the clergy, however, the general feeling grew that God would not have allowed mortals to assume such powers as witches were traditionally supposed to have acquired. There was also a growing revulsion not only against the formal persecution of witches, but against the kind of local cruelty practised in many parts of Europe. Reginald Scot (1538-99), at the age of 46 published *Discoverie of Witchcraft*, a powerful attack on the childish absurdities of the witch-craze. However, although King

An invitation to a Rosicrucian meeting, dated 1771, is inscribed within the movement's "Hill of Knowledge" triangle. The symbol of the "Rosy Cross" rises above the text, which is expressed in deliberately obscure terms.

James I (notably hysterical about witchcraft) had Scot's book burned by the public hangman, it was to be enormously influential over the next century. Yes, witches existed, Scot believed – but they were either simply crazed, and used poison rather than magic to injure people, or pretended to be able to effect cures in order to make money. He did not believe in any supernatural influence.

From the beginning of the nineteenth century, the idea of witchcraft as a serious diabolical plot against humanity almost vanished. The conviction that some "wise women" – occasionally referred to as witches – knew much about natural medicine, the healing properties of plants and potions, remained; as did a superstitious addiction to charms and "good luck" formulae. But witchcraft in the true sense of the word was dead – if perhaps only temporarily.

MAGIC SOCIETIES UP TO THE PRESENT DAY

After the Age of Reason in the eighteenth century, when the influence of scholar magicians like Robert Fludd dwindled and almost died, the Romantic movement of the early 1800s saw a rebirth of interest in magic. In 1801 Francis Barrett published *The Magus*, a brilliantly illustrated work that brought the magic of the grimoires and the earlier magicians to a new public. Barrett was familiar with alchemical texts, the work of the philosopher magicians of the Renaissance, and the Christian Caballah, and his book had a wide influence both in England and the USA. Soon afterwards, in Europe, the strange figure of Eliphas Lévi (1810-75) had an even greater effect. Born Alphonse Louis Constant, the son of a cobbler, Lévi studied for the priesthood but broke off his studies shortly before he was due to be ordained. After some years as a revolutionary socialist, he became interested in the occult, especially the Caballah, and began to experiment with ritual magic. He published his conclusions in the

important *Dogme et rituel de la haute magie* and was regarded as the leading magician of his time. Lévi based his work on the "Law of Correspondence", which was derived from the ancient belief that man was a microcosm (small universe) corresponding in every detail to the macrocosm of the great universe; the genitals, for example, were equated with the zodiacal sign of Scorpio, red was the colour of Mars, and the soul of man was the "magical mirror of the universe". He also believed that the human will was, if properly directed, all-powerful. Most important, he held that formless, invisible "astral light" (a concept borrowed from Paracelsus) pervaded nature, and could be moulded into visible form by human will – as witnessed in spiritual seances.

Lévi's influence grew after his death, and played a part in the revival of the Rosicrucian (Rosy Cross) movement under the Marquis Stanislas de Guaita (1861-97). There seems to be some connection between the Rosy Cross and Freemasonry, but in the late 1800s the movement suffered from internal dissensions. A leading member, Joséphin Péladan (1858-1918), denounced the order, refusing to "rub shoulders with spiritualism, masonry and Buddhism", and the movement became fatally split.

The Order of the Golden Dawn was formed by some disenchanted members of the Rosicrucian Order, led by S. L. MacGregor Mathers (known later as Count McGregor of Glenstrae). A Temple of Isis-Urania was set up in London, and the whole organization was shrouded in secrecy (any member who revealed information about it was to be subjected to a magical influence which would result in his falling dead – though there are no attested examples of this actually occurring).

The Order attracted some well-known members, including the poet W. B. Yeats, the actress Florence Farr, the author Arthur Machen and the Astronomer Royal of Scotland. It involved a considerable amount of ritual, and each member had to show an interest in and knowledge of such techniques as the making of sigils and talismans, divination, reading the Tarot and writing in the Enochian language.

Mathers, who became the head of the Order (he named himself Adeptus Exemptus, and thus holder of the highest degree available to human beings) was clearly a remarkable modern magician. When Yeats first visited him, he was told to hold a coloured cardboard sigil against his forehead, and immediately began to see visions – of a desert and of the ruins of an ancient city. There are many other recorded examples of Mathers using drawn or written symbols to invoke extraordinary visions.

Aleister Crowley was initiated into the Order of the Golden Dawn in 1898, and by 1900 had become an Adeptus Minor. He claimed that many of his writings were directly inspired by, even dictated by, occult powers; sometimes he asserted that he could not himself understand them. He said this of the blasphemous and vicious *Liber Legis*, or *Book of the Law*, which he claimed was dictated to him in Cairo in 1904 by the angel Aiwass (one of his followers committed suicide after attempting to interpret the Book). In 1906 he visited China, and in 1913 travelled to Russia (accompanying a music hall act called The Ragged Ragtime Girls), where he wrote a gnostic catholic mass which included references to several saints created only within his own imagination – among them were one of the Borgia popes and "Sir" Aleister Crowley himself. In 1916 he visited America, where he published anti-British propaganda and crucified a toad while reciting blasphemous references to the New Testament; this, he believed, raised him to the rank of a Magus.

He formed his own magical Order – the silver star – and for several years ran an abbey at Thelema, near Cefalu in Sicily, whence came rumours of bisexual orgies of the utmost salaciousness, and of the sacrifice of babies. Several of his closest associates died in mysterious circumstances, including his wife and child. He became a drug addict and possessed by ambition to be (as he called himself) the Great Beast, "the wickedest man in the world".

Nevertheless, there are many who point out that Crowley was capable of considerable personal kindness, and that he certainly was not a fraud because he believed in his own system of magic. His influence and that of the Golden Dawn have grown since his death, particularly in the USA. Dr F. I. Regardie, formerly Crowley's secretary and, until quite recently, a well-known practitioner of alternative medicine in California, has done much to emphasize the more positive aspects of Crowley and the Golden Dawn of MacGregor Mathers. Many contemporary American magicians have drawn on Regardie's work, which makes use of mystical doctrines from the Hindu Tantra and the Chinese Tao, as well as those of nineteenth-century magicians (whose work itself derives from much earlier sources). The growth and development of modern witchcraft deserves separate study, and we discuss it later in Chapter Ten.

*Aleister Crowley (**right**) developed an influential doctrine of "magick". Based on teachings from the Golden Dawn order, which Crowley had joined, it included Oriental occult practices, varieties of sexual magic, and a new religion of "Force and Fire". Crowley's seal (**above**) and one of his designs (**opposite**) contain details of his so-called Law of Thelema.*

2.

The Spirit World

The world has always seemed to be full of spirits – unseen agencies working for or against man. We have seen how in the very earliest times hunters tried to evoke the spirits of animals they wanted to track; it was not long before they came to believe that other spirits had a peculiar interest in men and women themselves – perhaps to entrap them into evil, or to encourage them towards good, and almost invariably either to combat or satisfy their human desires.

Magicians throughout the ages sought to achieve their aims – knowledge, power, wealth, healing and so on – by invoking the unseen spirits who inhabited the supernatural world, and enlisting their help. Sometimes this help was freely given; at other times, great danger was involved. Magicians had to use elaborate devices and rituals to protect themselves from the awesome powers which might at any moment be turned against them.

SPIRITS OF THE NATURAL WORLD

Early civilizations were very close to nature, and man expressed this dependency by developing a belief in spirits which lived in, controlled, or were associated with natural phenomena; for example, Greek nymphs, the god Pan, or animal gods. Even today, herbalists collecting elder flowers or berries always apologize to the tree, so as to placate the spirit dwelling within it. Perhaps the most familiar nature spirits, which still carry a powerful superstitious influence in the West today, were the "little people", or fairies. Fairies were supposed to live deep in the countryside, but were occasionally seen by humans as they danced in rings. They were best left alone. Sometimes they played jokes on servants, and even stole a child, leaving behind a

*The angelic, demonic and human worlds interpenetrate (**opposite**) according to many occultists. Special rituals, including the speaking of certain words, the use of special plants and the forming of a magic circle, may induce an other-worldly entity to manifest itself on Earthplane.*

This photograph of a fairy, faked at Cottingley, Yorkshire, in 1920, convinced writer Arthur Conan Doyle (creator of Sherlock Holmes) of the existence of the "little people".

substitute which would inevitably grow up as a feeble-minded weakling.

The best way of keeping fairies at bay was by ensuring that your house and its occupants were clean and tidy. It was also wise to leave food and drink for them, in some convenient place, as well as water and towels for their convenience.

Belief in fairies remained remarkably strong in some areas of Europe, particularly in the regions with Celtic populations, until well into the 20th century. The "little people" were tenacious denizens of the countryside for millennia. The magic wrought by fairies was largely country magic – evil spirits were blamed for evil deeds, good spirits praised for happy events and good fortune. Sometimes they were tricksters – like Puck, a generic name in Germanic folklore for various malevolent spirits, whose best-known appearance is in Shakespeare's *A Midsummer-Night's Dream*. Such characters could be positively dangerous, inflicting men, women and beasts with sickness and disease. People believed in them implicitly. John Aubrey, the English antiquarian, said that when he was a boy country folk talked much of them. In 1670 he carefully recorded the appearance near Cirencester of an apparition which, "Being demanded whether a Good Spirit or a Bad? returned no answer, but disappeared with a curious Perfume and a most melodious Twang. Mr W. Lillie believes it was a fairy."

The astrologer William Lilly (1602-81) made several attempts to contact the Queen of the Fairies, and in his delightful autobiography tells how on one occasion he invited "a very sober, discreet person, of virtuous life and conversation" to his house at Hersham, when

> *the Queen of the Fairies was invocated; a gentle murmuring wind came first; after that, amongst the hedges, a smart whirlwind; by and by a strong blast of wind blew upon the face of the friend – and the Queen appearing in a most illustrious glory, "No more, I beseech you!" quoth the friend "My heart fails; I am not able to endure longer." Nor was he: his black curling hair rose up, and I believe a bullrush would have beat him to the ground: he was soundly laughed at.*

The fairies' reputation held until comparatively recently; anyone who grew up in rural England in the 1930s will remember grandmothers' tales of fairy rings and the misdoings of pixies or elves – tales half-humorously told, but with a nervous system of their own which could produce a twinge when one walked through a dark lane at midnight, by moonlight. And even today one can find people who will not wear

Nymphs and satyrs coexisted with humans in the classical world of the Greeks and Romans. The goat-legged satyr has obvious affinities with devils in later, Christian, demonology.

green – it is unlucky. Green is the colour favoured by the "little people".

Fairies and other nature spirits were seldom regarded either as good or evil. They could be mischievous and spiteful, but on the whole would not harm man as long as they were treated with respect.

Much more serious consequences could ensue if an unwary magician should trifle with the powerful spirits of good and evil: the gods and goddesses, angels and demons. The concept of a malign, destructive supernatural force developed very early on in civilization, and gradually individual spirits came to be associated either with good or with evil.

The Greek and Roman myths populated the invisible world with gods and goddesses in whom human virtues and failings were raised to mythic status; these figures are heroic, vicious, generous, amorous, noble and ignoble – reflecting recognizable human traits, but on the broadest scale. The all-powerful Zeus is all too recognizably human, with qualities of generosity but also of spite.

In many religions, it is recognized that the existence of evil on earth predicates a god to whom evil is a necessity. This cannot be the creator, for were he "responsible" for evil, he would be without that innate and utter goodness which is his main property. So in some cases his opposite, a god of evil, a devil, was imagined, served by legions of devils.

GOD AND THE DEVIL

In the Judaeo-Christian tradition, the forces of good are represented by a single God, attended by lesser spirits known as angels. God is opposed by a spirit of evil known as the Devil, or Satan, or The Evil One, who is himself a fallen angel and is attended by others of his kind. There is a constant battle between these forces of good and evil for the possession of human souls. The magician who attempts to call upon the forces of evil to help him achieve his ends risks paying the ultimate price: the loss of his immortal soul.

It is only in the Book of Revelation (AD 81-96) that the idea of fallen angels is clearly set out: "And his [Satan's] tail drew the third part of the stars of heaven [the angels] and did cast them to earth . . . and Satan, which deceiveth the whole world; he was cast out into the earth and his angels were cast out with him." A cardinal archbishop of Tusculum actually counted the fallen angels – there were 133,306,668 of them – and named a few: Shemhazai, Armaros, Samsaweel, Kawkabel . . .

The Book of Genesis (eighth century BC), on the other hand, records that some angels "saw the daughters of men . . . and took them wives", and that is what resulted in their demotion – one manifestation of the early Christian writers' preoccupation with the idea of sex as *the* original sin (they also ascribed to the fallen angels the discovery of "necklaces, armlets, rouge, and the black powder for the eyelashes").

As to Satan himself – his biography has often been written. Originally he was the twelve-winged chief of the seraphim, who "wore all the angels as a garment, transcending all in glory and knowledge", as Gregory the Great put it in the sixth century. He only emerged as the prince of darkness in New Testament times – but since then has ruled undisturbed as the principle of evil, under various names.

Satan could appear in as many guises as he had names: as almost any animal (except the lamb, ox or ass, too closely associated with Christ); but usually he preferred to masquerade as a serpent, dragon, goat or dog. Sometimes he impersonated a priest or theologian, sometimes a beautiful youth or girl. In his own person he was not a pretty sight, indeed he was exceptionally ugly; he had cloven hooves, and was lame because of his fall from heaven, his knees were twisted backwards, he had an extra face on his belly and buttocks, no eyebrows, and an inordinately large nose and phallus. He often had red hair (so of course had Judas) – and usually a charcoal black skin. Despite all this, he nevertheless found it extremely easy, in one way or another, to seduce both men and women.

The Devil was given charge of anything regarded as improper or sinful: for instance pagan temples and the countryside (closely associated in the mind of early Christians with pagan gods, and latterly with witchcraft). Any mysterious feature of the landscape was usually associated with him – hence the many Devil's dykes, bridges, gorges, ditches. Happily, he was not always regarded with the respect his position demanded; in 1648 a broadsheet was published "for the confutation of those that believe there are no such things as spirits or devils", describing how

> the Devil was seen there, in a Cellar, in the likeness
> of a Ram; and how a butcher came and cut his
> throat, and sold some of it, and dressed the rest for
> him, inviting many to supper, who ate of it. Attested
> by divers letters of men of very good credit in the town.

The Devil had a great number of associates – his demons: so thick in the air that a needle dropped from heaven could not but strike one of them before falling to earth:

> Smooth Devils, Horned Devils,
> Sullen Devils, Playful Devils,
> Shorn Devils, Hairy Devils,
> Bushy Devils, Cursed Devils,
> Foolish Devils,
>
> Devils, Devilesses and Young Devils,
> All the progeny of devildom,
> Come from your devilish tricks
> Quicker than light,

invited a magician in a fourteenth century passion play.

The idea of devils is not specially Christian, however; in classical Greece, every individual was supposed to be allotted a particular demon, who would record his actions, and was neutral rather than urging either to good or evil. But there were many devil sects in various parts of the world – devils were *Eblis* or *Jinns* in Arabia, *Maskim* in Chaldea, *Duyel* in Holland, *Typhon* in Egypt, *Rakshasas* to the Hindus, *Pookas* to the Irish, *Asuras* to the Persians, and so on.

But as to the devils recognized by Jewish theologians, the Talmudists counted

*Satan's face glowers from a fresco of
Hell in the Campo Santo, Pisa, Italy.*

*Demons thrive in all cultures. A Mughal painting of demons at the Topkapi Museum, Istanbul (**above**), displays them in a jocular, if somewhat sinister aspect. A depiction of "The Evil One" (**opposite**), by the 20th-century illustrator Frank Papé, presents an altogether darker view of the demonic world, and one in keeping with the Christianized Western version, where humour is not considered appropriate.*

them, and arrived at a total of 7,405,926 – rather fewer than the fallen angels counted by the cardinal archbishop of Tusculum. However, if Rabbi Rav Huna is correct, the cardinal was nearer the mark, for he suggested that every human being has a thousand devils on the left side, and ten thousand on the right. They were also divided into various grades: at their head stood the Trinity of Evil, the Devil and his two lieutenants – one of the sea, one of the earth. Out of the mouths of that diabolical Trinity came three unclean spirits in the form of frogs; then a great legion of minor devils in a giant rout, appearing as horses with men's faces, lion's teeth and women's hair, with crowns of gold and breastplates of iron, barbed and pointed tails.

FRANK C PAPE

SPIRITS OF GOOD AND EVIL

Angels were the god's good spirits, and therefore his servants in a true sense – indeed,
divine (the Sanskrit *angiras* means a divine spirit; the Persian *angaros* and the Greek
angelos signifies a messenger – of good, no doubt). Both angels and devils were considered capable of being "raised", conversed with by men, and therefore useful for
magical purposes. God, on the other hand – the moving spirit of the universe, in
whatever shape or persona he was imagined – was considered too powerful, too unknowable, for man to attempt conversation with him; his power could only be
approached through intermediaries (the Devil, however, could be "raised", though
that would be a perilous undertaking).

The most famous Englishman to devote much time to spirit raising was John Dee
(1527-1608), a very great man indeed, an authority on mathematics and navigation,
an alchemist who formed the first great library in England, and Astrologer Royal to
Elizabeth I (having narrowly escaped being burned as a witch by Queen Mary). He
was the alchemist in Ben Jonson's play of that name, and some say the original of

*Spirit-raising requires self-discipline as well as knowledge, as illustrated in an early 19th-century depiction of a magician in his oratory (**above left**).*

*The Elizabethan sage and magician, Dr Dee (**above right**) used methods derived from the Caballah (**above**).*

Prospero in Shakespeare's *The Tempest.* Dee was fascinated by magic. His preoccupation was with the secrets of nature, and he regarded his work as scientific rather than magical (neither the first nor the last occasion on which the two have been confused). A profoundly pious man, he passionately hated ignorance – and so, evidently, did the angels with whom he conversed, for one of them told him:

> *Ignorance was the nakedness wherewithal you were*
> *first tormented, and the first Plague that fell unto*
> *man was the want of Science . . . the want of Science*
> *hindreth you from knowledge of your self.*

Dee employed the Caballah to raise angels, in a complex system using their Hebrew names, often in anagrams, and *gematria*, a system in which numerical values assigned to the Hebrew letters were juggled and carefully arranged. He worked with a medium, a dubious character called Edward Kelley, who had called on him and claimed to see visions in his crystal. Later Kelley became an alchemist, who failing to produce gold for the mad Emperor Rudolph II of Prague was imprisoned by him and died trying to escape. It was Kelley who claimed actually to see the angels Dee raised, and contributed to their raising by recording a special language, Enochian, with a proper alphabet and grammar in which they must be addressed. This – and the angels' names – had to be spoken backwards (because they appeared backwards in the crystal the two men used).

To record the language, Kelley sat in front of the crystal, and the Angel Gabriel appeared to him with a wand and a board on which were written various letters and figures. Gabriel dictated 49 tables, each of which contained 49 rows of 49 small squares each holding a letter of the Enochian alphabet. Kelley, looking into the crystal, would "see" an angel pointing to one of those squares, and call out its reference number to Dee (as though it were a map reference). Dee would then find the square and write down the letter. Thus, the calls were "given" by which the angels could be summoned.

What eventually resulted from a long series of conversations were books written *backwards* in Enochian. Transcribed, the sentences read literately – and even if the text seems meaningless, it is almost impossible to believe that Kelley had the ability to memorize the entire system and use it to produce readable prose. Clearly, something extremely odd was going on.

An early success was in raising Uriel, the spirit of light who told Dee that there were 49 good angels who would be happy to appear at his command. His main informant was Madimi, who appeared to Kelley and Dee for seven years:

> *A spiritual creature, like a pretty girl of 7 or 9 yeares*
> *of age, attired on her head, with her hair rolled up*
> *before and hanging down long behind, with a gown of*
> *changeable green and red, and with a train she*
> *seemed to play up and down and seemed to go in and*
> *out behind my books.*

Madimi was a lively little spirit, who "went up and down with most lively gestures of a young girl, playing by herself, and divers times another spake to her from the corner of my study by a great perspective-glass, but none was seen beside herself."

Other angels occasionally did appear, however, some of them "merry and naughty", eccentrically dressed, holding peacocks' feathers, telling silly and often bawdy jokes, which rather upset the serious-minded Dr Dee. The last word may perhaps be left with Madimi, who on one occasion pointed out that there were no secrets in the universe "save those that lie buried in the shadow of men's souls".

Conversation with angels was a serious matter, and "it is not everyone, or every person, that these angelical creatures will appear unto", William Lilly reminds us soberly, "though they may say over the call, over and over; nor indeed is it given to very many persons to endure their glorious aspects." Certain men had forfeited the right to fairy favours – a man called Gladwell, for instance, brought to Lilly by Sir Robert Holborn, had formerly had sight and conference with Uriel and Raphael, "but lost them both by carelessness; so that neither of them both would but rarely appear, and then presently be gone, resolving nothing."

ANGELS AND SAINTS

Christianity, Judaism and Islam all incorporate the idea of angels: high-ranking spirits which serve God and assume individual responsibilities and embody specific powers. Saints are the immortal souls of the righteous, who are believed by Christians to have performed miracles during their lifetimes and to have the power to perform miraculous deeds when invoked by the faithful.

Angels are the senior spirits, as to age; they were really born in Babylon, whence they were adopted by the Persians, then by the Hebrews. Only two angels (or demons, as they were also called) are named in the Old Testament – Michael and Gabriel, who both originated in Babylonian mythology; Raphael, the third oldest angel, appears in the Apocryphal Book of Tobit.

In the very earliest Christian times many angels were named by Enoch, but although they also appear in documents contemporary with the New Testament gospels (round about the first century AD), they are ignored there, more often being invoked in books or Jewish mystical works.

It was between the eleventh and thirteenth centuries that for obscure reasons angelology became a veritable craze, and thousands of angels were identified. Various views were taken of them: Catholic theologians believed them to have been created at the beginning of the world; Jewish theologians believed they were "new every morning", and continued to be formed with every breath God took.

The angelic hierarchy was somewhat confusing. According to St Ambrose, Pope Gregory and other authorities, angels were lowest in the supernatural order of things: the seraphim and cherubim were highest, together with thrones; next came dominions, powers and virtues, then principalities, archangels and angels. But elsewhere there were other rankings and other names: in *The Greater Key of Solomon* (a very ancient source) and the *Mishna Thora* by the Jewish rabbi and philosopher Maimonides (1135-1204) the "ten choirs of holy angels" were given in the following order: chaioth ha-Qadesh, auphanim, aralim, chashmalim, seraphim, malachim, elohim, beni elohim, kerubim and ishin.

In Jewish theology most angels are male, though in Arabic legend *benad hasche*, daughters of God, are not uncommon. The great exception, for Jews, is *Shekinah*, "the bride of the Lord", who can be compared to the *shakti* of Shiva. She is named by Jacob, in Genesis (c. eighth century BC) as "the angel which redeemed me from all evil"; she appeared to Moses (though Aaron is said to have died as the result of her kiss); and she is said to bless all unions between Jewish husbands and their wives.

Angels have always stood guard over the marriage bed, and even assisted in its rites: of the 301,655,722 angels which the Caballists believed to exist, 47 were particularly charged to assist in various phases of lovemaking. Others had other specific duties: for instance, governing the twelve months of the year – January was guarded by Gabriel, February by Barchiel, March by Machidiel, April by Asmodel, May by Ambriel, June by Muriel, July by Verchiel, August by Hamaliel, September by Uriel, October by Barbiel, November by Adnachiel and December by Hanael.

*Angels dance in a paradise garden: a
detail from the painting, The Angels,
by the mystical Florentine monk, Fra
Angelico (1400-55).*

The "Cherub of the Sephiroth" features in a grimoire prepared by the 19th-century magician Eliphas Lévi.

These angels also took the twelve Zodiac signs under their wings:

Aries – Machidiel
Gemini – Ambriel
Leo – Verchiel
Libra – Uriel
Sagittarius – Adnachiel
Aquarius – Gabriel
Taurus – Asmodel
Cancer – Muriel
Virgo – Hamaliel
Scorpio – Barbiel
Capricorn – Hanael
Pisces – Barchiel

Naturally, each planet (except for the most recently discovered ones) also has a guardian angel. According to Francis Barrett in his seminal work *The Magus* (1801), Raphael rules the Sun, Aniel Venus, Michael Mercury, Gabriel the Moon, Kafziel Saturn, Zadkiel Jupiter, and Sammael Mars. But there are various theories of the planetary guardians. Perhaps because of the importance of the planets in all forms of magic, *The Secret Grimoire of Turiel* allotted them no less than nine "spirits, messengers and intelligences".

Each day of the week was guarded by two angels with the exception of Monday, which was ruled solely by Gabriel, the senior angel of death and resurrection, mercy and vengeance, who also presides over paradise. The archangel Khamael and the angel Zamael rule Tuesday, while Wednesday is guarded by Michael and Raphael. Thursday is governed by Tzaphiel and Sachiel, Friday by Haniel and Anael, Saturday by Tzaphiel and Cassiel, and Sunday by Raphael and Michael.

The hours of each day also have an angel ascribed to them. In using the system normally put into practice, it seems that a rather curious and not uncomplicated device is used to discover the relevant hours of the day and night, which have nothing to do with the conventional twenty-four hour clock. To find the hours of the day at any time of the year, one must take the number of minutes from sunrise to sunset, and divide this by 12, this gives the number of minutes in any hour of that day. For instance, on 3 August, 1991, in London, England, the sun rose at 5.26 a.m. and set at 8.46 p.m. There are 840 minutes in 14 hours, to which must be added 34 minutes (the time between 5.26 a.m. and 6 a.m.) and 46 minutes (the time between 8.00 p.m. and sunset). The total is 920, and dividing this by 12 gives us 76 minutes for each "hour" of that particular day. So the fourth hour of that day, for angelic purposes, would begin at 228 minutes past sunrise, or 8.34 a.m. The hours of the night are calculated in the same way, taking the time from sunset to sunrise. The hours of the day and night, incidentally, are also ruled by the astrological signs and planets according to a precisely organized system.

Some angelic names are very familiar to us, of course – Gabriel, Michael, Raphael . . . others are less well-known; but about each, something is known. Cassiel, for instance, is one of the princes of the Order of Powers, the angel of solitude and tears, who rules the seventh heaven and sometimes appears as the angel of temperance; Aniel, one of the seven angels of creation, governs the second heaven, and being the angel of the star of love (Venus, the evening star) is much concerned with human sexuality; and Tzaphiel must (according to *The Greater Key of Solomon*) be appealed to by those who wish to procure and make use of a magic carpet.

It is often believed that fallen angels become demons (though as we have seen, the names were originally interchangeable: it seems to have been "the Angelic Doctor" St Thomas Aquinas who first used the word "demon" in a pejorative sense).

Then there is the matter of the saints, human beings who have often during their lifetime been credited with magical acts of healing (perhaps explicable in modern terms, when healing arts are still practised) but also of levitation or being in two places at once – and these are in relatively recent times. It is also believed that saints may be used as intermediaries with God; and may certainly be invoked and asked for help, whether in such major matters as sickness or peril, or in minor matters such as finding lost articles. They clearly possess magical powers, though the term would probably not be used by the pious.

POSSESSION

The idea of the Devil "entering into" someone was for centuries a standard explanation of unusual or unstable behaviour; and since it was so easy for the Devil to enter into a human soul, it was an acceptable explanation of the presence of evil.

In Christian societies, devils in various guises were assumed to be used in particular to torment monks – which they did according to a careful battle plan, suiting the temptation to the age and temperament of the monk concerned – elderly monks would be tempted by sloth, food and drink; younger ones by sex. Sometimes the devils were simply instructed to make themselves a general nuisance – for example St Anthony's contemplations were interrupted by devils in the form of lions, bears, leopards, asps, scorpions, wolves; at least once he was physically assaulted by a pack of demons who left him senseless in the road. St Hilarion was troubled by noises from cattle, babies crying, and lions roaring. Other monks were disturbed by singing, whistling, even loud farting.

A considerable difficulty in combating devils was that they could make themselves so small they were impossible to see, and enter one's body in the air one breathed – especially through the nose. Sometimes this made one sneeze; when it was important to have someone nearby to say "God bless you". (Perhaps we still breathe them in, calling them germs rather than demons.)

Devils disported in the jetstreams of the human sneeze, according to medieval sages.

The horrors of demonic possession (left), vividly captured in a 19th-century engraving, were recognized by civilized as well as primitive societies. Exorcism in the 16th century at Laon, France (opposite and below), was carefully regulated by the canon law of the church. Holy water, incense, and loud noises of all kinds were recommended by most authorities.

Even if one caught sight of a visiting devil, it was not always easy to distinguish him from an angel. Monks were specially instructed in techniques which would reveal the difference, but the easiest option was simply to confront the intruder and ask him outright whether he was angel or devil. If the first, he would reveal himself; if the second, he would flee, gibbering. A true saint, though frequently troubled by demonic visitors, in the end always vanquished them.

The saints were not spirits of course, but human beings who, after their deaths, became spirits and could be invoked by the living to intercede for them with God.

Medieval theologians were sure that men and women could be possessed, their bodies literally inhabited, by demons; is not the Bible full of such incidents, and had they not experience of actually seeing the tormented and writhing bodies of those suffering under such possession? Today, the churches are less certain – but it is unusual to find a priest willing to state unequivocally that possession is not possible.

Exorcism is usually the means of persuading spirits to leave the body of the person they are currently possessing. Both Christians and Muslims have practised this technique over the centuries, and a minority of priests and clergy in the Roman Catholic and Anglican churches still practise it; nonconformist ministers also, though less formally and using their own natural powers of persuasion rather than ritual.

It is when a bridge of some kind has been built between the demon and the exorcist or psychiatrist treating the possessed person that the cure or successful exorcism begins. Frequently, the signal of the beginning of the end comes when the demon identifies itself in response to the exorcist's command. In the Bible, Jesus enquired the name of an "unclean spirit" possessing a man, and received the reply, "My name is Legion, for we are many."

The simplest form of exorcism is the pronouncement of one simple sentence: "I command thee to leave the body of X . . ." However, more complex ceremonies are needed in extreme cases. A comparatively recent case required many hours of work to drive out no fewer than 13 devils.

There are possible dangers in taking possession so seriously as to seek exorcism.

DEO
ET SVMMO IESV CHRISTI VICARIO
IOCHANNES BOVLÆSE PRESBITER
ET CIVIS LAVMDVNENSIS PAVPER
COLLEGII MONTIS ACVTIPARISIENSIS
1566

La Croisée de l'Eglise.

*Guardian spirits of the harvest receive
offerings to ensure cooperation from the
Mehenaku people of Brazil.*

There have been cases of subjects, after an attempted exorcism, physically attacking
other people in the most diabolical way, perhaps because they were persuaded by all
the attention paid them that they were indeed possessed by a devil who "needed" to
commit crimes. Either the devil was thus encouraged to flex his muscles, or the
psychologically troubled victim had the delusion reinforced and in the form of self-
fulfilling prophesy offered new proof of his or her situation.

Though many will come to the conclusion that diabolic possession is more likely to
be a delusion than a fact – that it is unlikely that a devil actually enters the body of a
human being in order to use it for his own evil purpose – a number of serious-minded
people who have studied the question would disagree. They are in no doubt that diabolic possession is a matter of fact; and psychiatrists would no doubt admit that the
minds of some patients are indeed possessed – if only by an idea, an idea sufficiently
real and powerful to unbalance them. Once more, magic and the imagination meet,
and may be indistinguishable.

If the status or indeed the existence of devils is uncertain in our modern world,
what are we to say about angels? The attitude of the Christian church towards these
entities is one almost impossible to establish, for it seems to depend very much on the
individual viewpoint. It is certainly not the case, as far as we know, that any Christian church has pronounced that angels do not exist, although it has been argued that
it is neither necessary nor particularly desirable to have any intermediary between
man and God, and that angels should not be regarded as such (though in the past that
was the view). On the matter of personal guardian angels there are also various views
and when one comes to the question of spirit guides, there are as many opinions as
there are questions.

We have already looked at the conventional angelic world; and perhaps all that
need be said here is that there is absolutely no reason why anyone should not choose a
"personal" angel to whom to appeal, through whom to channel prayer; and if this is

magic, it is benign Christian magic and carries the usual caveat: that while in both cases the supernatural plays a dominant part, a chief difference between religion and magic is that in the former one requests, in the latter one commands.

Angels perform a multitude of tasks, not only serving God by chanting prayers and tunes of glory, but acting directly as guardians, comforters, guides and counsellors – even, in the past, as cooks and matchmakers! So there is no reason not to seek out a sympathetic angel and ask its help (angels seem to be sexless).

Much the same is true of the saints, who are more readily accepted as intermediaries where conventional religion is concerned; that is, they are on the whole recognized as more closely concerned with the relationship between man and God, conveying the former's prayers to the latter. Again, choose your saint – perhaps the patron saint of your profession, and address him or her personally.

But is there a difference between the guardian angel or saint, and the spirits said by clairvoyants to accompany us through life? Most spiritualists prefer the term "doorkeeper" to "angel" or "saint" though the concept is much the same. These spirits, they say, have never been embodied in flesh: though they are "souls" just as we are, they are souls which have never been incarnated on earth. (Christian theologians would dispute this: angels, they say, have nothing in common with us – not even a soul, in any sense we would understand.)

Perhaps a personal guardian angel does not guard us in any literal sense, holding off enemies with a flaming sword or actually preventing us from doing evil, but exists to guard us from evil thoughts and deeds by suggestion; in other words, it is our conscience. Spiritualists claim that the "door-keeper", who is in a one-to-one relationship with a particular living person, stands between this world and the next; but agree with conventional Christianity that it represents our better self – a self we may not even be capable of recognizing except with supernatural assistance.

There are other somewhat similar spiritual beings who are believed to accompany us through life – or at least to be available as guides and advisers. A step up, as it were, from the individual guardian angel are what spiritualists describe as the guardians of the threshold. One of these – the lesser guardian – represents everything in our past which might restrict our spiritual growth – the sum of those attitudes and predilections, those desires and ambitions, with which we must come to terms, for which we must perhaps forgive ourselves before we can make spiritual progress. (This is a good and helpful psychological notion – it is interesting how often traditional magical or religious invocations tally with the latest psychological theory.)

It is believed that we can get in touch with our personal guide, perhaps through meditation, and ask for help in our way through life. It has been argued that such a guide has been appointed to work with us for its own benefit as well as ours, and while the guide will be more knowledgeable or wiser than us, it can benefit as much as we can from the contact.

There are many unanswered, and presumably unanswerable questions about spirit guides. For some reason, a large proportion of them seem to be American Indians – but as yet, no one has ever been able to explain the significance of this . Many people claim to know their guides very well, to see them about the house, to be able to converse with them as freely as with a friend (we once dined with a friend and hearing a slight scuffle outside the door as she was bringing in the main course, enquired what had happened: the spirit guide had apparently been standing there, and there was insufficient room to pass him with the tray).

There is always the possibility that these guides may be the result of vivid imaginations, and it must be admitted that attempts to prove their existence have been less persuasive than the arguments advanced for the existence, say, of ghosts. But even where this seems likely, the simple faith of those who converse with their spirit guides often convinces one that they are as real to them as their friends and neighbours; and with spirits as real as that, who is one to draw a line between one's own "reality" and theirs?

3.

Spells, Sigils &
Talismans

As we have seen, magic involves calling upon supernatural powers in order to achieve specific aims. In order to do this, the magician needs to choose his spirits wisely and call upon them using mystical combinations of words, numbers, signs and sounds. These combinations, or coded messages, are what we know as magic spells. In some languages, the word for "spell" is the same as the word for magic – in Maori, for instance, Skarakia means both. And spells have always been crucial to the performance of magic.

THE POWER OF SOUND

When we think of magic spells, we usually think of spoken words, or incantations, and it is certainly true that sound has a very important role to play in the creation of magic spells. In its spoken form, a spell is simply a series of sounds – and in using sounds the magicians of the past were, perhaps unconsciously, tapping a strange power which is still relatively unexplored. We know that sounds can have odd effects, and that at a basic level these are at least partly physical in nature – make certain sounds near a sensitive surface covered in fine sand, and that sand will arrange itself in the most subtle patterns, while a high-pitched sound can shatter glass. It has been calculated that a noise measuring 90 decibels (produced, perhaps, by a car horn sounded a few feet away from one) can cause the amount of blood pumped through the heart each second to double.

Men have always instinctively recognized the power of sound. The historian Eusebius (AD 260-340) reported that a loud noise was produced by the king of Alba's troops before a battle by striking their bucklers with their swords. This was meant to encourage the gods to channel their power through the bodies of his soldiers – but

*The power of the word (**opposite**) is crucial to the effectiveness of magical activity. Spells, whether spoken or written, bind their object with their secret force, involving the mysterious properties of sound and symbol.*

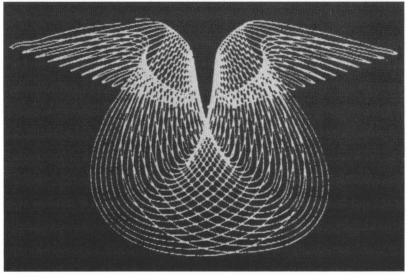

*Sounds take particular forms through the vibration of
their utterance, indicating that the word has force in a
literal, specific manner. The Theosophical "thought
forms" (**above**) are developed from sounds.*

also incidentally struck terror into the hearts of their enemies. The "rebel yell" of the Confederate troops during the American Civil War had much the same effect, and even today recruits training with bayonets are trained to scream wildly as they charge at the straw targets.

This is of course psychological – sound can produce that effect, just as more complex spells can. More recently, sound has been used in various ways as a means of torture. The impact of continuous loud noise upon a human being is imperfectly understood, but can clearly be both psychologically and physically terrifying. The use of sound in the theatre, not only in the form of music, but sound effects, can leave no one in doubt of the effect it can have on our emotions.

But for many people interested in magic and religion, the chief significance of sound is mystical. Sound, they claim, is at the very core of the universe: it is omnipresent. Tantric yogis say that the Divine Mother sings the symphony of the universe; the Christian Bible suggests that when God created the universe he did so by invoking sound – he spoke a Word, casting as it might be the first and greatest spell.

The effect of music on the emotions is so mysterious as to seem magical. There is no logical explanation why a particular combination of musical notes, whether in the form of a tune or of a simple chord, can affect the heart. Nothing in nature has perhaps so persistently resisted explanation. In modern rock music, basic rhythm (perhaps in some way connected with the sound of our beating heart) may be responsible for an effect on the senses. But what is responsible for the ecstacy which both a simple folk tune and the complex music of, say, Bach or Mozart provokes in the listener?

The miracle of the evolution of musical style seems to satisfy at least one definition of magic – it can release powers of the mind of which many people are unaware – as those who "discover" great music late in life will testify. And it is not impossible that there is a connection between the mysterious way in which that happens and the mysterious effect of the magical sounds of spoken or chanted spells.

Magicians and theologians alike – and the two are not mutually exclusive – have from time to time turned their attentions to the thought that it might be possible to discover that single apocalyptic first Word – for the Jews, the secret name of God. As published in the Old Testament, the name Jehovah (or Yahweh) is certainly not secret, but was considered to have great power (it was derived from the Tetragrammaton, or four-letter word, Y H V H – the original pronunciation is unknown). Another published "secret" name of the Almighty is the Shemhamforash, the name Moses pronounced when he divided the Red Sea. This name has 72 letters, and again its pronunciation is unknown. Names more easily pronounceable were Adonai and Elohim, published in the Old Testament and used by magicians.

Instructions for the use of such potent sounds as that of the secret name of the Creator resemble the use of *mantras* as an aid to meditation by Buddhists and Hindus. Certain sounds, repeated again and again, are believed to be useful in healing, to ensure command over others, and even to bestow the power to levitate and travel through time and space.

Tantric texts suggest that sounds can bring one closer to the centre of all things, and in ancient times many potent mantras were devised for that purpose. The best-known of these, of course, is OM, considered to be the ultimate mystic sound, which repeated sufficiently often and with sufficient intensity produces complete harmony of body and spirit.

Tantric scripture holds that certain *bija* mantras (seed sounds) correspond to the seven chakras (energy centres) located up the spine, from the sacrum to the crown of the head. Proper recitation activates each chakra of the human body, so that the *kundalini* (coiled energy) moves from the *Muladhara* (earthroot) chakra to the *Sahasrara*, or chakra of 1,000 lotuses. In ancient India there were seers who claimed they could see the shapes produced by mantras in the ether of space. One of the reasons why in yoga there is great emphasis on breath control is that it is considered that each breath is in effect a mantra – the *ajapa mantra*, or cosmic breath. As with more conventional Western "spells", considerable patience is involved in the proper use of mantras, which must often be repeated a great number of times; one authority has commented somewhat acidly that if he instructs an Indian pupil to recite a mantra 100,000 times, he simply settles down to do it, whereas a Western student complains if even 1,000 repetitions are asked.

In one way, a mantra is a kind of spell whose intention is to work on the inner consciousness of the person who utters it. Other spells, of course, are external, recited not to benefit the person who invokes them, but to affect others, or perhaps to raise supernatural spirits. These are closer to what most of us mean when we talk about "magic spells". Not that such spells, written down and considered in cold blood, seem often on the face of it to mean much more than disembodied sounds.

The sounds and words used in spells are intimately connected with the effect the spell is intended to have. Pronouncing a spell to make a fishing boat successful, for instance, a tribal magician will use the names of various kinds of buoyant woods which float especially well; and other words which mimic the sounds made by the waves and winds. Similarly, a spell for successful hunting will use words which imitate the sound of running animals or wounded or dying beasts.

The magician Reginald Scot inscribed "the characters of the angels of the seven days, with their names" (**right**) *in his book* The Discoverie of Witchcraft *in 1584. Accompanying them are the "figures, seales and periapts" which, correctly used, bestow magic power. A 16th-century grimoire or "black book"* (**opposite**) *displays pictures of the ruling angel, possibly Samael. The page also illustrates a variety of demonic sigils, along with corresponding names. Grimoires were magicians' textbooks, often containing codes to prevent their use by the uninitiated.*

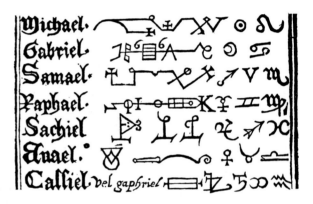

SECRET LANGUAGES & MAGICAL TEXTS

The tradition of secrecy in magic is a very old one. The spells used in the most ancient societies were carefully kept secret from neighbouring tribes or from the magician next door. The invocation, known, would lose its effect. Spells were passed down with the greatest care and ceremony from one generation of magicians to the next, frequently in language understandable only to a very select few. The Etruscans are believed to have got their magic from the Lydians, for instance, who used a form of writing which no one else understood. In their secret magical texts, the questions posed by people consulting them would be written in ordinary script, the answers in ancient, sacred and secret characters. The Egyptians, always regarded as great magicians, relied on the fact that no one outside the priesthood could interpret their books. Lucius Apuleius (c. AD 155), an African fascinated by magic (which plays a great part in his novel *Metamorphosis*) studied it in Egypt, and when he progressed to the first degree of initiation, found that the books it was necessary for him to study were kept by the priest in the most secret part of the sanctuary of the temple, that the most important part of them were written in unknown characters, and that even these were disguised by being interspersed with meaningless hieroglyphics.

Magicians frequently used carefully constructed codes to protect their spells from rivals. Some even went to the lengths of inventing whole secret languages, like the Enochian language which John Dee claimed had been dictated to his assistant Kelley by an angel (see p.39).

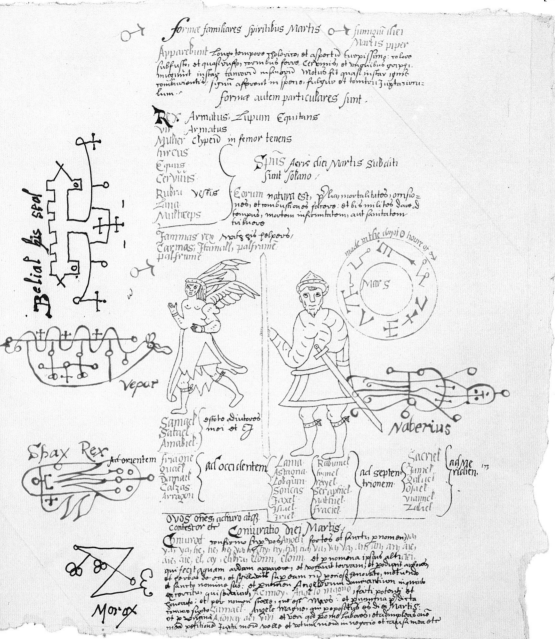

GRIMOIRES

The reason that we know anything about the spells which were used by magicians so many centuries ago is that some of them have come down to us in written form, contained in magical texts known as grimoires (the word means "black books"). These grimoires are often very difficult to understand, as they may be written in code or even in a secret language like Enochian.

One known grimoire is *The Chaldean Oracles of Zoroaster*, a book which seems to have existed for at least 1,500 years. This enshrines many "barbarous words of evocation", possibly sounds rather than words, for they consist of connected syllables which have no meaning recorded in the dictionaries of any known language. There are a number of other famous grimoires. *The Grimoire of Honorius*, for instance, which appears to advocate cannibalism among the practices essential to obtaining the utmost spiritual power over one's adversaries.

Honorius (who was probably a priest), answers to the description of "a black magician" if that phrase is to be used at all. His spells were largely magical sigils or signs which he advised writing on vellum, using a quill pen made out of a feather from a black cockerel sacrificed at sunrise after the celebration of a Mass of the Holy Ghost. For ink, wine consecrated at a Mass of the Angels should be used.

The Key of Moses is yet another grimoire whose power was considerable. Moses was regarded by magicians in the first century BC as a potent magician, and his name is to be found in a number of Graeco-Egyptian papyri. This is quite understandable considering the marvels the *Book of Exodus* describes him as accomplishing. However, the grimoire published under his name is one almost of evil – or at the very least, bad taste. For instance, he advises this spell "to make a woman submit":

> *Write your name upon your door with blood drawn*
> *from your hand. Then write your name on paper*
> *with blood drawn from your finger. Then say the*
> *following prayer: "I conjure you strong spirits in the*
> *name of God, IH, IHVH, IHVH. Truly this is the*
> *Sword of Moses with which he accompanied his*
> *miracles and mighty deeds. May the Sword be*
> *effectual and may the Lord of it approach to serve me."*

"She will come to you soon," the writer assures us.

Anyone who experiments with these grimoires should do so with the utmost care, for there are many recorded occasions on which some kind of unpleasant power seems to have been released as a result of such experiments. A book called *The Sacred Magic of Abra-Melin*, for instance, gives instructions for the inscription on vellum of a number of words of power (words which seem meaningless but have an unpleasant ring – "Surmy, Delmusan, Atalsloym, Charusihoa, Liamintho"). A magician who at the turn of the present century prepared such a slip of vellum found his house filled with "tangible darkness", so that on the sunniest day he had to work with a lamp lit, and was followed about by shadowy figures. In 1927, another unwise researcher in a similar experiment raised an invisible creature of dreadful power, which resolved itself into a demon with serpents for hair. She had to consult a white witch before she was released from her hallucinations – if that is what they were. In the 1930s a well-known magician and composer, Peter Warlock, was found dead by his own hand, an Abra-Melin spell tattooed on his arm.

The grimoires frequently offer simple spells or charms for use on specific occasions and for specific purposes. *The Boke of the Mervayles of the World*, allegedly written in the thirteenth century by Albertus Magnus or St Albert of Cologne, a Dominican friar and teacher of St Thomas Aquinas, provided a number of useful charms – a white henbane root hung about the neck will cure the colic; the smoke of an extinguished lamp will provoke the early birth of a child; the heart, brain or eye of a lapwing hung about the neck will "sharpen the understanding"; any stone hung about an ass's tail will stop him braying.

But there are more curious spells. For instance:

> *Associate with two fellows in the 28th day of*
> *October, and go into a certain wood with dogs as to*
> *hunt. And carry home with thee the beast which thou*

A modern English grimoire features
a red gemstone (probably signifying
Mars), demonic seals, a special
clasp and a skin cover.

shalt find first. Prepare it with the heart of a fox, and
thou shalt understand the voice of birds and beasts.
And if thou wilt also that any other understand, kiss
him, and he shall understand.

The tongue of a frog, boiled and placed between the breasts of a sleeping woman will ensure that she speaks the truth; and "to put any man in Fear in his Sleep, Put under his head the skin of an ape."

THE MAGIC OF NUMBERS

We may think of spells as being a collection of sounds or words, but in many cases numbers are also an important element: either as part of the spell, or as a means of calculating the propitious time to prepare or cast the spell.

Numbers have been considered to have magical significance for thousands of years. Man was aware, very early in the history of thought, that there was something mysterious about numbers – but the sixth-century Greek philosopher Pythagoras is the earliest person we know to have been, intellectually, seriously preoccupied with them. Indeed, he once said "all things are numbers", a pardonable exaggeration when one looks at his lifetime study of them. Certainly he believed numbers to be intimately connected with the structure and even the "idea" of the universe, and with religion: "Number is the ruler of forms and ideas, and is the cause of gods and demons," he wrote in his *Sacred Discourse*.

He looked closely at the association between numbers and music (mathematicians still speak of "harmonic mean" and "harmonic progression", terms he coined). Putting forward the theory that the earth and planets revolved around the sun, he suggested that they must make sounds associated with their different positions relative to it – the so-called "music of the spheres".

He also considered numbers in terms of their form and appearance, and even their physical shape, speaking of "cubes", "squares", even oblong, triangular and pyramidical numbers, which were devised by counting the number of pebbles used when piled up to make those shapes.

But from our point of view, the most important consideration is that numbers seemed to Pythagoras and others to be eternal, divorced from earthly time – thoughts in the mind of God. Plato (c.428-c.348 BC) believed Him to be a geometer, and Sir James Jeans (1877-1946) expressed the belief that He was addicted to arithmetic.

The difference, almost an emotional one, between odd and even numbers much preoccupied Pythagoras and his disciples; they thought of even numbers as powerful and male, odd numbers as less powerful and female – after all, the division of an even number is complete, whereas division of an odd number leaves "one over". Also, adding an odd and an even number together results always in an odd number.

Religious philosophy has tended to combine mathematics and theology; and from an equally early date magicians and those concerned with magic have seen something special in the idea of numbers and the strange ways in which they seem to "work". Their occult significance is age-old – the number 13, for example, has been considered unfortunate since long before the Christian era (the presence of 13 men at the Last Supper merely reinforced the idea).

The early occult associations of numbers presumably arose for very natural reasons. The importance of the number seven may have arisen because there were seven known planets, seven primary colours, and the apertures of the head – eyes, nostrils, ears and mouth – totalled seven. The Old Testament records an obsession with seven – Joshua marched six times around Jericho with his army, and on the seventh day seven priests sounded seven trumpets seven times, at which the walls collapsed. God created the world in six days, and on the seventh He rested. And so on.

Arabic magic had its own systems of numerology and occult geometry, as seen in this magical square, probably related to the square for Saturn, from a scroll in Kuwait.

But each number had its own significance, proposed almost as early as the various planetary qualities were proposed by astrologers. The number one symbolized aggression and action; two, compliance; three, versatility; four, persistence; five, sensuality; six, harmony; seven, intellect; eight, possessions; and nine, the spirit.

The pseudo-science of numerology was developed by the cabbalists who, noting that God created the world by giving names to everything in it, considered that those names must be of the greatest importance, and that therefore much could be divined from a numerical study of them. The 22 letters of the Hebrew alphabet were therefore numbered, and it was then easy to calculate the basic number of a name – by adding the numbers of the letters together, and then simplifying the total: that is, if the letters in a name totalled 129, those numbers were further added together to make 12, and 1 + 2 = 3, so the basic number of the name was 3.

The "astrological series" they devised deals with the numbers between one and twenty-two, using the letters of the Hebrew alphabet and associating them with the planets and signs of the Zodiac. When adapted to the English alphabet, some letters must of course be doubled, giving the following table:

Aleph	A	1	Mercury	Lamed	L	12	Pisces
Beth	B	2	Virgo	Mem	M	13	Aries
Gimel	G	3	Libra	Nun	N	14	Taurus
Daleth	D	4	Scorpio	Sameck	X	15	Saturn
He	E	5	Jupiter	Ayin	O	16	Mars
Vau	V U W	6	Venus	Pe	F P	17	Gemini
Zain	Z	7	Sagittarius	Tzaddi	Ts Tz	18	Cancer
Cheth	H	8	Capricorn	Quoph	Q	19	Leo
Teth	Th	9	Aquarius	Resh	R	20	Moon
Jod	I J Y	10	Uranus	Shin	S	21	Sun
Caph	C K	11	Neptune	Tau	T	22	Earth

The cabbalists spent many weary hours over biblical texts, finding numerical meanings out of them much as, later, some scholars puzzled over the word *honorificabil-itudinitatibus* in Shakespeare, in attempts to prove anagramatically that Bacon was author of his works.

Perhaps the most notable of numerical cabbalists was Giuseppe Balsamo (1743-95), better known by his more grandiloquent assumed name, Count Alessandro di Cagliostro. He was an Italian occultist who travelled to Germany and France and had an enormous success there as a fortune teller and amateur psychologist. It was said that he had an infallible gambling system, sold a Parisian aristocrat three winning lottery tickets, and, numerically analysing the names of the king and queen, forecast unfortunate deaths for both Louis XVI and Marie Antoinette.

Cagliostro used his own numerological system, which assigned the following values to the letters: A, I, Q, J and Y were valued at one; B, K and R at two; C, G L and S at three; D, M and T at four; E, H and N at five; U, V, W and X at six; O and Z at seven, and F and P at eight.

Attention was given to numbers throughout the world: four was the divine *tetraktys* for Pythagoras (we still have four seasons, four elements, four geographical directions). The number five had great importance, especially among the Chinese and Hindus. This perhaps arose because of the frequency with which the number occurs within the run from one to ten. If you add pairs of numbers together, for instance, running towards the centre of the row, ten (5 x 2) is always the result: $1 + 9$, $2 + 8$, $3 + 7$, $4 + 6$; five itself is left, at the centre. Then, if you add all the numbers of the row together you get 45 (9 x 5); add the odd numbers and you get 25 (5 x 5); add the even numbers and you get 20 (4 x 5).

The Chinese spoke of the Five Useful Things, the Five Punishments, the Five Ways; and, of course, attributed the useful things (earth or clay, wood, metal, fire and water) to the five planets as then known (Saturn, Jupiter, Venus, Mars and Mercury, in that order).

Nine is another number which has always had great significance, partly because of the numerical tricks that can be played with it. Multiply any number by 9, and the sum of the digits will also add up to 9 ($5 \times 9 = 45$, $4 + 5 = 9$). Reverse the digits, and the number (54) will also be a multiple of nine. Take any number – say 73 – and divide it by 9; the remainder (1) will always be the same as the remainder you get when you add the digits ($7 + 3$) and divide by 9 – this is why mathematicians check their calculations by "casting out nines". The Egyptians respected the *Enneads* (a triple triad); Dante described the nine circles of Hell – in the Middle Ages nine was "first and foremost the angelic number". And still, today, the number plays its part in some civilizations. Kyoto, in Japan, is divided into nine sections. In Beijing, the emperor would within living memory mount to the Altar of Heaven, nine grades of mandarins performing a nine-fold bow, and stand at a point where nine rings of paving stones radiated out in concentric multiples of nine above nine-rowed terraces.

In Burma at the present time the dictator Ne Win governed his life by the number nine. He overthrew a pro-democracy coup on the 18th day ($8 + 1 = 9$) of the 9th month, gave his party the 9th, 18th and 27th ($2 + 7 = 9$) entries on official electoral ballots, and at one stroke brought economic chaos to the country in 1987 when he insisted on withdrawing all bank notes and replacing them with 45- and 90-kyot notes. Nine, he clearly believes, is a powerful number which he must conquer if it is not to conquer him.

The western "astrological series" of numbers seems to have arisen quite independently of the cabbalist series, and perhaps predates it. In this system (which does not refer to the alphabet) each number was given a specific symbolic meaning, interestingly it was not so distant from the cabbalist meaning.

one was traditionally the symbol of the Deity – but also of the Sun; it is the basis of all numbers, and the basis of life itself.

two (ruled by the Moon) was the symbol of duality, of pairs of opposites – anima and animus, yin and yang, but also of procreation.

three (Jupiter) was connected with the principle of Life, in Christianity with the Trinity (but in earlier religions with, for instance, Osiris, Isis and Horus); it represented past, present and future – the three elements of Time – understanding, harvest and plenty, fatherhood. It had a special relationship with the planet Jupiter, always important in numerology.

four (the Sun) was the number of the square, the cube, the cross, and stood for intellect, opposition, rebellion, explosion – it was a number much associated with alchemy.

five (Mercury) on the other hand was the number of versatility and adaptability, of criticism and analysis, of communication.

six (Venus) was associated with partnership, harmony, sex; ancient numerologists saw a very weak side to this number – even, when repeated, an evil one (hence "the beast 666", a title assumed by Aleister Crowley – which stemmed from the "Book of Revelations", suggesting that 666 was "the number of the beast or the number of man").

seven (the Moon) was the number of revolution, freedom, but also separation; many "sevens" affect our lives – seven prismatic colours, seven days of the week, the seven seals, the seven ages of man. . . It is a mystical number – the number of magic, much used in ceremonies of various kinds. Domestically, it was strongly associated with childbirth.

eight (Saturn) ruled old age, death, time and space: the Greeks called it the number of Justice, and it appears symbolically in many Books of the Old Testament – Noah was the eighth in descent from Adam, eight prophets descended from Rahab, there were eight sects of Pharisees, and so on; some occultists considered three eights (888) to be the number of Christ.

nine (Mars) was the number of protest, energy, courage – but could also be foolishly pigheaded.

ten stood for infinity, the unknowable, Divinity – but also restriction, imperfectibility – the infinitely great and the infinitely small.

To continue beyond the mystical **ten**, briefly, **eleven** represented compassion, universal love; **twelve**, universal understanding; **thirteen**, new beginnings; **fourteen**, natural forces, growth; **fifteen**, fate; **sixteen**, passion, anger; **seventeen**, immortality, understanding; **eighteen**, material things, opportunism; **nineteen**, pleasure, happiness; **twenty**, spirituality, faith; **twenty-one**, achievement, authority; **twenty-two**, vanity, self-aggrandisement.

In general, these numbers can be interpreted by looking at the astrological interpretations of the signs and planets associated with them. This is a useful shorthand for interpretation – but only the planets are used: the "sex" of the number is sometimes replaced by the words "negative" or "positive", where "negative" stands for female, "positive" for male – the terms, of course, are no more chauvinist in intention than in electricity! Where no sex is indicated the number is androgynous (Mercury is famously so, hence so is 5).

Letter	Number	Sex	Planet
A I J Q Y	1	M	Sun
B C K R	2	F	Moon
G L S	3		Jupiter
D M T	4	F	Sun
E N	5		Mercury
U V W	6		Venus
O X Z	7	M	Moon
H F P	8		
Th Ts Tz	9		Mars

Anyone with a rudimentary knowledge of astrology will spot some strange anomalies: the Moon rules two groups of letters, one masculine, the other feminine; two groups remain "unsexed" though governed by Mars and Venus, about whose sex there is no astrological doubt!

We give the above tables and attributions in case readers like to try out these ancient systems: today, it is more common for numerologists to number the Western alphabet in order, A being valued at one, counting on to I at nine, then J is one again, in a simple table (see p. 208). But as with magic in general, the rule is to make it one's own, and if the cabbalistic or astrological systems work for one, there is no reason not to use it.

TALISMANS & MAGICAL OBJECTS

Many spells take the form of spoken incantations, but some of the most potent spells are – and for proper effect must be – written down or inscribed on objects. There are several different types of magical object which are carried about the person either to give power or offer protection. Broadly speaking, a talisman is a source of power, an amulet offers protection, and a sigil is rather vaguely defined as either a seal or a "device with mysterious powers".

Through the ages, there have been some very strange and macabre examples of such magical devices. A piece of the hangman's rope by which some poor wretch had been suspended was considered to have very great power indeed as an instrument of natural magic, and the hangman could make a considerable amount of money by selling his rope piecemeal. But perhaps the most macabre of charms was the Hand of Glory – a hand chopped from the corpse of a hanged man, pickled in salt and nitre, then dried in the sun between the end of July and 15 August.

The Hand of Glory was used in various ways – in particular by burglars, for if you made a reversed sign of the cross with it over a sleeping person, his sleep became so profound that you could empty his house of valuables without the slightest risk of his waking. As late as 1831, burglars disturbed in a house at Loughcrew in Ireland were found in possession of such a hand. In some cases, secret rituals would be performed by the light of such a hand, its fingers lit to flame like torches.

The hand of a man who had been hanged was believed to have special efficacy, provided that it was acquired at the right season. Known as the Hand of Glory, it favoured the activities of malefactors.

Death seems to have sanctified such charms to magicians over the ages: pieces of shroud, coffin nails, dead men's fingernails or hair have all been prized for magical use. A coffin nail hammered into the footprint of a victim with a prayer to the Devil would dispose of your enemy without further ado; while the *Gremorium Verum*, a not very reputable eighteenth century grimoire, claimed that the head of a human corpse stuffed with black beans was an essential element of a spell designed to render the magician invisible.

In China, talismans represented calligraphic spells of Taoist magic, which were severely practical and intended to help men and women cope with everyday life – with making their living, profiting from a good harvest, finding the right partner, or ensuring the safety of their homes. Taoism, an ancient religion of China, relates to the whole principle of how nature works. Tao is the Way – but not a Way which involves following strict rules, as in so many other religions – on the contrary, Tao emphasizes relaxation, spontaneity, intuition; and calligraphic talismans and charms were designed to help one through life by positively intervening in it through the spirits inhabiting them.

These talismans were certainly in existence before AD 1190, for well over 1,000 of them are preserved in a book of that date, the *Taotsang*. They were prepared by Taoist priests, faith-healers, sorcerers – and the very spirit of the person who so carefully wrote – or rather drew – the words on them (for much of the point of them is in the beauty of their calligraphy) was transferred to the talisman itself. If you possessed such a talisman, you were able at any moment to communicate with the spirit that inhabited it.

Not only the calligraphy of the talisman was important, but the material on which it was inscribed and the very colour of the ink: yellow represented the centre, blue the east, red the south, white the west and black the north. Since red symbolized blood, a talisman written on red paper would protect a whole family from sickness. Peach wood might be used, special paper or silk, even gold or jade tablets. The Five-Colour talisman (worn as a protection against illness and plague) would probably be written on silk of various colours. The Red Spirit talisman, which prevented death or wounding in battle, bore writing in red cinnabar on yellow paper.

The preparation of a talismanic spell was extremely careful. An astrologer would first be consulted to fix the precise date and time for the ceremony, and the names of the people likely to be present were carefully scrutinized to ensure that the date and times of their birth did not conflict with the time fixed. This depended on the nature of the spirit to inhabit the talisman: that of Chung Kuei, the devil-catcher, could only be "caught" in a talisman prepared on his name-day – the fifth day of the fifth moon, between 11 a.m. and 1 p.m., the hour of *wu*.

We may find it difficult to understand just how reverently these talismans were regarded. They were not mere good luck charms; they were treated with the greatest respect. When you went to receive them from the priest who had prepared them, you were introduced to them as though to an honoured senior. You had to recite your name, bow deeply, and perhaps speak a specially prepared formula. The talisman could then be placed on your person, hung on the gate of your house, fastened on a door or roof-beam, set up at a crossroads or other public place, or perhaps even burned and the ashes swallowed.

As to the "language" used on the talismans, this was highly symbolic. There is a multitude of calligraphic symbols to be seen on them, and apart from their magical power they are beautiful works of art. Their inscriptions certainly always in some way represent the oneness of Heaven and Earth (in the earliest talismans thin lines represented Heaven, thick lines Earth); later, rounded writing represented *yin*, the female principle of the universe, and squarer writing *yang*, the male principle. Dots represented stars (the gods of the stars were efficient antagonists of evil spirits). They often carry drawings of gods (though usually only rough and emblematic – merely showing a hand or a foot, for instance) as well as the names of guardian spirits. Both gods and

A doublepage from Francis Barrett's
The Magus (**above**), published 1801,
contains a portrait, sigils and
description of Cassiel, the angel who
rules Saturday according to Barrett's
version. A design for the Great Seal
(**opposite**) of Dr Dee, the Elizabethan
scholar and magician, contains lettering
both in Roman script and in
"Enochian", the language of angels.

spirits were chosen from among the generals of the celestial armies.

Far from being examples of silly superstition, such talismans were regarded with at
least as much veneration as that shown by Christians for the relics of the saints. They
enabled man to be in constant touch with the spirits both inside and outside his body,
and helped him to participate in the perfect union of good and evil which, provided it
remained in balance, resulted in perpetual equilibrium.

Though important in the history of magic, talismans, sigils and amulets produced
in the West have never been regarded with quite the same reverence. Nevertheless,
if only a minority would now regard them as important sources of power and protection, there was never in the past any doubt that their influence was great, and the
care with which they were produced was meticulous.

One of the best literary sources on talismans and amulets is that extraordinary
book The Magus, or Celestial Intelligencer, which its author, Francis Barrett, described
when it was published in 1801 as "a complete system of occult philosophy".

It is indeed a remarkable (if, now, almost unreadable) book, which deals among
other matters with alchemy, numerology, the raising of spirits, the Cabbalah, and innumerable other aspects of magic. Barrett concentrates in particular on "images,
seals, rings, glasses" through which the powers of "the celestial bodies" can be channelled, and goes in great detail into the images of the planets which he found in
various ancient sources: using a talisman of Venus, for instance, "to obtain the love
of women", one would engrave on lapis lazuli, "at the hour of Venus":

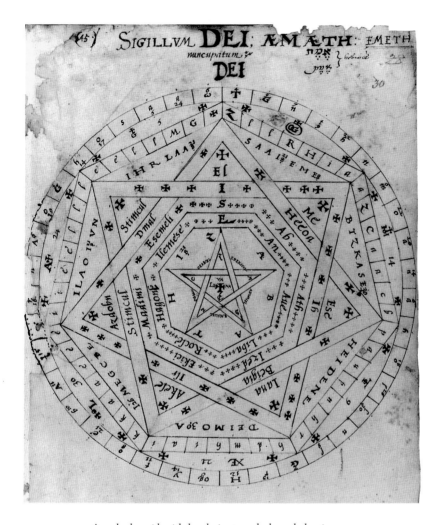

A naked maid with her hair spread abroad, having a looking-glass in her hand and a chain tied about her neck – and near her a handsome young man holding her with his left hand by the chain, but with his right hand doing up her hair, and both looking lovingly on one another – and about them is a little winged boy, holding a sword or dart.

Barrett also describes the twenty-eight "mansions of the Moon", and provides figures for each of them – for instance, the twenty-third, produced to injure an enemy, is "the image of a cat having a dog's head; this must be engraved on a piece of iron, and perfumed with dog's-hair taken from the head."

But the chief thrust of this part of Barrett's book is the preparation of magic seals or talismans of the sun and five planets. He is careful about the times when these must be prepared – "To make anyone fortunate, we make an image at that time in which the significator of life, the giver of life, or Hylech, the signs and planets" are fortunate. This means that an astrologer must advise a time when a planet considered to be specially apposite to the person commissioning the talisman is in a propitious position. Barrett gives technical advice on this – and on the proper time to prepare a talisman to injure an enemy, "to chase away certain animals (from any place) that are noxious to thee, or to attract the love of another person".

These instructions are extremely complicated, and someone without a training in astrology would find them impossible to follow. For instance, a talisman prepared "for gain" must be made when

> *the lord of the second house, which is the house of*
> *substance, [is] joined with the lord of the ascendant in*
> *a trine or sextile aspect and let there be a reception*
> *amongst them; thou shalt make fortunate the eleventh*
> *and the lord thereof, and the eighth; and if thou*
> *canst, put [the] part of fortune in the ascendant . . .*

A modern astrologer will find this difficult enough to follow; to someone without astrological knowledge it is mere gobbledegook. Fortunately, for those who wish to try making their own talismans, modern followers of the occult advise much less complex instructions, and we shall be dealing with these in Part Two of this book. The theory underlying such careful preparations is clear, however – a talisman made of material associated with a particular planet, and bearing its symbols, would be an effective channel for the *spiritus* or essential influence of that planet.

There has always been a clear association between the planets and certain substances. This is based on the theory of correspondences which has always had such importance in magic: the idea that everything in the universe is connected with everything else. So when it is seen that Mars has always been associated with iron, a talisman made of iron will be the most effective channel for its influence.

Talismans sometimes took the form of seals. It was with a seal that, according to Jewish occult writers, Solomon controlled an army of demons; and there have not unnaturally been attempts, from time to time, to reconstitute it – perhaps most notably by the Frenchman Alphonse Louis Constant (1810-75), better known as Eliphas Lévi, a remarkable experimenter who, if contemporary records are to be believed, had some notable and frightening successes in raising spirits.

Lévi's version of the Great Seal of Solomon does not seem to have been a practical success, though it incorporated many symbols frequently used in magic: notably the pentagram, the five-pointed star. When drawn with a single point at the top, this represents the spirit of man; with two points at the top, however – which become representations of the Devil's horns – it symbolizes the power of evil. Apart from which, the number associated with it – five – stands in magic for the power of nature. The pentagram was almost always drawn around the rim of the magic circle within which the magician was safe from opposing evil forces.

According to the *Key of Solomon* itself, the pentagram (sometimes called the pentacle) should be inscribed on virgin calfskin, prepared when the moon is rising in Virgo, and only on a Saturday or Tuesday night in an atmosphere scented with alum, cedar wood, aloes and resinous gum. Once made, the pentagram must be worn on the front of the magician's robe, just before his heart.

Almost as celebrated as the Great Seal is the *Amadel of Solomon*, instructions for the preparation of which were discovered in manuscript by Sayed Idries Shah and is printed in his *The Secret Lore of Magic* (1978). This talisman is made of wax, and is used in conjunction with a silver or gold seal; both must be very carefully prepared – angels can be raised and invited to help the magician.

The inscriptions on talismans are frequently very difficult to decipher, and often seem meaningless. But they were usually prepared according to very strict rules indeed (just as there were rules about the material on which the symbols or words were inscribed). It was important to know which symbols would raise which spirits – and there were plenty to choose from, even among those whose symbols were known to man: the grimoire called the *Lemegeton* or "Book of the Spirits", another book attributed to Solomon, listed 72 genies, 18 of them kings, 26 dukes, 15 marquises, 12 presidents and 5 earls. All these had names, and could be asked to help in particular cases. A number, including Dantalian, Gaap, Gomory and Beleth, would be useful in matters of love; Belial and Orias, among others, could help win promotion; Bune and Shax would bring riches, Bathin and Gaap help one to fly, Berith and Zagan were useful to alchemists, and Valefor to thieves.

The inscriptions on seals or talismans often embodied a sort of verbal magic, or at least trickery – such as the palindrome (a word or sentence which is unaltered if read backwards).

The palindrome was considered extremely powerful magic, and could be used for various purposes. The best-known one is probably the legend 'Sator arepo tenet opera rotas'.

S A T O R	*Written in bats' blood on a special parchment, and hidden under the threshold of a house, this palindrome charm compelled those who stepped over it to dance uncontrollably.*	C A S E D	*Worn round the neck, this talisman in palindrome form was believed to offer powerful protection against witches, who would be forced to leave the room.*
A R E P O		A Z O T E	
T E N E T		S O R O S	
O P E R A		E T O Z A	
R O T A S		D E S A C	

One early eighteenth century book (written by Master Aptolcater, Mage of Adrianople) prints one which can be used to instigate violence. Procuring a piece of lead, you scratched on it with an instrument of iron, the characters

Inscribed on metal, this talisman stirred up violent conflict if the wearer turned to each point of the compass and shouted the words "Roudmo!" and "Pharrua!" seven times. This would cause bystanders to fight viciously, but peace could be restored if the wearer uttered the word "Omdor!".	H D H D H
	I D I D I
	D H D H D
	D I D I D

PREPARING A SPELL

Given all that has been said, preparation is therefore an involved operation and has always been a vital part of any magic spell. If the spell was incorrectly prepared, the chances were that it would not work. Preparations for casting a spell had to be meticulous, and this included not only learning the correct words, but – if the spell was to be in written form – using the correct materials and choosing the correct time.

Just occasionally, a spell has come down to us "in clear", as they say of secret codes. In the British Museum, for instance, is an Egyptian papyrus which bears a spell to raise the dwarf god Bes, the god of dreams, also associated in particular with childbirth. This spell had to be written in a liquid composed of ordinary ink to which had been added mulberry juice, frankincense, myrrh, rain water, mercuric sulphide, and the juices of mugwort and vetch, the whole thickened with cow's and pigeon's blood. A sketch of Bes was then drawn on papyrus together with the question which the god was to answer, while the querant chanted the spell:

> Send the truthful seer out of the holy shrine, Lampsuter,
> Sumarta, Baribas, Dardalem, Iorlex, Anuth, Anuth, Salbana,
> Chambre, Breith . . . Come this very night.

The querant then wrapped around his left hand one end of a piece of black cloth consecrated to the goddess Isis, passed the other end around his back, and settled down to sleep. Bes would appear in his dreams, and answer his question.

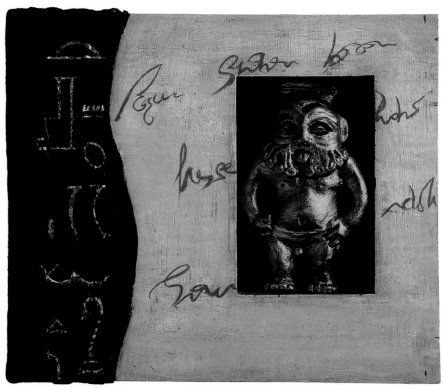

The ancient Egyptian god of dreams, Bes, often has a lion's head. Correctly invoked, he will answer the dreamer's questions.

FOLK CHARMS

The difference between the simplest of Albertus Magnus' spells and the "charms" which our grandmothers remembered and used is often negligible. Simple actions married to a simple spoken formula are easily memorable, and some are of the greatest antiquity. The Anglo-Saxons had a spell for destroying an enemy, which in one form or another survived for centuries. Originally, it ran:

> *May you be consumed as coal upon the hearth,*
> *May you shrink as dung upon a wall,*
> *And may you dry up as water in a pail.*
> *May you become as small as a linseed grain,*
> *And much smaller than the hip-bone of an itchmite,*
> *And may you become so small that you become nothing.*

In living memory, a German peasant cutting himself would mutter:

> *Sprach jungfrau Hille*   (Call on the maiden Hille and
> *blut stand stille*   blood shall stand still)

The charm dates from pagan times, Hille being the Valkyrie Hilda.

Among the most ancient and long-lived charms are the innumerable spells to do away with warts. Probably every reader could recite one. Take a beanshell, rub the wart with it, then bury it under an ash-tree with the words:

> *As this beanshell rots away*
> *So my wart shall soon decay.*

The same could be done with a little raw beef. In Ireland, when a funeral passed by, people would rub their warts and mutter, three times, "May these warts and this corpse pass away and never more return."

Sometimes village "wise women" devised their own spells. An old woman in Shropshire in the 1880s, for instance, used to take as many sprigs of elder as there were warts; with each sprig she touched a wart, saying, "Here's a wart", then touched a place where there was not one, saying, "But here's none". Then she buried the sprigs, and within a week or two the warts were gone.

Well, yes, of course, they might have gone anyway. Most warts, if left alone, will disappear. But medical authorities now agree that suggestion therapy, whether performed by a lay or medical person, is often successful.

If we do not wish to get caught up in the kind of magic which involves extremely complicated preparations and rites, the world of simple charms is available to us all. Perhaps happily, the most serious and even dangerous spells are for a number of reasons relatively inaccessible. But we can all, should we wish, try out the simplest charms. For example: "To see your lover", you must sit with an unmarried person of your own sex, by yourself, in complete silence, from midnight until one in the morning – then take as many hairs from your head as you are years old, and put them in a cloth with a piece of *herb paris* or "truelove" and, when the clock strikes one, burn each hair singly in the fire, with the words

> *I offer this my sacrifice*
> *To him/her most precious in my eyes;*
> *I charge thee now come forth to me*
> *That I this minute may thee see.*

Your lover will then appear, walk once round the room, and vanish. Your friend will see his or her lover, and not yours.

A simpler method may be to peel an onion, wrap it in a clean handkerchief, and put it under your pillow with the words

> *Good St Thomas, do me right*
> *And bring my love to me this night*
> *That I may look him in the face*
> *And in my arms may him embrace.*

Your lover will then appear in your dreams. Such charms may seem silly, but we know enough about dreams to recognize the fact that one can often invoke a dream one wishes to have; the unconscious is perfectly capable of producing the required image – perhaps even that of a lover on whom one's conscious thoughts have not yet fixed!

Not all traditional charms are as simple or as efficacious, of course. There is a spell to make one invisible, which is said to be infallible. At midnight on the Eve of St John the Baptist (June 23), one must take a plate and catch upon it some fern-seed as it falls – a simple matter, except for the stipulation that the fern must not be shaken; the seed must fall of its own accord. Take the seed and concealing it about your person, recite the words

> *Fall free, fall free*
> *Where none shall see,*
> *And give the same*
> *Great gift to me.*

You will then indeed become invisible, or so it is claimed. But the conditions are almost impossible to fulfil, which may be one reason why the efficacy of the spell has rarely been tested.

4.

Rites, rituals & superstitions

In order for a magician to make contact with the spirit world, and enlist its help, it is necessary not only for him to select and prepare the correct spells and objects, but also to perform the correct ritual. Without ritual to empower the spell, the spirits will not lend their aid and it will not work. The magician himself must also be mentally and physically prepared, and the ritual must take place in a favourable environment.

Rituals are a combination of complex elements which have developed over the centuries, as magicians discovered that magical spells or charms worked best when pronounced under very carefully organized circumstances. Belief in these rituals has been so strong that even in a sceptical society like ours they survive, albeit diminished to the level of superstition. For most superstitions are little everyday rituals which we perform, often almost unconsciously, to ward off danger and bring ourselves 'good luck'. We might hardly consider them to be magical, and yet like all magic rituals they are an attempt to change the nature of things by involving supernatural powers. In performing these minor rituals, we are linking ourselves to a long tradition of folk magic through the ages.

The idea of good or bad luck is never far from magic, though somewhat down the scale from "serious" magic. When people call a talisman a good luck charm, they are devaluing it somewhat, suggesting that to carry it is not a really earnest attempt to influence events, but merely a nod in the direction of hocus pocus. Here is the difference between a carefully contrived symbol of good fortune, made and consecrated at the proper time, and a rabbit's foot – and often the difference between magic and mere superstition.

The idea of luck – that good or bad luck can arise from something we may do or fail

*The elements of ritual (**opposite**) provide the context within which magic can operate. Magicians use colour, movement and dance to create suitable conditions, and stress the importance of timing.*

to do, carry or fail to carry – is a sort of bulwark against the apparent formlessness of life; it is a sign that we recognize that much in life is irrational, and that we are power-less to do anything other than continually expect the unexpected and hope that it does not harm us too much. In some civilizations, the gods have been dangerous, always seeming to have something nasty in mind with which to test or torment mere mortals. Not surprising, then, that we devise ways in which we can perhaps safeguard ourselves. The Greek philosopher Theophrastus (c.372-c.287 BC) in his book of *Characters* sketched the typically superstitious man:

> [He] is one who will wash his hands at the fountain, sprinkle himself at the temple font, put a bit of laurel leaf into his mouth before going about for the day. If a weasel runs across his path, he will not continue his walk until someone else has passed along the road, or until he has thrown three stones across it. When he sees a serpent in the house, if it be a red snake he will immediately build a shrine on the spot. He will pour oil from his flask on the smooth stones at the crossroads as he passes, and will fall to his knees and worship them before he leaves.

The means the Greeks and Romans used to attempt to prophesy the future were more to do with superstition than magic (the line between them is so thin as sometimes to vanish altogether), though many of their superstitious amulets and gestures were rooted in their own religious beliefs. Christianity later took the view that any re-cognition of gods other than the Christian God was improper, and that therefore any idea that "luck" could somehow be summoned in assistance was a heresy. Through-out the last 2,000 years a long list of heretical beliefs grew, including confidence in magic cures, spells and charms.

Yet Christianity adopted many superstitions, and proved quite unable to root out the history of illogical and irrational beliefs which had grown up over thousands of years. The internecine warfare between different sects of Christians also had its effect, for the beliefs of the Catholics (in relics, mortifications, holy water) were con-sidered dangerous superstitions by Protestants. Voltaire said the Protestants regarded "almost all the rites of the Roman church as a superstitious dementia".

No one would deny that superstition and the idea of luck are still very much alive at the end of the 20th century, and may even be taken seriously. During the Gulf War fighter pilots were just as prone to carry good luck charms as were the archers at the battle of Agincourt, and the slogans painted on their aircraft echoed those scratched on the blades of ancient swords.

In our everyday lives we still pay tribute to superstition, guiltily throwing salt over our shoulders, avoiding walking under a ladder (or, just as culpably, carefully walking under one to "prove" that we are not superstitious!). We excuse our lack of success in life by "bad luck", just as, if we are modest, we may attribute our achievements or prosperity to "good luck".

The superstitions of Western Europe are legion, as one might expect, for they re-flect centuries of unquestioning belief in the power of witchcraft, spirits and demons. It would require a huge volume to collate them all. Here, however, are a few of the most common or curious.

Getting out of bed on the right side This is a superstition which dates at least from the sixteenth century; but there is no trace of any explanation of how the idea rose. The "wrong" side of the bed seems to be the one you don't normally use. It used to be said that getting out of bed backwards meant good luck – but only if you did it without thinking.

Telling the news to the bees It is a very ancient convention that if you keep bees, any piece of important news should be told to them before anyone else in the family hears about it. This especially refers to news of a death.

Blacksmiths and horseshoes Blacksmiths were often regarded as "lucky" in country districts, and were said to be able to cure sick children. The association between horseshoes and good luck is immemorial. It is especially lucky (if, these days, uncommon) to find a horseshoe; but acquiring one from a smith and nailing it to your front door is the next best thing. Reginald Scot (c.1538-99) in his *Discoverie of Witchcraft* (1584) wrote:

> To prevent and cure all mischiefs wrought by these
> charms and witchcrafts . . . nail a horse shoe at the
> inside of the outmost threshold of your house, and so
> you shall be sure no witch shall have power to enter
> . . . You shall find that rule observed in many
> country houses.

The heel or open part of the shoe should always be pointing upwards, or there will be trouble. As recently as 1983, a small boy in Essex explained to Iona Opie, co-author of *A Dictionary of Superstitions* (1989) that if you hang the shoe with the heel pointing downwards "the luck drips out".

Bleeding The traditional notion of dropping a key down the back of the neck to stop a nosebleed seems to have no medical foundation, any more than the many quasi-religious charms which were supposed to staunch a flow of blood.

The Sortes Virgilianae Stemming from the use of a book by the Roman author Virgil, this is the term for the judgement offered by opening a book at random and stabbing the page (eyes closed) with a pin or a finger. The words indicated are supposed to have a bearing on the query or problem in mind. The earliest recorded report of this practice in England dates from AD 379. The Bible was very often used for the purpose, and so were the works of Homer. The method has something in common with the ancient Chinese *I Ching*, where the verse is chosen according to the falling of some tossed yarrow sticks or coins.

Carrying the bride over the threshold A custom dating at least from Roman times, the origin of this is uncertain. One notion is that it shows how unwilling the bride is to lose her virginity: she must be forcibly carried into her man's house! Another is that the household is sacred, and the man (the owner and governor of it) must first carry his partner into it if she is to live there happily.

Throwing the bride's bouquet The idea of the bride throwing her bouquet into the crowd as she leaves her wedding reception, and the girl (man?) who catches it being next to marry, seems to have originated in America sometime in the early 1900s. But the explanation of the custom is unknown. In Lancashire, the idea was for the bridesmaid to throw the bride's shoe: the man it hit would be next to wed.

"Something borrowed, something blue . . ." A bride should wear "something old, something new, something borrowed, something blue". The rhyme seems only to be about a century old, but the ideas it enshrines are older. While wearing splendid new clothes for a wedding, the idea of also wearing something borrowed from a happily married woman sprang up centuries ago. The idea of "something old" seems more recent – on the eve of her marriage a bride was sometimes dressed by her bridesmaids in her oldest nightgown. The colour blue has been associated with a happy married life for at least 600 years (it is mentioned in Chaucer).

Cats Cats have been associated with magic since ancient Egyptian times, and the number of superstitions attached to them are legion. Ordinary cat behaviour is often associated with weather forecasting: a cat washing itself is apparently an infallible sign of rain; if it sits with its back to the fire there will be a frost; if it rushes illogically about, a storm. Like the behaviour of cows (who when they lie down are said to fore-tell rain) this may be based on observation of some sort. Less readily explained is the belief that if a cat washes behind its ears, one will soon see a stranger.

Cruel recipes for curing sickness (especially in children) involve roasting cats' hearts or heads; more innocently, the tail of a black cat rubbed across a running or itching eye will certainly cure it. The belief that a black cat running across your path brings good luck is precisely balanced by the contention that it will bring ill luck. The idea that cats have nine lives may relate to their ability to land on their paws, but the number nine also has numerological significance.

Carrying a caul To be "born with a caul" (a portion of amniotic sac sometimes covering a child's head at birth) is believed to be lucky. The superstition usually refers to the caul being twisted in some way about the baby's head, in which case good luck will follow. To carry one's own caul into battle was to be magically protected from injury or death – and the belief died hard: cauls were advertised for sale as recently as during World War I, when they were particularly sought after by sailors, as they had always had the reputation of protecting one against drowning.

Clocks It is an ancient and tenacious idea that a clock will often stop at the moment of a death in the family. Only one or two coincidences of this sort would of course be sufficient to start the superstition off, but by the nineteenth century it had certainly gained currency through Western Europe and America.

Four-leaved clover This may be a case of relative rarity making the leaf a lucky one – the tradition has existed in England for at least 500 years. It was said that if one carried a fourleaved clover, one could see fairies invisible to others.

Coal, lucky In the nineteenth century in England, most burglars were found by the police to be carrying a piece of coal "for luck". It was also believed that to "turn over" a piece of coal on a fire was a way of invoking the protection of good spirits against evil ones.

Touching the corpse Fear and horror of death has provoked many superstitions, among which is the belief that to touch a dead body prevents one from dreaming about the deceased; if a tear falls on any part of a dead person, its ghost will walk; a corpse unburied over a weekend, or at the beginning of a new year, brings bad luck; a hand cut from a corpse can be used for all kinds of curative purposes, especially warts and other growths; if a corpse is carried to burial through a field, nothing will subsequently grow well there.

Crossing your fingers Crossing your fingers for luck may seem a very ancient superstition; yet the oldest reference to it so far found appears to date only from 1912. Crossing the legs for luck, however, has been current for at least 300 years.

Crows Two crows seen together bring good luck; more than two, ill luck. This is an old superstition – and the crow itself has been thought an unlucky bird in many cultures for at least 2,000 years.

The donkey's cross A hair from the "cross" on a donkey's back is supposed to cure whooping cough.

Elder trees The elder, the curse of the gardener, has attracted many superstitions: it is unlucky to cut down an elder tree, and one should apologize even when pruning it. Burning green elder is very unlucky, and bad luck is associated with anything made from elder wood; though it is said to cure saddle sores and be a protection against lightning.

Fire Fire is so important to man that it is unsurprising that many superstitions attach to it: if a fire burns low, it is a sign of difficulty and dissent; if it burns on one side it can be taken for the sign of a wedding, a move away from a neighbourhood, or a death; if still burning the following morning, it presages illness; sparks mean news. It is very unlucky to let a fire go out on New Year's Eve – or to allow anyone to "borrow" a fire (i.e. start their fire with a flame from yours). You should not spit into a fire, for fear of bad luck – or poke anyone else's fire unless you have known them for at least seven years.

First-footing The first person to enter your house in the New Year suggests the sort of luck you will have during the ensuing twelve months. Ideally, the first-footer should be dark, and male.

Friday This is for some reason considered an unlucky day (because of the alleged association with the crucifixion?). It is unlucky to begin a venture on a Friday, to set out on a journey, go courting, get married or move houses on that day. Friday the 13th is especially unlucky.

Hair Hair has always been considered strong magic – witches casting an evil spell needed a piece of hair from the victim to make it truly efficacious. If a bird picks up a piece of your hair and uses it to build a nest, the consequences can be extremely unpleasant for you. It is very unlucky to burn your hair, though sometimes this was done as part of a spell to raise a vision of a possible lover.

Hangman's rope Hangmen traditionally made a considerable profit by selling pieces of the rope used at an execution: among other things, such a talisman could cure headaches or the ague. A piece of a suicide's rope provides marvellous protection against bad fortune.

Rabbit's foot A rabbit's or hare's foot traditionally brings good luck, protects one from witches, and is an efficacious charm against the gout or rheumatism.

Heather The idea that heather is lucky may spring from Queen Victoria who gave her prospective daughter-in-law, Princess Alexandra, a piece of heather allegedly picked by the late Prince Consort, saying that it would bring good luck. The news, being reported, inspired many people to copy the idea.

Walking under a ladder This superstition seems to have arisen during the eighteenth century, and may be connected with Tyburn Tree (the famous London gallows) and the ladders used there. It was believed that anyone who walked under a ladder would remain unmarried for at least a year. Spitting three times after passing beneath a ladder may alleviate bad luck.

Unlucky magpie Magpies have sometimes been considered as unlucky as crows, presaging evil events.

Seven years bad luck The idea that breaking a mirror brings bad luck may be associated with the notion that magicians commonly use magic mirrors to raise spirits. The magic in mirrors has often been stressed, from Biblical days onward ("now we see through a glass, darkly"). The extent of the bad luck which follows a breakage varies: it can be death, or merely seven years' misfortune. Mirrors were often covered with a cloth in a sick room, lest the invalid should see his or her face.

Mistletoe Kissing under the mistletoe may be pleasant, and may be lucky; originally, activity of another sort, taking place under a mistletoe bough, made it certain that the lady would conceive.

The moon Superstitions cluster around the cycle of the waxing and waning Moon: enterprises started under a waxing moon are more likely to be successful; vegetables and other crops should be harvested under a waning moon; it is unlucky to point at the moon (it offends the Old Man who lives in it); the light of the full moon causes or exacerbates madness; to sleep in moonlight is dangerous to the health. On the other hand its light washes away warts. You should always bow to the new moon when you first see it; if you see it first on your right-hand side, that means good luck. Seeing it first through glass is unlucky.

A roasted mouse This will infallibly cure whooping cough.

Fingernails and toenails The clippings have much the same uses as hair (see above). It is very unlucky to cut your nails while on shipboard – or on a Friday or Sunday. They should always be clipped on a Tuesday.

The robin Oddly, ill-luck has always been attached to the robin – perhaps because of the blood-like red breast. It is thought of as a harbinger of death, and believed to tap three times on the window of a fatally sick person. It has nevertheless often been considered "sacred", and not to be injured.

Salt This essential, like fire, has collected many superstitions about it from ancient times (when it was often deemed holy). It is unlucky to spill it, unless one throws a pinch over one's shoulder afterwards. It can be a protection against witches or evil spirits; it is dangerous to lend it; throwing a handful on to the fire will disarm a witch; strewn on a corpse it will prevent the ghost from walking.

Sneezing It has been suggested that a sneeze was one of the first signs of the plague, which was why we cry, "God bless you!". But a similar cry went up when someone sneezed in ancient Rome. It seems now just to be an excuse to exchange a friendly word or greeting. An old rhyme suggests:

> *Sneeze on a Monday, you sneeze for danger;*
> *Sneeze on a Tuesday, you'll kiss a stranger;*
> *Sneeze on a Wednesday, 'tis for a letter –*
> *Sneeze on a Thursday, something better.*
> *Sneeze on a Friday, sneeze for sorrow,*
> *Sneeze on Saturday, see your love tomorrow.*
> *Sneeze on a Sunday, the Devil will have you!*

The spider This creature has always been considered a bringer of good luck – and indeed money; it is very unlucky to kill one. The Roman natural historian Pliny suggested that a spider's web should be applied to a wound – a recipe which has some basis in medicine; webs have also been said to cure whooping cough.

Spitting Until our own cleanly day, spitting was common and regarded as an extremely useful prophylactic against witches, spells, forged coins, and magic in general. The Romans spat in the street to nullify the effect of seeing a deformed person or a beggar; spitting could also cure sickness. Spitting at a known witch would prevent her from injuring you.

Umbrellas The idea that it is unlucky to open an umbrella in the house is a relatively modern one – and certainly cannot be older than the umbrella itself – the middle of the eighteenth century in Europe (though it was known in ancient China). Held over one's head indoors, an open umbrella presages death.

We accept that superstitions are rituals – what can they tell us about magic rituals themselves? They tell us what is important to ritual: colour, movement, timing and the relationships between events that bring certain things about.

ELEMENTS OF RITUAL

Movement and ceremony have, like sound and symbols, been associated with magic since before written records began. We have no means of knowing when man first began to believe that magical spells or charms worked best when summoned under very carefully organized circumstances, but the evidence of cave paintings suggests it must have been at least 20,000 years ago.

Ritual itself is of course important to us in everyday life: when we shake hands we are performing a little ritual of friendship; when we make a rude gesture to a driver who cuts in, we are performing a ritual which is a sort of curse; and so on. These rituals often involve not only words, but sounds, movement, even dress. Early cave paintings suggest that dancing was associated with magical rites very early in our history; and of course it is now recognized that rhythmic movement together with percussive sound can put us into a state of mind which makes us highly receptive to the kind of emotional experience which is often linked with magical or indeed religious experience. The chanting and rhythmic shouting and clapping which accompany religious services in both primitive Africa and urbanized North America bear witness to the importance of this kind of behaviour in producing an atmosphere conducive to worship of one kind or another. Both witch-doctors and priests have always worn specially designed clothing – at Star Carr in England an antlered skull has been

"The Sorcerer", a paleolithic painting of a masked and antlered man from a cave in the Pyrenees.

found drilled with holes which enabled it to be worn as a head dress; and a prehistoric cave at Les Trois Frères in France has on its wall a brilliantly lively drawing of a shaman or witch-doctor dressed in antlers and skins.

Ritual, traditional movement and gesture sanctified by age and custom (whether in wild primitive dancing or the carefully choreographed motions of respect and veneration of the Roman Catholic Mass) have a tremendous significance in magic and religion. Music, whether that of simple native drums, the tuned cymbals of the East, or the instrumental compositions of the most sophisticated Western composers, has often been crucial to such ceremonies; and the shaman's drum is probably his most important attribute in summoning denizens of the spirit world.

Particular rites with particular purposes – specific ceremonies composed of special movements, objects and colours, sometimes extremely complex – have developed in all societies, sometimes associated with a specific national religion, but very often with "rogue" religions of one kind or another. "Sacred" objects associated with rites of one kind or another have been discovered at ancient religious sites in many parts of the world; and of course have often been found, and still are to be found as central to religious and magical experience, whether the crosses associated with Christianity, the phallic symbols or lingams now most common in Eastern religions, or the strange symbols of traditional witchcraft, many of which may derive from "lost religions."

And, of course, in the realm of what most people call magic rather than religion, a multitude of ceremonies, some simple, some elaborate, some touching, some bestial, have been devised for multifarious reasons. Here, we look at some of the actions and ceremonies, the atmospheres and contexts which have accompanied the use of magic, to cure sickness, raise spirits, or cast spells.

The ritual of Candomblé, at Rio in Brazil, recalls the practices of West Africans brought to South America as slaves. It combines elements of the old African religion with Catholicism in a heady mixture, climaxing with an invocation to Iemanja, Queen of the sea.

COLOUR

At the simplest level, colours have often been used – not so much to focus magical powers, it seems, as to put the would-be magician into the proper mood. There are indications that colour was used in medical and religious rites in ancient Egypt, Chaldea, India and China – and psychiatrists today accept, even if they do not fully understand, that colour can affect us deeply. We all know this, indeed – most of us "feel good" when dressed in one colour rather than another, and though fashion consultants have recently attempted to show that this is because one is an "autumn" person or a "summer" person, the truth is more likely to be that one's feelings about particular colours stem from deep within one's own psyche.

On the other hand, these feelings are sometimes clearly linked with the collective unconscious, and sometimes with entirely understandable superstition – in the past century or two, in western Europe, green has on the whole been considered unlucky

*The heavenly bodies and the zodiac (**opposite**) were closely studied by magicians in planning the content and timing of their rituals.*

because of its association with the "little people" of the countryside, who were at best mischievous and at worst positively malicious. More recently, green has been associated with safety ("the green light") as well as with the green movement (there, the association is with vegetation) while red has come to represent danger – but also sex (can it be coincidence that areas of cities where prostitution is concentrated are known as "red light" districts?). In many countries blue is associated with safety, law and order and the police forces.

Particular colours have been associated with particular planets, and with some spirits (they should be used in preparing certain talismans, for instance, and certainly – as we have seen – in the preparation of Tao talismans). But perhaps it is in Tantric yoga that the magic of colour is most thoroughly used.

As in so many areas of magic, science is beginning to dig up some reasons for ancient beliefs. Tantra has always taught that red is associated with sexual activity; it is now known that red light stimulates the male reproductive organs and increases muscular tension. It also, incidentally, has an effect on the mind: students working in red light have shown greater skill at solving mathematical problems than when set to work in ordinary light. Tests show other effects, too: in red light, objects seem heavier than usual – under green light, they seem lighter; red and yellow light appear to make time pass more slowly, while green and blue light accelerate its effect.

Magicians must have sensed some at least of these properties when they associated particular colours with the effects they wished to obtain from various spells or ceremonies; here is another example of magic beginning to "come true", at least in the sense of an experimental basis being discovered for traditional beliefs.

In Tantric yoga, there are exercises which specifically use the *idea* of colour: students are taught, while sitting in full sunlight and using the breath control so vital to yoga, to imagine their bodies soaked first in red, then in yellow, then in blue, and finally in white light – this concentrates *prana*, "the seven-rayed emanation from the sun", and is of inestimable value.

But is this magic? Not for the first time, we are unsure. After all, the effects of sun- and moon-light have long been recognized, and the former (though recently its dangers have been emphasized) is used to treat depression. In China, men have for centuries been advised to sunbathe naked to increase their *yang*, while nude moon-bathing for women increases their *yin*. Light as well as colour is clearly of importance.

THE PLANETS

Not only the sun and moon but also the planets have always had a close association with magical practices. No doubt the association originally sprung from the belief that the planets themselves, those mysterious bodies seen wandering about the sky in front of the fixed pattern of the stars, were in fact gods. Though it seems to be the case that some of the attributes of the planets, the effects they have on human character, can now be demonstrated empirically, there can be no doubt at all that in the early centuries of astrology belief in their magical powers was compulsively strong. Hence the conviction that those powers had a crucial part to play in almost all areas of magic, from the summoning of spirits to the making of talismans.

The "correspondences" of the planets were of vital importance, and were laid down in the earliest times. From remote ages certain metals, stones, colours and body organs were connected with particular planets (Uranus, Neptune and Pluto of course had not yet been discovered):

Sun	gold	topaz	yellow	the heart	fatherhood
Moon	silver	crystal	white	breasts	motherhood
Mercury	mercury	agate	grey	lungs	intellect
Venus	copper	emerald	green	kidneys	love
Mars	iron	ruby	red	sex organs	aggression
Jupiter	tin	sapphire	blue	liver	religion, philosophy
Saturn	lead	onyx	black	bones	old age

Though we can only conjecture, it seems fairly clear how these associations or correspondences occurred: the silver white of the Moon and its effects on the female cycle strongly suggest its sphere of influence, while the warm golden glow of the Sun, the fiery red of Mars and the relatively quick, darting motions of Mercury seem equally to suggest the influence they might have on humankind. The association between various gemstones and the zodiac signs almost seems to have developed separately, for the two often clash when one looks at the planet and sign relationships. As one might expect, the planetary list seems to rely primarily on colour rather than anything else.

Priests, shamans and magicians were quick to attempt to make use of planetary forces, in every way that suggested itself. Priests in Egypt timed certain ceremonies by the movements of the planets, and there is a strong suggestion that certain stone circles and megalithic structures such as Stonehenge in England, or Newgrange in Ireland, were astronomical "clocks" built in order to enable ceremonies to be properly timed. Shamans or magicians attempting a spell to assist a woman eager to become pregnant would wear white robes, hang their working environment with white, use a wand tipped with silver, and perform their ceremonies at the full moon.

There was an early association with medicine too: herbs and plants used to treat particular illnesses were plucked when the planet governing them was in a propitious position – Nicholas Culpeper's *Herbal*, first published in the 1640s, and perhaps the most important book in the history of European herbalism, is specific on the point. Aconite is "under the government of Saturn", agaric "under the government of Mercury in the sign of Leo", all-heal "under the dominion of Mars, hot, biting and choleric, and remedies what evils Mars afflicts the body of a man with . . .".

The planet and zodiac signs associated with the relevant part of the body having been consulted, the proper herb would be picked at the proper time, and administered at the most propitious hour.

Again, the extent to which all this can be called "magic" is debatable – Culpeper would have called it a combination of empirical knowledge and common sense.

A pentagram designed by Eliphas Lévi, the influential 19th-century magician, contains elements of the Cabballah combined with the ritual magic of the grimoires. Lévi was not afraid to reorganize traditional magic rituals in a way that reflected his own personality.

TIMING

Talismans, certainly magical in origin and intention, were made at keenly specified times and of the astrologically proper metals, and featured the glyphs and signs associated with the planets in question. Apart from this, they had to be sanctified or consecrated with the proper rites. In comparatively recent times the Order of the Golden Dawn, the magical society active at the end of the last century, diligently researched the ceremonies considered proper, using colours, perfumes, the names of the gods of Egypt, Greece, Rome, and of Jewish and Christian spirits.

The researchers had to delve into a vast library of books and manuscripts, cluttered with instructions about times, places, circumstances and actions. The most complex probably had to do with times – and these were so complicated that even the author of that most influential magic textbook, *The Key of Solomon*, tried to simplify them. But first, there were other considerations. You must, for instance, decide which planet to use in your magical experiment.

This, at least, was relatively easy. Solomon (if we accept for the moment that he was indeed the author of his *Key*) gave a list: naturally, you consulted Venus in cases of love, but also of friends, journeys and pleasure; Mars in cases of war, but also of disharmony, death, and "to obtain fortune in army affairs". Saturn helped you with building, business, property, fruit and vegetables, and "gaining familiar spirits to speak to one in one's sleep". Jupiter dealt with riches and physical health; the Sun with money; Mercury with art and science, the discovery of a thief, and eloquence; and the Moon with travel, reconciliation and messengers. (There were of course many other possibilities.)

Now came the importance of the hours associated with the planets. You chose those governed by Saturn, Mars or the Moon to raise spirits; those associated with

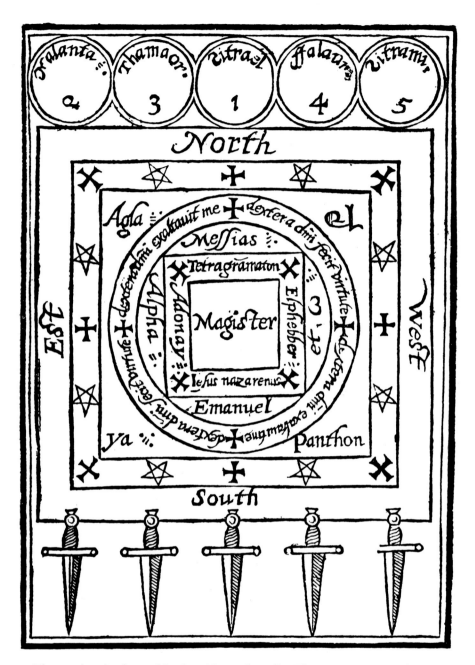

This ritual circle, designed by the 16th-century scholar-magician Reginald Scot, was specifically intended to bring about the "inclosing of a spirit in christall". The names written in the five circles at top signify the "five infernall kings", whose assistance was essential.

Mercury for setting up practical jokes or detecting thefts; Mars' hours were best to "raise souls from the inferno", and Jupiter's or the Sun's for "works of invisibility, love and well-being, and all unusual experiments".

The positions of the planets (and in astrology the Sun and Moon are for convenience called planets) must also be considered – which in the days before computers made planetary positions easily available, took some doing.

PREPARATIONS

Once all this had been accomplished, the subtle and often dangerous rites themselves could begin. Most crucial – and this is stressed again and again in magical textbooks – was the physical and spiritual state of the magician. Fasting was in general a prerequisite (and, interestingly, fasting has been used in every civilization by witch-doctors and shamans of all kinds, to raise them to the properly intense state of spirituality necessary for the exhibition of their powers). The extent of the fasting varied, but frequently could be as long as six or eight days and sometimes longer. Solomon suggests that complete abstinence from food might be undertaken for only three days – though the magician should abstain from "all unworldly and sensual things" for at least nine days. He should be scrupulously clean and properly robed, preferably in silk – though linen would do – woven by a virgin girl. On his robes and shoes certain signs should be woven, and magical marks should be inscribed with a pen dedicated to this purpose.

Next came the setting up of the proper environment: the decking out of the room to be used in the proper colours, and the collection of the proper accessories. Then, as crucial as the preparation – and this is also stressed in every textbook of magic – came the necessary protection which would allow the magician to deal with evil or potentially evil spirits without his soul being captured by them. Pentacles must be drawn, under very special conditions (in particular colours on special parchment at a specific time); and then the all-important magic circle must be set out.

There are various surviving instructions for this vital exercise, some involving black stones, some recommending that the circle be described in flour spilled on the ground, some involving metal. Solomon again is most particular: the circle must be inscribed using a rope nine feet in length, and the best place to lay it down is in a graveyard. Inside this circle, another circle one foot less in diameter should be drawn (while reciting from the Psalms).

Between the two circles and the east and south points of the compass, I H V H (the Tetragrammaton) must be inscribed, and the Names of Power (AHIH, ALVIN and ALH) in the other three sections. A double square must then be drawn to enclose the circle, the corners directed towards the four compass points, and at those corners should be four more circles one foot in diameter, and within them written four more names: ADNI, AGLA, IH and AL. The Tetragrammaton is again written between the squares.

SPIRIT-RAISING RITUALS

When a fire has been made on which perfumes can be burned, and the magician is safely esconced within the circle, the spells can be recited with which it is hoped to raise the spirits proper to the occasion. Even with the protection of the pentacles, the special clothing, and above all the magic circle, this could be a chancy business. But that it was performed in all seriousness cannot be doubted. One of the most dependable accounts of an attempt at spirit-raising has come down to us not from a magician but a layman, the artist Benvenuto Cellini (1500-71). In his autobiography Cellini recalls that when he was in Rome he got into conversation with a renegade Sicilian priest who offered to demonstrate spirit-raising. The two of them, with Cellini's friend Vincenzio Romoli and an accomplice of the priest, went off to the Colosseum one night, where the priest inscribed the necessary protective circle, lit a fire, burned perfumes, and spent an hour in various incantations.

Cellini reported that several legions of spirits appeared, till the Colosseum was filled with them. Urged by the priest to ask something of them, the artist invited them to reunite him with a Sicilian girlfriend who had recently deserted him.

There was no reply that night, but a few nights later the party returned to the

Colosseum, Cellini bringing at the priest's request "a virgin boy" apparently necessary for success. When the priest had again made his preparations and recited incantations in Hebrew, Latin and Greek, Cellini, his friend Romoli, and another friend, Agnolo Gaddi, saw the place filled with "demons". The boy also saw them, and was terrified, though protected by a pentacle which Cellini held over him. The ensuing furore included demons leaping and shrieking among flames, the small boy crying that four giants had appeared to attack them, and Cellini's friend Agnolo becoming so terrified that "he shat himself". Nevertheless, in spite of these distractions the spirits were heard to promise Cellini that he would find himself with his girlfriend Angelica, within a month.

Some time later, Cellini to his surprise, came across Angelica in an inn near Naples, where

> *she gave me an unimaginably passionate welcome. I stayed with her from about two hours before nightfall till the next morning, tasting greater pleasures than I had ever known before. And while I was enjoying myself so delightfully I remembered that the month expired that very day, as the demons in the necromancer's circle had promised me. So anyone who meddles with spirits should bear in mind what tremendous risks I ran.*

We must take this account as it comes, of course; but Cellini's manuscript was not written for publication – and indeed was not published until the eighteenth century; there seems no reason why he should have been romancing. He must surely, to put the circumstance at its lowest, have thought he saw what he recorded. And his witnesses? Alas, they left no record.

There are other accounts of attempts to raise spirits, and by no means all of them from remote centuries. The most dramatic of nineteenth-century records concerns the Frenchman Alphonse Louis Constant (1810-75), the son of a shoemaker who used the Hebrew version of his name and became well known as Eliphas Lévi. Educated for the priesthood, he was expelled from his seminary for unorthodox views, and took up with semi-professional magicians. In time, he became a highly professional student of the occult and published a number of books on the subject, including *The History of Magic* (1860). He was an impressive man, handsome and well-mannered, with a great talent for oration – though also with a lack of interest in the merits of soap and water, and an enthusiasm for food and wine which was sufficiently robustly expressed to upset some of the more ethereal of his admirers, according to some contemporary observers.

Eliphas Levi (1810-75)

The account he leaves (in his book *Transcendental Magic*) of a ritual over which he presided in London in 1854 is one of the most convincing we have of such an occasion, at least in terms of detail, minutely and painstakingly described. It took place under the aegis of the poet, diplomat and statesman Bulwer Lytton (1831-91), whom Lévi met in Paris when the former was consul there. Through an intermediary (for Lévi at first declined to give any kind of magical demonstration for the members of Lytton's occult club) the diplomat provided the somewhat impoverished magician with the magic vestments, rare books and instruments he needed in order to "converse with the dead".

The experiment took place in a carefully designed room, evidently furnished at some expense. The cabinet prepared for the evocation, writes Lévi in his *Transcendental Magic*,

*was situated in a turret; it contained four concave
mirrors and a species of altar having a white marble
top, encircled by a chain of magnetized iron. The
Sign of the Pentagram was graven and gilded on the
white marble surface; it was inscribed also in various
colours upon a new white lambskin stretched beneath
the altar. In the middle of the marble table there was
a small copper chafing-dish containing charcoal of
alder and laurel wood; another chafing-dish was set
before me on a tripod.*

Lévi, who had fasted for seven days (and gone without meat for twenty-one) entered
the room clad in white, crowned with vervain leaves, with a sword in one hand and
the "Book of the Ritual" in the other, and prepared to call up the ghost of Apollonius, the first century Greek magician and philosopher.

Like all good magicians, Lévi is less than specific about the ceremony which followed, except that he tells us that he used the book of *Magic Philosophy* of Patricius,
which itself was based on the writings of Zoroaster and Hermes Trismegistus.

After the final incantation, the flames he had lit flickered and rose, and the huge
figure of a man momentarily appeared before the altar. After further incantations,
from safe within his magic circle, Lévi saw the figure of a man

*wrapped from head to foot in a species of shroud,
which seemed more grey than white. He was lean,
melancholy and beardless, and did not altogether
correspond to my preconceived notion of Appollonius.
I experienced an abnormally cold sensation, and
when I endeavoured to question the phantom I could
not articulate a syllable. I therefore placed my hand
upon the Sign of the Pentagram, and pointed the
sword at the figure, commanding it mentally to obey
and not alarm me, in virtue of the said sign. The
form thereupon became vague, and suddenly
disappeared . . .*

Lévi after a while managed to raise the spirit a second time, but

*experienced such an intense weakness in all my limbs,
and a swooning sensation came so quickly over me,
that I made two steps to sit down, whereupon I fell
into a profound lethargy, accompanied by dreams, of
which I had only a confused recollection when I came
again to myself.*

The spectre would answer specific questions only by the word *Death!*, which Lévi
found somewhat unhelpful; but on a further two occasions he got better results, including the revelation of "two cabbalistic secrets which might change, in a short
space of time, the foundations and laws of society at large, if they came to be known
generally". Alas, they have not.

Lévi's account of his experiences is strangely convincing, and it is difficult not to
accept at least that he believed he was reporting them accurately. Sadly, though he

*Flickering flames illuminate "sky-clad"
figures dancing to the sound of lute and
horn: an artist's reconstruction of a
spirit-raising ritual.*

had invited two other people to be present during the experiments, they lost their nerve and asked to be excused.

It is interesting that educated people in the middle of the last century could accept such an experiment as permissible. But then, the public attitude to magic has always been equivocal, even that of the church. Of course during the witch-craze it was taken for granted that converse with the Devil, or devils, was evil. On the other hand, built into the rites and spells used by magicians to raise spirits were often prayers and psalms of a conventional nature; though it is sometimes far from clear whether the spirits they hoped to raise were good or evil, angels or devils.

Solomon in the famous *Book of the Spirits* lists a number of personalities on whom one could call for various purposes. A number of sorcerers made use of his work, which indeed was for centuries a standard textbook. By consulting it, a magician knew that if a spirit was needed to find hidden treasure, Purson was the proper one; that Valefor would be helpful in curing illness, Bathin would bear off an enemy, and that Ose (who appeared as a handsome leopard) could cause insanity.

Witches dance around the horned god in this 18th-century engraving, encapsulating most of the age's prejudices.

THE DARKER SIDE OF RITUAL

All magical rituals involved an appeal to supernatural powers. However, a clear distinction should be made between rituals which were relatively innocuous (though might involve the magician in some personal danger), and those which were positively unpleasant, being pornographic, sadistic or even murderous.

The Black Mass itself is a relatively modern rite, dating back only to the seventeenth century, although black (meaning evil) magic had been in existence for many centuries before then.

A lot of nonsense has been written and talked about such ceremonies, usually inaccurately described by the catch-all phrase "the Black Mass", and ignorantly associated with witchcraft. The modern media are specially culpable, connecting almost any incident involving sadistic torture or murder with "black magic". The notorious case in the United States in 1969, when Charles Manson, a mad semi-literate sadist, was involved in a multiple murder, was widely associated with witchcraft, when he was really the leader of a weird and entirely self-inspired Satanist cult.

The fact that traditional witches, and indeed magicians, have scarcely ever been

associated with what is called "black magic" does not mean of course that it does not exist – that people have not from time to time tried to take hold of the supposed powers of "black" forces; and because those forces themselves are assumed to stem from evil and to take their power from it, evil means – involving the infliction of obscenity, pain and death on animals and even humans – have sometimes been used in attempts to command them.

The Black Mass itself – to dispose first of the most famous black ritual – was virtually unheard of until King Louis XIV of France (1638-1715) set up an enquiry into reports that certain secret societies were for various purposes using poison on a wide scale. The enquiry indeed uncovered a large ring of poisoners.

Either because of the vivid imaginations of those concerned, or because there really was a scandal, the members began to hear of priests saying Mass over the bodies of naked girls and joining in orgies of ritual copulation which involved the murder of infants and the drinking of their blood, and other loathsome practices. These blasphemous masses may have been called black simply because of their black nature – though black clothing is said to have been worn.

The king eventually came to the conclusion, as more and more elaborate descriptions of wickedness were produced, that the whole thing was the product of overheated minds, and in 1682 put a stop to his enquiry and ended all prosecutions.

If anything like these Black Masses went on, one must suspect that rather than being serious attempts to raise the Devil or his ministers, they were really cases of outrageous insults to the Christian religion offered by people who were opposed to it and wished to parody it by producing ceremonies or rites totally opposite in nature to, for instance, the

Gilles de Retz's castle of Tiffauges, France, was supposedly the site of black magic rituals and the murder of children.

ritual of Holy Communion. If the word "fun" is certainly too lighthearted to apply to such goings-on, it might perhaps be applied to the less vicious proceedings of the Hellfire Club in England in the next century, when Sir Francis Dashwood got together a number of friends (including Benjamin Franklin) to enjoy food, drink and wenching in the grounds of his house in Buckinghamshire.

Dashwood and his friends were accused of blasphemy and obscenity, but were far from being magicians, and it is doubtful whether they believed in the possibility of magic any more than they believed in God or the Devil. Rationalists to a man, they simply believed in having a good time, and by all means did so. That the devout among Dashwood's neighbours believed they practised black magic only sharpened their amusement and increased their pleasure.

The history of the world has produced plenty of men and women who believe in the power of evil with the same passion with which others embrace good; and in the realms of magic this has resulted in patterns of pure horror. If one had to fix on the patron saint of "black magic" in its traditional sense, it would be difficult to dismiss the claims of Gilles de Laval, Baron de Retz (1404-40).

De Retz, a rich and ambitious Breton, seems to have believed completely that magic could help him in this course. Retiring from his position as Marshal of France at the age of 25 after an admirable career as a soldier (he played a notable part in the campaign against England led by Joan of Arc), he began to experiment in black magic with the aid of a disreputable Italian priest called Prelati.

After about eight years, the regular disappearance of young children in whichever area of France de Retz happened to be staying drew attention to his practices, and in 1440 the bishop of Nantes began to collate a dossier of information about him. Among the stories he recorded was that of de Retz's attempt to raise a spirit called Baron, reputed to dispense great wealth to those he favoured. De Retz attempted to flatter Baron by offering him a child's heart, eyes and blood, contained in a crystal glass. The bishop was keenly interested, and when the Duke of Brittany reported the disappearance of over 150 children, de Retz was arrested and tried simultaneously for heresy and murder by church and civil courts.

De Retz's confession was obtained by torture, but there seems little doubt that he was guilty of at least some of the enormities ascribed to him. He was hanged and burned, though Prelati escaped. Reading the confessions, and what the court made of them, one must wonder to what extent de Retz's activities were the result of a genuine belief in magic and to what extent he was simply engaging in sexual pleasure. There was no doubt an element of both; and we will never know which was the stronger in the activities of de Retz.

This is the case where most "black magic" is concerned and sexual activity is involved – which is in most cases. For orgasm, providing one of the keenest and most explosive of human experiences, has always been considered a source of magical power. Puritans have naturally regarded the sexual practices of so-called "black magic" with a certain amount of horror, often for psychological reasons. But it is certainly the case that there can be confusion when one considers certain rites which at the very least contain unattractive elements.

Some Tantric rituals involved meditation while sitting among decomposing corpses or inside small stockades built of human skulls; and it was not uncommon for the sexual unions which are the culmination of several Tantric rites to be practised in the same place.

The object of such rituals, real or imaginary, was to strengthen the magical power which would fuel the *chakras*, the seven centres of psychical energy embedded in the body. After much practice, the Tantric could bring into play the supreme energy of the *kundalini*, a sort of psychic snake inhabiting the lowest *chakra* in the body. This, while powerful enough to destroy the body, can rise throughout the passages of the spirit and bring about complete ecstasy, oneness with the universe – the state which the alchemists desired, of golden fusion with all things.

5.

The story of witchcraft

The dictionary defines witchcraft as "the use of magic or sorcery", but to most of us the word calls up a more precise image. The archetypal witch, as described in countless fairytales and children's books, was an old woman, living alone in her cottage, usually with a cat (to which there certainly might have been more than met the eye). She would cure your warts, give you a charm against toothache, or put a spell on a neighbour's cattle, should he have upset her in some way.

The witches of old Europe seem always to have had a close relationship with nature and the seasons. They may have something in common with the shamans of traditional societies (sometimes known in Africa as witch doctors), whose influence on the community arose from an ability to achieve communion with the spirit world. The power to fly, for instance, and the use of animals in ritual, as familiars or "allies", as well as in the preparation of potions and medicinal ointments, are characteristics shared by both shamans and witches. However, shamans do not usually assemble in ritual meetings, whereas European witches have often worked in covens or Wiccas, pooling their energies when possible.

In traditional societies, the shaman is seen as someone whose contact with the spirit world enables him (or sometimes her) to play an important role in the community. In Australia, for instance, the aboriginal *kurdaitcha* has been successful both in curing disease and in inflicting it through cursing the unfortunate victim. In Zaire, the *mganga* or *mufumu* acts not only as doctor but as conjurer, herbalist and magician, expelling evil spirits, foretelling the future and bringing rain. In Brazil, the Tupi people employ a *pajé* to search for the missing souls of dead relatives, and after his own death he may become a jaguar spirit. But remarkable though these people are, they are scarcely witches in our meaning of the word.

*A traditional witch (**opposite**) would have been little more than the village healer and spell-caster, deriving her lore* | *from pre-Christian beliefs. The medieval witch-hunt frenzy drastically changed this role.*

A Siberian shaman's costume (**above**),
with accessories, contrasts with an
American shaman's cave (**below**).

In fact, witches tended to be village healers as well as spell-makers who worked in response to requests from local people. Despite the lurid fantasies of clerics, few people seriously suspected them of killing children in order to drink their blood, or having intercourse with the Devil at wild nocturnal meetings.

Witches' knowledge and apparent power inevitably isolated them from the rest of the community, and, whilst they were often respected, they were also feared. This fear grew to a peak of hysteria during the medieval witch-hunts, when witches were universally believed to be in league with the Devil, and many innocent people were tortured and executed.

Historically, a witch was someone who used sympathetic magic (which works on the principle of like affecting like), and had – or claimed to have – the power to fly, to heal or harm, to cast spells, change his or her form, communicate with animals and raise spirits. Sex, the universal life force, was believed to be an important part of their rituals. Traditionally, witches met and held festivals at certain important times of the

African witch-doctors share some of the attributes of traditional Western witches. The Dinka witch from Sudan (**left**) stands within a protective circle to receive a spirit. A Cameroon witch-doctor (**far left**), wears a costume that identifies him with his leopard "ally", recalling the cat familiars of many European witches.

year: Halloween (the day before All Saints' Day), Candlemas, May Eve (the day before May Day), Midsummer's Eve – all of which are the dates of key religious festivals of pre-Christian cultures, notably the Celts', and clearly indicate a pagan survival of the "old religion". Witches prefer to call these festivals by their old Celtic names: Samhain (year's end) for the day before All Saints' (November 1), Imbolc for Candlemas (February 1), Beltane for May Eve. These, with the August festival of Lammas, relate to the four "quarter-days" of the year, marking a division of time that probably goes back to the Bronze Age.

It seems likely that most activities were harmless: the witches invoked the spirits of earth and air, of whatever gods were apposite to their purposes – and in early centuries these almost certainly included the pagan gods, whether of Greece and Rome or of Northern Europe. The life force being so powerful, it is very likely that sex in one form or another was used to strengthen the force of the powers witches believed they were releasing.

But that takes us nowhere: what, actually, is a witch, and what does (s)he do? First and foremost it should be asserted firmly that most witches have been concerned with natural and sympathetic magic, and apart from a little ill-tempered cursing of an unpleasant neighbour's cows or ducks, have been on the side of good rather than evil; they have not on the whole been Satanists, have rejected the Black Mass, have very rarely attempted to invoke evil spirits, and have more often engaged in helping, healing and blessing than in cursing.

So whence their bad reputation? Is there really smoke without fire? Were the many

thousands of people tortured and burned during the witch craze as innocent as babes? The sad answer is, yes, many (perhaps most) of them were.

The idea of witchcraft is indivisible from the idea of spell-casting, which itself is based on the idea (now once more fashionable) that the known universe is one – that no force exists without being connected to all other forces, and that therefore one force can be made to affect another force. So in the earliest ages it was believed that by performing a particular ceremony corn could be encouraged to grow more richly; by performing another, a woman could be made fertile; by damaging a wax model of someone, the person it represented could be injured. Spells were based largely on sympathetic magic; hence the "poppets" or miniature portraits of men or women at whom a spell was directed.

*Witches of every culture have made images of those they wish to affect. These images may contain something from the victim's body, such as hair or nail clippings. Thus the image takes on the identity of the targeted person. Known as "poppets" (**below left** and **right**) by Western witches, they are used by African witch-doctors (**opposite left** and **centre**) and practitioners of voodoo in Haiti (**opposite right**). The basic features of voodoo were brought by slaves from West Africa, especially Dahomey, where the name originated. From left to right they represent: A European in Benin, West Africa; a "juju man" in Southwest Cameroon; a voodoo doll from Haiti, with a pin in its heart; an American curse-doll, speared to a tree with the victim's name attached; and an English poppet in a miniature coffin.*

We are still closer to the idea of sorcery than we may sometimes imagine. We smile, perhaps, at the idea of the aborigine witch-doctor who invokes rain by performing a special dance accompanied by a particular form of chanting. But one still hears prayers for rain from Western pulpits – the main differences being the absence of dancing, a rather different form of words, and a technique of supplication rather than invocation. It was the opinion of the Inquisition that if a witch caused rain – by dipping a twig in water and sprinkling the water in the air – she could not be praised for breaking a drought, but should be condemned because while it was God, and not she, who made the rain, she had brought it forth as a result of a pact with the Devil. A witch was, from the start, a loser.

A witch-doctor from Zimbabwe, southern Africa, in full regalia, poses for the camera with an assortment of implements, including a gourd used for preparing magic potions.

The word "witch" can be traced back to the Indo-European *weik*, which is vaguely connected with magic, and produced such derivatives as the Old Norse *wik* (holy) and the Old English *wigly* (sorcery), *wicca* "witch" (a term still used by many modern witches) and *wiccian* "to work sorcery" or "bewitch".

Witches have always been outsiders, which is perhaps the chief reason why in every age they have been regarded with suspicion, particularly by the religious and social establishment. At one end of the scale they have been horrendously persecuted; at the other, it was still possible in an English village not too long ago to hear it said of almost any lonely old woman who for some reason eschewed society, "Ah – she's an old witch."

A witch-doctor from southern Africa prepares to cast a spell. As with Western witches, self-discipline and careful preparation are essential for successful results.

WITCHES IN WESTERN SOCIETY

We have seen how witchcraft in its common forms – stemming from a desire to pro-cure advantage (a good harvest, a handsome husband) or to revenge oneself for injury – arose among the earliest tribes of primitive man, and was performed among them much as it was until very recently performed throughout Africa and South America or among the aborigines of Australia. Indeed, it still survives in apparently similar forms in parts of the world so far only partially influenced by "civilization".

Among the Babylonians and Sumerians, at the dawn of history, witches began to acquire their reputation as workers of evil: failing to understand the mysterious spread of disease or the nature of infection, men assumed that most illnesses were the result of a curse. Similarly, it was in a sense comforting to believe that if one had worked hard from dawn to dusk, but the result had been blighted crops or a barren herd, some witch must have been working against one.

The magic employed by the witches of Babylon, Sumeria and Mesopotamia was relatively simple: there was great reliance on sympathetic magic, especially image-making. Small pottery figurines have been found which were clearly made as repre-sentations of living humans on whom the witches wished to have an influence; some of them damaged by fire, for after reciting a spell over an image it was frequently des-troyed by burning. An even simpler method of gaining control over a victim was to spit on the ground in front of him as he walked; if he trod on the spittle, he im-mediately fell under the influence of the spitter (though one could escape by using one or two specially devised spells which would counter the influence).

Though in early centuries witches were often confused with spirits – such dange-rous spirits as the *lilim*, or children of the monstrous demon, Lilith, or the *Lamia*, a vampire who drained Greek and Roman men of their sexual vigour – it is surprising how quickly the conventional idea of a witch became standard, and surprising, too, how universal that idea was. Both in primitive African societies and in the great civilizations of Greece and Rome it was the case that suspected witches were usually lonely old women, said to be capable of flying and of changing their shape, given to eating children, often accompanied by an animal "familiar" (frequently a cat), and meeting in groups at night to enjoy orgies of one sort or another.

Some of these ideas are remarkably tenacious: the idea that witches can fly, for in-stance, appears in almost every civilization and almost every age – one of the earliest extant pictures of a witch, from Mexico, shows her in a traditional pointed hat and mounted on a broomstick. (Broomsticks are still used, symbolically, in modern Wicca ceremonies.) In the tenth century it was claimed, in Europe, that "wicked women in the dead of night ride upon certain beasts with the pagan goddess Diana, and fly over vast tracts of country".

It was in classical times that the association between witchcraft and demonology began; the Greeks believed that all witches worked closely with demons (though these could be good as well as evil). Similarly the idea that witches' meetings were orgiastic probably sprang from Greece, reflecting perfectly accurate reports of the feasts of Dionysus, which involved dancing, chanting and enthusiastic sexual activity. In Rome, such feasts became Bacchanalia (Bacchus being the Latin name for Dionysus), and descriptions of them (before they were outlawed in 186 BC) are re-markably similar to accounts of what went on at sabbats or witch-meetings.

It may be that a degree of envy, as well as fear, attached itself to growing con-demnation of witches (who had formerly been regarded as useful, if somewhat dange-rous). The stronger the powers of these outsiders were rumoured to be, the more they were persecuted, especially by governments and heads of governments. Most Roman emperors, for instance, clearly felt that their influence was too strong for comfort – and not only outlawed them but, as so often taking things to extremes, made life ex-tremely uncomfortable for anyone who seemed more than usually superstitious. Time was when a person could be executed for a simple gesture such as touching wood for

*Goya's etching (**opposite**) portrays two witches in combat.*

luck or placing his hand on his breast and repeating the seven Greek vowels, though this was only the equivalent of taking an alkaseltzer, for it was supposedly a cure for stomach discomfort.

The early Christians suffered from similar persecution, as had the followers of Dionysus before them; when the former religion spread throughout the western world, the Christians, once themselves outsiders, began to suspect that witchcraft might be improper – though they were at first reasonably tolerant, for during the early Middle Ages an old woman found mumbling an incantation was only ordered to do penance for three years.

WITCHES AND CHRISTIANITY

In the West a witch was anyone with "strange powers" which did not derive from the church or its offices. If these "powers" were not derived from God, it was believed they must come straight from the Devil. No third way was possible.

A witch, through simple existence, challenged orthodoxy and God Himself. This view was a pressure within society waiting for some outlet. For many years the church and witches coexisted, if uneasily.

The growth of the Christian concept of the world as a battleground between God and the Devil made the position of witches more difficult. Sorcerers – and the word steadily became more and more generally a synonym for witches – communicated with the Devil or devils, whom they could instruct to perform evil deeds. Christians invoked angels and saints, who were in the same sense spirits, but who could not be instructed but merely supplicated. They had no domination over men – while a devil, once one had asked a favour, had one within his power. Those who dealt with

*Christianity could not tolerate the "old religion" of witchcraft. In Giotto's painting (**opposite**) St Francis of Assisi empowers a monk to cast out devils from Arezzo, Italy. At Bamberg, Germany (**above**), the bishop's palace was the command point where medieval witch-hunts were organized.*

evil, it was said, were themselves evil. An edict of AD 900 condemned those women who, "led astray by the Devil, believed themselves capable of riding out at night, mounted on strange beasts" (though it is worth noting that word "believed" – it seems that at first witches were accused of having their minds perverted by the Devil, rather than of actually being able to fly).

Gradually the attitude of the church authorities hardened. It is at this point – at the beginning of the so-called witch craze of the two centuries after about 1450 – that we first find extensive accounts of what witches allegedly did. We hear of witches making pacts with the Devil, repudiating Christ, taking part in orgies, desecrating the cross and the Host, murdering infants and drinking their blood . . .

In repeating descriptions of the behaviour of witches one must always remember that these were largely recorded by people preoccupied with making them as repugnant as possible, or were drawn from unwilling tongues by the most awful tortures. It would be a brave person who would say that enormities never took place, but it seems likely that infanticide was in fact extremely rare, while recorded incidences of the actual appearance of the Devil are at least equally rare. This does not mean that a number of people did not believe that they had come to an arrangement with the Devil, which would naturally have involved the repudiation of Christianity and very probably desecration of one kind and another. And while Dionysus may have been replaced by Lucifer, erotic temptation remained quite as urgent.

Tales of nocturnal orgies were common in the Middle Ages from as early as 1022, when one of the first executions for heresy took place at Orleans. There, it was alleged, heretics met at night in underground caverns to which they welcomed evil spirits, on whose appearance all lights were extinguished, and at a cry of "Mix it!" each person present seized the nearest human being – brother, sister, parent – and had sex with them. Any children born as a result were sacrificed.

Burning with slow fire formed part of the torture of a suspected witch, Herr Lutzen of Rheinbach, Germany, in 1631. Not all those arrested during the witch craze were females.

Relatively speedily, other alleged incidents of witches' meetings or Wiccas emerged, and became common coinage at witches' trials throughout Europe. It was claimed that an introduction to the Wicca invariably involved the killing of an infant (one was invited to bring one to the meeting for the purpose) and the adoration of the male leader of the Wicca (who might or might not be the Devil himself) by kissing his buttocks. As a result one would be given unusual powers, taught spells and shown rites, given the recipe for ointment which would enable one to fly . . .

Some or all of the worst enormities may or may not have happened; many of those forced under torture to confess to them no doubt did so because they had heard reports of such goings on – others, perhaps themselves deluded by hysteria, may have believed they had taken part in such ceremonies; a few may actually have done so. The latter had no difficulty in rationalizing behaviour which others would find disgusting. There had always been some heretics who argued that it was only by experiencing the greatest depths to which man could sink that he could rise to the highest heights. The body was evil, sex was disgusting – therefore one should degrade oneself by performing the most obscene acts that could be contrived – and if one did so for theological reasons, one would be forgiven. There was also the comforting argument that man's law did not apply to someone possessed by the Holy Spirit – while if one was not possessed by that Spirit, one was damned anyway, and a few extra sins were of no consequence.

The increased importance of the Devil, during the Middle Ages, had a great effect on the public conception of witchcraft. Not only was it believed that a pact between an individual witch and the Devil was at the bottom of all serious witchcraft, but sexual intercourse with him – or at least his earthly representative – was almost taken for granted. It is difficult not to suspect that the reputation of some covens for seducing beautiful young virgins may not have had a basis in the knowledge that its leader had a virtual *droit de seigneur*.

While the word "witch" is used for both male and female (a "warlock" means a traitor or miscreant) it is certainly the case that most witches were female. Occasionally there were cases of homosexual intercourse between men and the Devil; but for the most part, he preferred women – not only because of his sexual proclivities, but because they were more stupid and easily led astray. We need not blame the Devil himself for being specially chauvinist; the view was that of the church in general, and is enshrined in that terrible document, the *Malleus Maleficarum* or *Hammer of Witchcraft*, a textbook for witch-finders first printed in 1486. Women, it explains, are emotionally immoderate and immature, insatiable in carnality, more credulous and talkative and less intelligent than men, usually liars, and being weaker than men more prone to revenge themselves (on, say, an erring husband or negligent lover) by witchcraft than by bodily strength. "The guilt of women is proven," say the authors firmly. Happily for the witch-finders, it is also the case that in the Middle Ages there was for one reason or another a large population of unmarried women, some of them desperate in poverty, half-crazed by loneliness, and natural targets for suspicion.

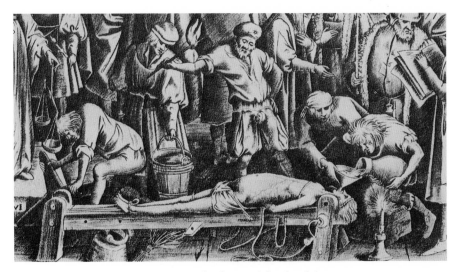

Water torture is the theme of this detail from a print by H. Cock. Entitled "Justice", it is taken from a 1559 drawing by Breughel the Elder.

WITCH-HUNTS AND PERSECUTION

It was at the end of the Middle Ages that anti-witch hysteria took hold of Europe, reaching its height between 1560 and 1660. The church was involved, most notably through the printing and wide distribution of *Malleus Maleficarum*, which went into 13 editions in 30 years, and was published not only with the approval of Pope Innocent VIII, but with a preface written by him – a Bull in which he states as fact:

> *Many persons of both sexes . . . have abandoned themselves to devils, incubi and succubi, and by their incantations, spells, conjurations and other accursed charms and crafts, enormities and horrid offences, have slain infants yet in the mother's womb, as also the offspring of cattle, have blasted the produce of the earth, the grapes of the vine, the fruits of trees, nay, men and women, beasts of burthen, herd-beasts, as well as animals of other kinds, vineyards, orchards, meadows, pastureland, corn, wheat and all other cereals; these wretches furthermore afflict and torment men*

and women, beasts of burthen, herd-beasts, as well as animals of other kinds, with terrible and piteous pains and sore diseases, both internal and external; they hinder men from performing the sexual act and women from conceiving, whence husbands cannot know their wives nor wives receive their husbands . . . and at the instigation of the Enemy of Mankind they do not shrink from committing and perpetrating the foulest abominations and filthiest excesses to the deadly peril of their own souls, whereby they outrage the Divine Majesty and are a cause of scandal and danger to very many.

The *Malleus*, apart from its historical interest, is fascinating for the information it provides about what its authors (Jacobus Sprenger and Henricus Institoris) believed constituted witchcraft. We cannot tell how they gathered their information but clearly most of it came from "ordinary people", credulous, prejudiced, frightened and sometimes vicious.

It was very easy, they concluded, to be caught in the Devil's snare: one had only to ask a casual favour of a witch – would she cure one's cow of a distemper, for instance, or help find a husband? The favour would be granted, but a condition might be that one should spit on the ground during the ceremony of Holy Communion – enough to place one under the Devil's influence; next one would find oneself willy-nilly whisked off to a Wicca where a formal pledge of allegiance would be demanded, sealed by the application of ointment made from the bones and limbs of murdered children and by copulation with Satan or his representative.

The *Malleus* describes how after being anointed with flying ointment witches were "taken up into the air, by day or by night, visibly or invisibly". Recipes for "flying ointment" survive, and though they sometimes contain obscene ingredients, they also often include aconite, belladonna, poppy seed and hemlock – all of which are toxic, and rubbed into the skin can produce hallucinations. Was this responsible for the apparently genuine belief, on the part of some witches, that they could fly? Such a talent would not have surprised most people in the Middle Ages. In some parts of Europe until comparatively recently there had been a strong belief in flying gods – the Valkyries,

for instance, and Wotan's horsemen; while after all, many saints were known to levitate. Angels flew, devils flew – so why not witches?

Ointments, generally made up from the most repulsive ingredients imaginable, are often mentioned as part of witchcraft ceremonial; but these have always been used in "magic" ceremonies of one sort and another – as part of fertility rites, for instance, when they were often massaged into the body by a member of the opposite sex in a manner calculated to be sexually arousing. The Greeks used ointment in this way, for the simple pleasure of it; from that to a belief that increased pleasure meant an increased chance of conception, is a short step.

The *Malleus* provides several anecdotes which supported the theory that witches and necromancers were often conveyed from place to place in a somewhat unconventional manner. There was for instance the citizen of Freising, Germany (his name is not given), who claimed that he had been carried by the Devil to remote corners of the earth – and a priest of Oberdorf confirmed this, for he had seen it happen: and the man "was borne on high with arms stretched out, shouting but not whimpering".

The *Malleus* is particularly informative about witchcraft and sexuality – partly perhaps because of the church's general reservations about the enjoyment of sex, but partly no doubt to fuel men's fear of the wicked women whose aims might include an intention "to impede and prevent the power of procreation", or even "to deprive man of his virile member". After a careful description of how a spirit can copulate with a human, the authors hedge their bets by remarking that though such spirits are often invisible, witches have often enough been seen lying naked upon the ground, "and it has been clear from the disposition of their limbs . . . as also from the agitation of their legs and thighs, that all invisibly to the bystanders they have been copulating with Devils . . . " The description will be familiar to those who remember the reports of the occurrences at the convent at Loudun, two centuries later. It was also reported that many men had seen devils "swiving their wives, although they have thought that they were not devils but men".

With *Malleus Maleficarum* in hand, amateur and professional witch-finders ranged through Europe in the Middle Ages determined to root out the evil women so endangering man and his church. It would be interesting to know how many of the hundreds of thousands of men and women who now suffered had any real interest in

*e power to fly, often on a
omstick (**left**) was an ability widely
ributed to witches, male and female,
ing the witch-hunt hysteria of the
h and 17th centuries. It may relate
a far older shamanistic tradition of
ht, as does the use of animals as
miliars". Copulation with the Devil
goat form (**right**) can be traced
k to the Greek god Dionysus.
duction and emasculation of males
r right) may also have its roots in
ssical folklore.*

witchcraft, let alone engaged in even the most innocent recital of traditional spells or charms. But the witch-finders had no difficulty in finding people to burn, arresting them on the slightest suspicion, often because some neighbour spoke ill of them.

The first step was to search the suspect for the Devil's marks. Almost anything would do – a strangely shaped birthmark, or perhaps any birthmark at all; a mole or a scar, anything that could be mistaken for a supernumerary teat at which the Devil could have been given suck . . . Then, the suspect might be given one of several tests. Witches were supposed to have insensitive areas of the body; so a woman might be pricked all over with a sharp instrument, in an attempt to find a spot where the pain was less than elsewhere. There are of course such areas of the body; it was a great mistake however not to simulate pain. Or the swimming test might be more convenient: bound hand and foot, the supposed witch would be thrown into deep water. If she sank, she was innocent (though, often, also dead); if she floated, or even strove to float, she was guilty, hauled out, and put to the torture.

Torture was strictly necessary, first for the victims' own good – for the only way a witch's immortal soul could be saved was by recanting before being burned at the stake. But it was almost equally important to extract information from her. How was she recruited? Which particular devil had been her lover? How had she made a pact with him? Just what happened at the sabbats where she and other witches met? What spells had she cast on others? And – very important – what were the names of the other witches in her coven?

Anyone who reached the torture chamber was necessarily guilty, and any means could be used upon her to obtain the information the witch-finder needed – most particularly, the names of other witches. In desperation, the poor tortured creatures always talked – sometimes paying off old scores by naming their enemies, sometimes in desperation involving aunts, nieces, cousins, even husbands and children.

The tortures used have been so often described that it is almost superfluous to speak of them; but the history of the world has produced no greater horrors, even in the torture chambers of the Gestapo or Saddam Hussein. Innocent men and women were subjected to the thumbscrew and the strappado, the rack and the water torture, the iron spike and the bath of boiling liquid.

There is an argument that the ceremonies most commonly written about from the twelfth century onwards are the invention of the witch-finders – it is they who set down what they supposed happened when covens met, they who reported how and why the Devil was roused.

But minutes of these meetings were not kept; there is no equivalent of the Book of Common Prayer – no written text for sabbats; the truth is that we cannot know what ceremonies took place. Some prayers or curses were no doubt employed; but most of them seem to have been used in private. As to what actually went on when witches were gathered together, we can only guess – and there may well have been very considerable variations between country and country, even village and village.

Sometimes they made these reports up; sometimes they extracted them under torture. On 24 July, 1628, for instance, Johannes Junius, of Bamberg, wrote to his daughter on the eve of his execution. He had confessed to worshipping the Devil, performing evil magic acts, seeing innocent neighbours at witches' sabbats. He confessed to being ordered by the Devil to kill his children, but said he had deceived him by killing a horse instead. This had not satisfied his torturers, so he further confessed to having desecrated the sacred Host.

"Whoever comes into the witches' prison must be tortured until he invents something out of his head," wrote the unfortunate Junius, scarcely able to hold a pen after the thumbscrews had been applied.

The evidence in such cases is not real evidence. And it is only a little safer to turn to the *Malleus Maleficarum*, based to some extent on confessions. But this at least enshrines what two distinguished members of the church and the Holy Inquisition believed about witches and their activities.

Encounters with the Devil dominated the medieval obsession with witchcraft.

The witches of Lancashire, England, held feasts with devils, according to 17th-century accounts by witch-finders.

They certainly believed that the main purpose of witchcraft was, by making a pact with the Devil, to make use of his power – sometimes in order to enchant others, sometimes simply for the sake of power, or for revenge, sometimes it seems for pure enjoyment; for what reason should witches wish to fly except for the joy of it? (though doubtless sometimes for the convenience).

In a masculine-dominated society it is not surprising that witches were supposed to be adept at attacking the virility of men – preventing erection, for instance, by various spells involving wax models, potions of herbs, or cocks' testicles. In some cases, the genitals were entirely removed by magic, leaving the body completely smooth – and there were cases in which a witch would "collect male organs in great numbers, as many as 20 or 30 members together, and put them in a bird's nest or shut them up in a box, wherein they move themselves like living members, and eat oats and corn, as has been seen by many and is common report." In fact, the *Malleus* tells us, there was a well-established case of a man who had lost his penis in an accident, and consulting a witch was told to climb a certain tree, when he found a nest in which there were several phalluses; told to choose one, he naturally chose the largest – but was told he could not have it, because it belonged to the parish priest.

Witches could change men into beasts; could possess the body and mind of a person; could cause "any bodily infirmity, even leprosy or epilepsy". Sickness was usually caused by "making a waxen image or some such thing . . . [or] making an image of someone by pouring molten lead into water". But the job could be done simply by a witch breathing into one's face. Epilepsy was caused by using "eggs which have been buried with dead bodies, especially the dead bodies of witches".

Just as at other times of persecution – when a word of protest might result in the protester finding himself on the rack – the hysteria continued unabated, except for a few honourable exceptions such as the Belgian doctor Johann Weyer (1516-88), who in 1563 wrote a book (*De Praestigiis Daemonum et Incantationibus ac Veneficiis*) in which he claimed that most old women accused of witchcraft were merely deluded and mentally disturbed. This infuriated the clergy, and Weyer was instantly himself accused of being a witch, escaping prosecution only because he was protected by the powerful Duke of Julich, in Dusseldorf, to whom he was physician.

Queen Elizabeth I of England (1533-1603) had an interest in the occult, regularly consulting the scholar-magician Dr John Dee. Nevertheless, it was in Elizabeth's reign that the first recorded English witch trial occurred, in Chelmsford, under a statute signed by the queen which recommended the death penalty for witches, enchanters and sorcerers (though since the crime was prosecuted under civil rather than church law, witches in England were at least hanged rather than burned).

At Chelmsford, Elizabeth Francis confessed to having learned witchcraft from her grandmother, and was eventually hanged. So were several other women accused at Essex, in 1579. But there was no idea that society was seriously endangered by witchcraft – except possibly in Scotland, where King James VI (1566-1625) was much impressed by the confessions of an elderly woman called Agnes Sampson, who after being kept without sleep for some days and nights, fixed to a wall with an iron instrument forced into her mouth with spikes pressed against her tongue and cheeks, confessed to sailing to North Berwick with several friends, in a sieve, kissing the Devil's buttocks when he appeared in a church there, and plotting to kill the king.

When James, a Calvinist, came to the throne of England in 1603 as James I, he brought with him a serious conviction that witches were prevalent in his land, and authorized a version of the Bible in which certain terms were carefully mistranslated in order to satisfy his known hatred of witches and witchcraft.

Later James was to soften his attitude, after several trials had been held at which the evidence was clearly rigged – but too late for 20 witches tried in Lancashire in 1612, who kept the Devil among them in the shape of a small brown dog, and performed magic secretly.

In many ways the most famous case of persecution was the case of a group of hysterical nuns in Loudun in 1633. The mother superior and nuns of the Ursuline convent of this little French town accused their confessor, Father Urbain Grandier, of bewitching them, and provided excellent evidence by rolling on the ground, moaning obscenities and generally behaving in an irreligious and profane manner. Several of them, when Grandier was arrested and relentlessly tortured, recanted; but too late – by now Grandier's enemies had extracted a confession and forged a pact with the Devil, which the unfortunate priest signed (the Devil having ratified it by drawing a pitchfork at the foot of the document). Grandier was burned at the stake. Mean-

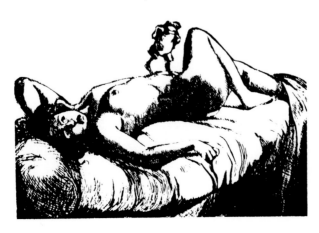

A *"lutin"* or goblin straddles the naked body of a young witch in this drawing by Michelet, 1911.

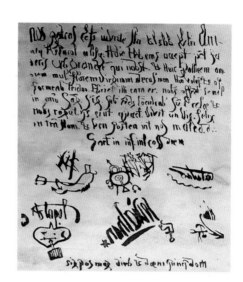

This "pact with the devil", was believed to have been signed by demons on behalf of Urbain Grandier, 1643.

while, unhinged by events, some of the nuns continued their obscene behaviour, though this seems not to have led anyone to suspect that Grandier might have been innocent.

During the English Civil War (1642-48), a Puritan witch-finder called Matthew Hopkins (d.1647) secured more convictions and condemned more witches than any other man in the country. He came to prominence in Chelmsford, and obtained confessions by means which, if less terrible than those common on the continent, were unpleasant enough.

Reading these confessions it is easy enough to see that the torturers expected their victims to report common beliefs about witches' activities: night meetings, orgies, child sacrifice, copulation with devils, and the friendship of familiars in the shape of cats, dogs, toads – Hopkins himself had seen these at work, assisting (for instance) a local pastor, John Lowes of Brandeston, to sink a ship by magic.

Trials continued after the Restoration – but the atmosphere had changed; convictions became rarer, and penalties no longer invariably fatal. With the coming of the Age of Enlightenment, witchcraft was out of fashion with authority – the last witchcraft trial in England was in 1731, when Jane Wenham was acquitted.

In America, the preoccupation with witchcraft was less pervasive than in Europe – with the exception of the case which, together with that of Loudun, is most famous of all: that of the witches of Salem. Salem was a small town in Massachusetts, where in 1691 two little girls experimenting with divination became hysterical. When a local doctor, unable to find the reason, suggested that the children might be bewitched, he started a local reaction which ended in tragedy.

The two original girls, no doubt enjoying all the attention they received, became more and more hysterical – and were joined by several friends who sought equal attention. Under questioning, they accused three local women of bewitching them. One of these, an Indian slave called Tituba, immediately confirmed the accusation, describing the Devil in some detail.

The neighbourhood was now terrified; more and more people were arrested and accused, and before the hysteria was over, no less than 19 people had been executed.

From this episode and so many others it has become apparent that, if we are unsure as to what a witch is, it is because "witch" has become a label to apply to outsiders; those that we are perhaps jealous or afraid of and would rather be without in our community. This might all read like nonsense: but there is a certain conformity about it –

throughout almost every description of witchcraft practices over 1,000 years, the same motifs recur again and again. Sometimes, this is understandable – the sexual act is such a keen and provocative experience that it is not surprising that its energy has often been employed; similarly, semen, the very source of life, has been at the centre of many ceremonies. But in other areas, the symbols and images are less explicable: why should toads in particular so often be cited as mystical mediums? Why cats, for that matter?

We have dealt with spells and rites elsewhere in the book. In this chapter, we have simply tried to outline the history of witchcraft itself without attempting the impossible – actually relating the true practice of the art. Some of the ceremonies outlined in the *Malleus* and elsewhere may have gone on; but whether the "ordinary" witch commonly, or even occasionally, indulged in such activities is doubtful. It would be surprising if even the most credulous old woman supposed that she needed to make a pact with the Devil in order to cast a spell on someone's goat, or to cure someone of toothache. The murder of infants, obscene rites in one form or another, may occasionally have happened – but not necessarily with the connivance of the kind of witch who lived in a country town or village, who tried to communicate with the powers of nature or of animals, and meddled a little in curative natural medicine or, cautiously, in whatever she thought of as magic.

"Real" witchcraft has probably always involved the kind of rites which are still performed in modern Wiccas or covens, and which we speak about in Part Two.

Anne Bodenham, a 17th-century wise woman, is recorded as having "drawn a circle with her staff", and called up a quartet of demons, who duly appeared "in the likeness of ragged boys," and danced with the witch's dog and cat.

6.

Plants & Animals

As we saw in Chapter Two, magic has its origins far back in pre-history when early man's survival was closely bound up with the natural world and the creatures who lived in it. So it is hardly surprising that rituals and beliefs involving animals and plants should be so common in magical lore.

One persistent belief about shamans (the earliest magicians) stresses their ability to fly. One explanation for this extraordinary ability is that they made use of so-called magical plants, which had hallucinogenic properties – mushrooms, fungi and so on. These were often made into ointments which were rubbed onto the body and absorbed into the bloodstream through the skin.

Plants considered useful for flying included hemlock, poppy and belladonna. Of these, hemlock is a poison (it was used in the execution of Socrates, the great philosopher sage of ancient Athens); and both belladonna and poppy are notorious narcotics. The flying ointment would have been fatal if taken internally!

Another explanation is that in the Middle Ages, when the witch-craze was at its height and there were many accounts of flying, there was also an epidemic of St Vitus' Dance – a disease produced by eating bread made from wheat infected with a fungus containing ergotamine. One side-effect of eating this fungus was that it produced hallucinations.

Many magical plants were believed to induce passion or love in the subject. Most of the herbs of love are traditionally linked with the ancient goddess Venus, and since September is the month when the sun enters Venus's sign of Libra, many of these plants are also associated with this month. According to the classical herbals, for instance, which reproduce pictures of "monthly flowers", the flower of September is the rose. Venus has always been linked with the rose, the flower of love, for she is of course the patron of sensuality and romance.

*The roots of magic (**opposite**), tapped for thousands of years by magicians and witches, derive strength from the secret properties of plants and animals.*

Numerous folk traditions reflect this association of Venus with the flower of love. A circlet of rose hips, pierced and strung like beads, may attract desire if worn round the neck or ankle, and rosewater may act as an aphrodisiac if sprinkled on the bedsheets or poured into a hot bath. The old texts usually require that the thorns should be removed from the stems before use as love aids – possibly as a sensible precaution but also, it is said, because the sharp spines are identified with the phallus, and the plucking is an act of sympathetic magic, a sort of "mental image" of coming gratification. For the rose is associated with love rather than carnal desire.

The Rosicrucians, a secret fraternity of Christian magicians which emerged in Europe in the sixteenth century, and strongly influenced occult tradition in the West, adopted as its symbol the red rose of Venus. The spined trailers, or stem, of the flower was represented in the form of a cross – the famous "Rosy-Cross" of the movement.

As the "flower of Venus", the rose pervades much magical tradition.

In the traditional herbal symbolism, the rose is either red or white, a reference to the dual nature of the goddess Venus herself. In the occult tradition, Venus was not only the goddess of love and feminine beauty, but also the ruler of feminine lust and immorality. The "good" or moral Venus was associated with the red rose, while her immoral aspect was linked with other plants and herbs symbolizing sensual or licentious passions. The myrtle, for instance, was regarded as a symbol of sensuality. A sprig of myrtle in a wedding bouquet secretly invited sensuality – and fertility – into the marriage bed of the newly-weds.

The mandrake or mandragora was another plant associated with the wanton and sensual Venus. This strange plant with its bifurcated root was considered to be magical for many reasons, not least because of its resemblance to the human body, and the medieval illustrators of herbals would present their mandrakes in the form of fairy-like or demonic creatures. When dragged from the earth, the plant was believed to emit a terrible scream that would prove fatal to those in the vicinity, so dogs were used to pull out the root.

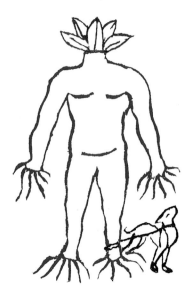

*The mandrake, with its strange resemblance to the human body (**right**), was credited with the power to induce passion, increase wealth and overcome barrenness. Its root was believed to emit a fatal scream when torn from the earth, necessitating the use of a dog (**left**).*

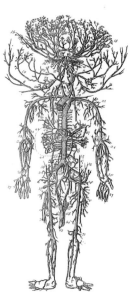

Once secured, the mandrake root could work powerful magic for witches and sorcerers, both as an aphrodisiac and as a narcotic, and other parts of the plant were also used for working evil. The flowers, and juice from the roots, were used in the manufacture of love potions, while the stems could be chewed, like licorice (another lust-inducing plant), or grated to a fine powder to make infusions.

The magical properties ascribed to the mandrake stress its effectiveness as a worker of evil no less than its potency as a sex herb. The mandrake has been associated with all kinds of witchcraft from the earliest times. In Arabia the plant is called "Devil's Candle" and in Germany "Sorcerer's Root". The manufacture of poppets, or witch-dolls, from the humanoid-looking plant was widespread throughout Europe, and many so-called "alrunen" plants have survived. As late as 1630, when witch-hunting was in decline in most of Europe, three women in Hamburg, Germany, were put to death just for having mandrake roots in their homes.

The mandrake root was expensive as well as illegal, coming as it did from distant Mediterranean lands. Cheaper substitutes with humanoid roots included the white bryony, which became established as the most popular of mandrake lookalikes. But this plant was also used as a purgative, so those who took large doses to increase their sexual prowess may have had a painful disappointment.

One of the most useful all-round plants in the herbals was the mugwort, sometimes called the artemisia. It was used for a variety of purposes, including astral projection and the power of prophetic dreaming. Nor were its clairvoyant properties confined to sleep, for a preparation of mugwort-water is traditionally used to

White bryony.

wash crystal balls suitable for scrying, and to this day many psychics grow the plant indoors in order to create an atmosphere conducive to clairvoyant work.

Mistletoe is still widely regarded as a magical plant, particularly at Christmas by those who wish to kiss and be kissed beneath it. One might assume it was connected to the love goddess Venus, but the ancient texts claim that it is a plant of the sun. The druids, the scholar magicians of the Celts, had a profound knowledge of herb lore, and they identified it with the moon, gathering it with a silver crescent-shaped knife. According to Pliny, the druids gathered the sacred mistletoe on the sixth day of the moon (when it was just on the full), sacrificing two white bulls and holding banquets beneath the oak.

Popular names for mistletoe, such as Devil's Fuge, Witches' Broom and so on, indicate a connection with evil-working. On the other hand, its power for good is suggested in names such as Wood of the Cross, Golden Bough, Holy Wood and All Heal. Its importance at Christmas, which is linked with the sun, suggests that it is a solar herb. And it remains the most popular of all herbs of love, for it is the one that allows man and woman to embrace during the most holy time of the year.

Mistletoe, the plant of the druids.

Magic techniques, dating back to shamanism, enable the practicioner to transfer animal attributes to humans.

ANIMALS

The conception of the world as a single living entity, no less than the theory of correspondences which sprang from it, meant that animals must be included in any magical system contrived by man. Sometimes the connection was a passive one – as in the silent appeal to the god of bison made by hunters when they inscribed drawings of the animals on the walls of their caves.

If, early in his history, man liked to see at least some of his gods as human in form, he also associated many of them with animals – using the association to explain their personalities: they had the bravery of the lion, the viciousness of the jackal, the nobility of the eagle. Anthropomorphism – the attribution of human characteristics to animals – came early to civilization, and is found at all levels of religious development from that of the Fuegians to that of the ancient Greeks. Various cults have developed through the millennia – pastoral cults, hunting cults, cults of dangerous animals or those accompanying human souls.

These had various attributes: in hunting cults, for instance, slaughtered animals were honoured; dangerous animals, when killed, could wreak revenge on their killers; human souls could take temporary refuge within the bodies of animals, so it was wise to treat all animals with respect in case the soul of a relative inhabited it. In some cases, in Europe and China, the spirits of vegetation could take animal form.

In many cases, the animals associated with certain gods were sacred because the god had originally been born in the shape of an animal. Dionysus was born a goat, Dagon a fish, Epona a horse, Tangaloa (in the Pacific) a lizard. And of course the sacred white elephant of Siam (Thailand) was believed to contain the soul of a Buddha, and was baptized, fêted and mourned after its death.

On the other hand, the god could have become associated with a particular animal. Siberian tribes showed the bear great honour, while the Tlinkit Indians of Northwest America revered the crow; the Bushmen honour the mantis, Cagn, and his other incarnation, the caterpillar. In Indian mythology the monkey-god Hanuman is important, while a sheep-god similar to Amun, god of Thebes, is found in Africa. In Nepal the tiger-god festival honours Siva and Durga; the Nosarlii of western Asia worship a dog; and serpent cults are found all over the world.

The Egyptians identified most gods with particular animals – they were shown with human bodies and animal heads; Amun wore the head of a ram or a goose, for instance; Anubis that of a jackal, Hathor that of a cow; the beetle was associated with Khepri, the vulture with Nekhbet, the snake with Renenutet, the falcon with Sopdu.

During Ptolemic and Roman periods literally thousands of sacred animals were mummified and buried in animal cemeteries carefully placed near the appropriate cult centres. South-east of Zaqawiq, in Egypt, lie the ruins of Bubastis, the town of the cat goddess Bastet and once the capital of Lower Egypt. Near the main temple are several large cat cemeteries; and at el-Ashmunein, the site of Hermopolis in Middle Egypt and the main cult centre of Thoth – a god shown with the head of an ibis – there are large cemeteries of mummified ibises. It is no exaggeration to say that several hundreds of thousands of them were mummified in ancient Egypt, together with cats and other animals. Worshippers would offer an ibis before the altar of a temple just as today one might light a candle in a church.

The same care shown in mummifying human beings was not generally shown where animals and birds were concerned; these were often quite roughly treated. But an exception was made for the sacred bulls of Memphis, Heliopolis and Hermonthus. The mummification and embalming of these animals – only one of which was allowed to live at any one time – was performed with the utmost ceremony, and they were buried in great state in an enormous catacomb at Saqqara, known as the Serapeum, one of the most impressive spaces in the whole of Egypt. Merely to stand within it is to understand just how important the bulls' human contemporaries must have thought their magical presence was to the health of the state of Egypt.

That certain animals and birds were divine in the fullest sense of the word meant that they were the repositories of great magical power – hence the reverential treatment they received. Looking at some of the representations of, for instance, Bastet with her noble cat-head, or Bes, with the head of a lion, it is easy to apprehend the awe they must have inspired even in the priests, let alone the ordinary people of Egypt.

As we saw in Chapter Two, animals are a vital part of the shamanistic tradition of magic. Shamans derive many of their powers from their animal "allies", carrying and wearing many animal talismans to endow them with the qualities they most admire in different animals: an eagle's feathers to give the power of flight, and so on.

In the Western tradition, too, animals have had an important role to play, though medieval Christianity tended to regard the close relationship between magicians with suspicion, evidence of a pact with the powers of evil. Indeed, animals such as goats and black cockerels are closely related to voodoo and black magic rituals, which often involve animal sacrifice; and of course the Devil is often portrayed in the form of a goat – the old symbol of lechery.

*Magical animals in the ancient world include the Egyptian beetle or scarab (**top**) and the ibis (**below**), associated with Thoth, the god of wisdom. The bee (**centre**) was revered by the ancient Greeks.*

CATS

It may be that the animal cults of Egypt, and in particular the prominence of the cat (in itself a creature with a somewhat mysterious and withdrawn personality) were partly responsible for the connection made throughout Europe between that animal and magic. The witch and her cat were a pair almost impossible to separate in the public imagination.

In the British Isles, one of the earliest appearances of a cat as the familiar of a witch was in the fourteenth century, when at Kilkenny in Ireland Dame Alice Kyteler was accused of witchcraft by her elder children (disappointed because she had announced her intention of leaving all her property to her youngest child). In 1324 Richard Ledrede, Bishop of Kilkenny, condemned her, finding that she had sacrificed various animals to demons, and in particular to her friend Robin Artisson, a minor demon who appeared to her as a cat (though also occasionally as a shaggy dog). This cat was Dame Alice's lover, and at night the two of them would gather a number of friendly demons, and blowing out the candles with a cry of "Fi-fi-fi, Amen!" would throw themselves enthusiastically into an orgy. (The idea of copulation between witches and their cats – unlikely and impractical though this might seem – is a theme which runs through the history of witchcraft.)

A black cat was often used to turn over a candle and extinguish it at the beginning of an orgy; there are records of this from as early as the eleventh century.

During the seventeenth century, witch trials revealed several cats as demonic companions and accomplices of their mistresses. One famous example was the great white spotted cat Sathan, the property of Elizabeth Francis of Chelmsford, England, tried in 1566. Or was she his property? – for Sathan, given to Elizabeth by her grandmother and nourished both with bread and milk and Elizabeth's own blood, was the Devil himself, in furry disguise.   Sathan helped her build up a fine herd of cattle, and inveigled one Andrew Byles into her bed, as a prospective husband. When he declined to marry her, Sathan killed him and arranged the abortion of his child. This busy puss arranged another marriage, then murdered Elizabeth's child when it proved too noisy and troublesome. When he was 16, Elizabeth gave Sathan to her friend Agnes Waterhouse in exchange for a cake. Agnes turned the cat into a toad, who helped her to bewitch cattle, drown cows, kill geese, and turn butter sour (what the cat thought of this liberty is not recorded).

The cat is by no means the only animal to enjoy this degree of notoriety. Conscientious witch-finders of European countries often made themselves fully conversant with the animals that the Devil could impersonate – not only cats and dogs, but squirrels, mice and moles. Witches themselves sometimes impersonated animals, for they could take the form of cats or wolves at will. During a trial in Scotland in 1662, Isabel Gowdie confessed that she had turned herself into a jackdaw and a cat in order to attend covens.

Cats, venerated in the ancient Egyptian and Norse religions, became an object of superstitious fear in the Middle Ages.

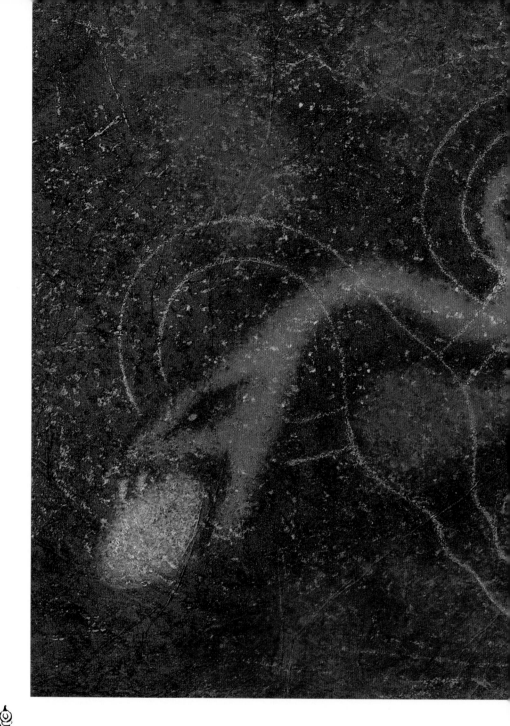

DOGS

The association between dogs and witchcraft is less strong, but widespread. They sometimes joined cats as extinguishers of light before orgies (the powers of witches as animal trainers are clearly not to be underestimated). A strange case in Germany, as recent as 1976, involved dogs, when an elderly woman, Elizabeth Hahn, was seriously accused of witchcraft, and of keeping two dogs as "familiars". A neighbour set fire to her house, killing the dogs and injuring the supposed witch.

*the dog Jarmara (**left**) was said to be a witch's familiar by 17th-century English witch-finders.*

*The snake (**above**), with cosmic egg in its mouth, was worshipped in the New World.*

SNAKES

The snake – so strongly identified in the old Testament with the Fall – appears throughout history, usually as an evil symbol. The male snake was always associated with lust (and would desert its mate for the female eel, more slippery and eager for copulation). Many snakes sprung from the spinal marrow of dead men who had led immoral lives, and some of them took strangely horrid forms – like the cerastes, a snake with horns like a ram, which hid in the sand with only its horns visible. One way of avoiding attack by the cerastes, or indeed by any dangerous snake, is to be naked – snakes which strike at a clothed man will hide modestly from a nude one. If a snake did bite one, the infallible remedy was to swallow the testicles of a hippopotamus in water – though even this might fail if one had been fixed by the serpent's evil eye.

Interestingly enough, the idea of the power of the snake's gaze is one of the few European myths that seems to have arisen, unbidden, in America, in connection with the rattlesnake. That animal is real enough, of course – but in the seventeenth and eighteenth centuries it was strongly believed to possess magical powers – the power of "fascinating" other animals. As Richard Blome put it (in *The Present State of His Majesty's Isles and Territories in America*, 1687): "They have the power, or art (I know not what to call it) to charm squirrels, hares, partridges, or any such things, in such a manner, that they run directly into their mouths."

Humans as well as animals were charmed in this way – if they were not careful. Samuel Williams, in *The Natural and Civil History of Vermont* (1794), recorded the adventure of a boy who met a rattlesnake and looked into its eyes:

> *The most vivid and lively colours that imagination can paint, and far beyond the powers of the pencil to imitate, among which yellow was the most predominant, and the whole drawn into a bewitching variety of gay and pleasing forms, were presented to my eyes; at the same time, my ears were enchanted with the most rapturous strains of music, wild, lively, complicated and harmonious, in the highest degree melodious, captivating and enchanting, far beyond any thing I ever heard before or since, and indeed far exceeding what my imagination in any other situation could have conceived. I felt myself irresistibly drawn towards the hated reptile; and as I had been often used to seeing and killing rattle snakes, and my senses were so absorbed by the gay vision and rapturous music, I was not for some time apprehensive of much danger . . .*
>
> *It was not without the most violent efforts that I was able to extricate myself. All the exertions I could make, with my whole strength, were hardly sufficient to carry me from the scene of the horrid, yet pleasant enchantment; and while I forcibly dragged off my body, my head seemed to be irresistibly drawn to the enchanter by an invisible power.*

MAGICAL ANIMALS

With such astounding powers being ascribed to commonplace animals, what chance had rarely glimpsed beasts from faraway lands of escaping occult significance or even total misrepresentation?

The phoenix occurs in the Bible, too – though this astonishing bird was born (perhaps in Egypt) as early as the eighth century BC as a symbol of the sun: only one bird lived at a time in the world, but survived for as long as twelve thousand years. The symbolism is powerful, and permeates the whole of European literature.

This is where the magic of these animals resides – in the power of their imagery. The venom of the basilisk, "king of serpents", was as legendary as the beast itself; while the unicorn became a powerful sexual symbol. He could only be captured by a female virgin: as Gerard Legh put it in *The Accedens of Armorie* (1562):

> *When he is hunted he is not taken by strength, but only by this policy. A maid is set where he haunteth, and she openeth her lap, to whom the Unicorn . . . yieldeth his head, and leaveth all his fierceness, and resting himself under her protection, sleepeth until he is taken and slain . . .*

*Capture of the unicorn (**opposite**) could only be effected by a virgin.*

Tapestries showing such a scene are many. The sexual significance of the unicorn stemmed from his horn, which (could one but obtain it) could be ground into the most powerful known aphrodisiac. It was also a remedy for most known poisons, and was efficient against diarrhoea.

Gradually, a combination of increased knowledge of the physical world and religious disapproval of myth resulted in the death of belief in the unicorn, and indeed in yet stranger creatures such as the centichora, the onocentaur, the ichneumon and the griphon. But belief in others died hard, particularly in their native countries.

Thus in Greece the satyr still seemed to lurk behind the trees of remote glades right up until the 19th century. He had the calm, gentle features of a handsome youth, but a body something like that of a goat (and certainly equally lustful). An early translator of the Bible rendered this creature as "the hairy one", and so he became decidedly devilish to Christians, though an exception was perhaps made for the satyr which appeared to St Anthony and asked for his prayers.

USING ANIMALS

We have seen the importance of talismans – spells in material form. If herbs and animals were *inherently* magical, or at least possessed wondrous properties, might not they be used for potions and amulets?

An aspect of "animal magic" we have so far ignored is the use made of them in medicine. This again was sometimes the product of the theory of correspondences – the Romans ate hyena heart to cure palpitations, and the ash from the incinerated jawbone of a wild boar to mend broken bones; but often one cannot imagine how the animal medicines came to be. Where did the Elizabethan landlord and brothel-owner Philip Henslowe get his prescription for curing earache, which involved frying earthworms in goose-grease, and dropping the result into the sore ear? Or his other recipe for the same problem: "Take ants' eggs and stamp them and strain them through a cloth, then take swine's grease or knot-grass, stamp the same, and take the juice and mix with other straining of the eggs and put into the ear"?

Presumably such cures sometimes worked simply because people believed in them; and in any case if they did not work it was not because they were inefficient, but because God did not will it, or witches had intervened to prevent it. One sometimes wonders what sort of trouble reliance on such remedies led people into. How many women became pregnant, for instance, because the Roman historian Pliny's absolutely reliable contraceptive – two small worms from inside the head of a hairy spider, tied in deerskin and used as an amulet – failed to work? Pliny recommended, again for pain in the ear, "the seminal fluid of a hog caught as it drips from a sow before it can touch the ground". It might seem difficult to obtain these ingredients – but at least it was easier, in the case of earache, to try centipedes boiled with leeks, or juice from the crushed head of a black-beetle. Vulture's brains were admirable against the headache, and itching genitals profited much from being massaged with the fluid from roasted ravens' lungs. And so on.

If these remedies sound rather worse than the afflictions they were meant to cure, there are worse: how eager would a shortsighted man be to swallow, at the time of the new moon, pellets of she-goat dung? Would someone suffering from cold be perfectly happy to place the dung of a horse fed with oats and barley in half a pint of wine, and swallow it at one gulp?

People did all this, and more. The argument used to justify the straightforward unpleasantness of such medicine was understandable: once more it was on the basis of correspondence, of treating like with like. Rather like modern Christian Scientists, many civilized people believed that sickness was evil, inspired by the Devil and spread by his demons. Such unpleasant ministers could only be driven out by similarly unpleasant means. Robert Burton (1577-1640), the author of *The Anatomy of Melancholy*, spoke of these "unclean spirits" which entered human bodies and "mixed with our melancholy humours, do triumph as it were, and sport themselves as in another heaven", infecting them often with sickness.

There was a weaker argument for the use of animal preparations as beauty aids. Rubbing your cheeks with bulls' dung to give them colour, drinking goats' gall mixed with sulphur to rid yourself of freckles, or eating cows' brains to thicken your eyelashes sounds radical enough, but then it is remarkable what people will go through for the sake of their personal appearance. Today, instead of enduring the pain and inconvenience of a hair transplant, it might be considered more convenient to swallow the ashes of burned ass's genitals, or to rub on one's bald head the grease of a boar mixed with laudanum and maidenhair.

Animals disport in the mysterious world of the "Garden of Earthly Delights", as seen in a detail from the visionary painting by the Flemish artist Hieronymus Bosch (1450-1516).

THE "TRUE" MAGIC OF ANIMALS

Indeed have we travelled so far, after all, from those days? Animals still have a sort of magic: the importance of pets, especially to the elderly and lonely, has long since been proven, while recent experiments have shown that hospital patients who are allowed to pet and cuddle dogs, recover more quickly.

Even the idea of correspondence has survived recently in the injections of monkey glands, which in the 1930s were said to permit old men to recover their vigour and youth. The novelist Somerset Maugham was only one of a number of enthusiasts for that treatment. Was that not almost as much a belief in magic as of medicine?

The most mysterious quality animals possess is the kind of magic mankind seems to have relinquished, or perhaps mislaid, over the centuries. Animals live in a sensory world which would seem magical to us could we inhabit it – with an astonishingly acute sense of smell (we have 5,000,000 sensory cells, a German shepherd dog has 220,000,000); enviable hearing (dogs can register sounds of 35,000 vibrations per second, while we can hear only sounds of 20,000 per second); and an ability – with other animals – to detect earth tremors much in advance of any human capability.

But they also have extra-sensory perception (ESP) which only relatively few humans have learned to exercise. As the distinguished veterinarian David Taylor writes (*The Ultimate Dog Book*, 1990): "Repeated testing under apparently stringent conditions has produced evidence to suggest that certain canines possess psychic/telepathic abilities: what is usually referred to in humans as a 'sixth sense'." This is how your dog knows you're going for a walk before you've even decided yourself!.

7.

Sexual Magic

*Those who attempt to use the power of sexuality for magical pur-
poses can be divided more or less into two types. First, there are
those who simply enjoy sex, want to have more of it, and see magic
as a means of obtaining it. There is little doubt that some people
have always involved themselves in witchcraft for this reason (and
have often been disappointed). Others have involved themselves in
obscene and sadistic rites, sometimes (like Aleister Crowley) for
genuine magical reasons; sometimes for sensual gratification. It
should be emphasized here that there is little evidence that, in the
1990s, those paedophile and other groups taking part in ritual
child abuse do so for any reason other than sadistic lust.*

More innocently (at least for the most part) there have been many attempts in previous centuries to raise amorous spirits, and experimenters have sought to discover
and use effective aphrodisiacs or spells which will attract or bind those with whom
they have fallen fruitlessly in love. And more seriously, we must look once more at
the area where religion and magic meet, and where those who regard sexuality as a
god-given gift use it as a means of apprehending the power and joy of the universe.

A strand of Christian thought, from St Paul onwards, has on the whole been of the
opinion that sexual activity is sinful – indeed, that it is the sin for which Adam and
Eve were turned out of Eden (although this is not the reason given in *Genesis*). It is
only comparatively recently that the idea of sex as a religious act has been accepted
by the Christian church, and even now sometimes reluctantly; some forms of sexuality are still regarded by many members of the Christian church as anathema.

Other religions have seen sexual activity as a celebration of one of the chief joys of

*The ancient Chinese Tao-ch'i symbol
(**opposite**) brings together the male
(yang) and female (yin) energies.*

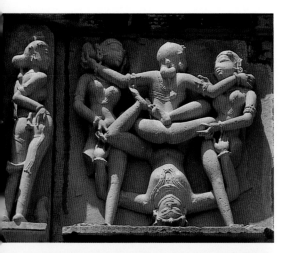

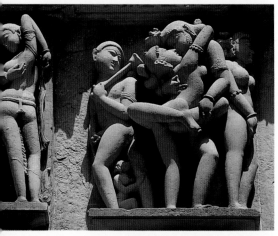

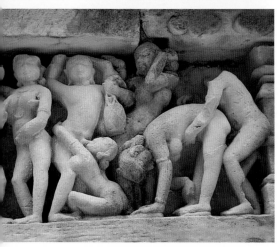

Hindu temple carvings at Khajuraho celebrate sexual energy in a divine context. As in Chinese Taoism, the followers of Tantra believe that the human sexual act reflects divine union.

life, and have wished to praise and revere it. The cult of Aphrodite – originating at Paphos, in Cyprus – is a case in point. She looked with approval on the happy consummation of sexuality and her sanctuary was sacred to sex, regarded (as Sir James Frazer put it in *The Golden Bough*) "not as an orgy of lust, but as a solemn religious duty performed in the service of that great Mother Goddess". Temple prostitutes served worshippers there, as elsewhere in the pagan world; in its grounds alcoves were tactfully placed every few yards so that worshippers could pay homage to the goddess in the way she liked best.

The other major religious system in which sex was and is sacred, is Tantric yoga, which sees the act as a physical metaphor for spiritual union, a means of approaching the principle of creation. It is centred on India, and is extremely ancient but still practised by a minority today. Tantric Buddhism also flourished in Tibet, Nepal and Mongolia, and Hindu Tantra in Cambodia, Java and elsewhere in Southeast Asia.

The theory and practice of Tantra is extremely complex – perhaps especially for Westerners; it involves metaphysics and mathematics as well as sexuality, and many of its rituals have never been recorded in writing, and can be learned only from a teacher or guru. In attempting to summarize it we can give only a faint idea of its depth and power.

The basic theory is founded on a positive approach to the universe: one must say yes to its joys and trials – which flow from male and female principles in reciprocal sensual interplay. The human body has its own relationship with the cosmos, and ideally human beings should identify with the cosmic energy that binds the universe in a continual state of ecstatic and all-embracing love: fatherly, motherly, sisterly, brotherly, and above all sexual.

This attitude to sexuality of course has much to do with texts such as the Kama Sutra and others which describe in detail so many varied positions to be adopted in intercourse; and the paintings, drawings and sculpture which illustrate them, often succeeding (as at the temples at Khajuraho) in conveying something of the subtle intensity of feeling to which they should lead. Studied with prurient interest by some Westerners, these are simply some of the techniques (and there are many of them) which aim to raise the male lover to a simulacrum of a male god, while the woman becomes the female principle itself.

These techniques are many and various, involving sound and colour, food and drink, meditation and yoga, massage with specially prepared scented oils, and complex rituals and mantras, presided over at *pujas*, or ceremonies of worship, by *devatas* – spirits human in shape, which are welcomed as representations of the sexual power of divinity and greeted with

sounding bells and music, offerings of flowers and perfumes, honey, liquid butter and milk. The happily
coupling devatas, differently coloured (to reveal their
qualities), often with many arms, each of which has a
different function, encourage human beings to emu-
late and identify with them as the first step towards
identity with the ideal.

The complete *Panchatattva* or ritual cannot be fully
described here, for reasons of space: in brief, and as
slightly adjusted for use in the West, it should take
place between 7 p.m. and midnight, in a comfortable
dimly-lit room, and accompanied by special objects
which include a silver tray of specially prepared food
(including meat and fish), some wine, and essence of
musk or patchouli.

The theory of sex as a means of approaching the in-
finite is also expressed in Taoism, the Chinese religion
which was first thoroughly expressed in an anthology
known as the *Tao-te Ching* and the *Book of Chuang-tzu*.
In this Chuang-tzu saw Tao as a quiet spirit pervading
everything. Man's (and of course woman's) body was
endowed with both *yin* and *yang* – the former being the
female principle, and the latter the male. *Ch'i*, the
vital spirit which gives energy to all things, is another
component of the living person, and is expressed in
human breath (the Taoist Chao Ping is said to have lit
fires, prevented boiling water from scalding, and
stopped dogs barking simply by the use of *ch'i*).

Sexual energy is another form of *ch'i*, and its correct
balance is crucial to a well-balanced spiritual life. The
Tao theory was that the sexual organs channelled the
vital forces of the universe – the earth, woman, and
the vulva being *yin* while heaven, man and the penis
are *yang*. United, these two bodily organs lead directly
to harmony – every time man and woman make love,
heaven is joined to earth – and the longer this religious
ritual can be prolonged, the stronger the magic.

In Taoism there are lucky and unlucky days for coi-
tus, favourable and unfavourable sexual positions, and
even positive and negative directions in which to lie.
For centuries, a ritual known as "deliverance from
guilt" was performed – it took place on the nights of
the new and full moon, and in it ritual dances ("the
coiling of the dragon and playing of the tiger") culminated in love-making between participants.

Tantric yoga and Taoist sexuality, seriously approached, place sex in what is ideally its proper place –
as a central revered power of the universe.

But of course there is a well-established darker side
to sex; and the compulsive itch of sex often had something to do with the depths to which some magicians
sank, either on their own behalf or that of their
clients. Abbé Guibourg, a notorious priest in Paris in
the seventeenth century, was known as the best person to approach if one wanted an "amatory mass" said

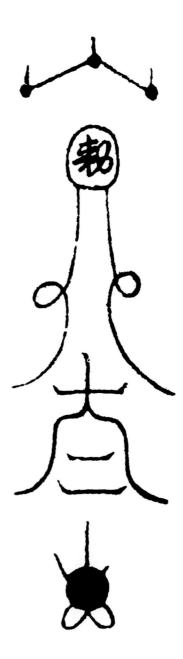

*A Taoist talisman
(**above**) illustrates a
means of curing illness
caused by excess of yin
influence by restoring
yin/yang balance through
sexual intercourse.*

on one's behalf, to engage the affections of another party. A similarly disreputable priest whose activities verged on the magical was Mariette, employed by Madame de Montespan (1641-1707), the French marquise and mistress of King Louis XIV. In 1667 she paid him for two masses intended to ensure that the king's wife remained barren and that the royal affections should remain fixed on his mistress. A little later two doves had their hearts torn from their bodies during a mass, and their blood, combined with wine from the chalice, was mixed with the king's food by the marquise, who also administered several aphrodisiacs. She had born him seven children, whom he had legitimized; but there were signs that she was being succeeded in his affections by Madame de Maintenon, their governess.

Growing desperate, she turned again to the Abbé Guibourg, and it is suggested that in 1673 he held a mass during which the chalice and paten were placed on the

*Mme de Montespan,
mistress of the
Sun King Louis XIV.*

belly of a masked, naked woman, and that after the consecration of the Host a child's throat was cut and its blood drained into the wine while a prayer was said to Astaroth, a demon who appeared in the shape of an angel, and Asmoday, another with three heads (of a ram, a bull and a man) who appeared riding a dragon.

Whether that story is true or not (and it was most thoroughly ventilated after the French Revolution by those who had a vested interest in discrediting all about the court), it is further rumoured that when Madame de Montespan became convinced that the king was about to reject her, she paid Guibourg to hold a "mortuary mass" at which menstrual blood and semen were ceremonially prepared, to be added later to the king's food. The ceremony came to an end when the police broke in; over 100 people involved in black magic of a similar nature were arrested and executed or imprisoned, though the marquise escaped all punishment.

APHRODISIACS

From the earliest period of history for which we have written records, it has been regarded as axiomatic that such a thing as an effective aphrodisiac exists.

Some foods, for very obvious reasons, have been positively regarded as aphrodisiacs – markedly, those that bear a physical resemblance to the male or female genitals: thus both the banana and the fig, as symbols of the penis and vagina, have at some stage been considered infallible raisers of the sexual spirits. (This theory of similarities was a serious one, known as the Doctrine of Signatures, and used in other areas such as medicine, when a food which resembled the diseased organ was supposed to help restore it to health.)

On this basis, the mandrake root was long considered an effective aphrodisiac, because of its likeness to the human body; sometimes eaten, it was also often worn as an amulet. Obtaining a mandrake root was a perilous business (as we have seen), for as it was dug from the ground it gave out a fearful cry of agony strong enough to kill. The solution to this was to train a dog to dig it up for you; the dog died, but you had the mandrake, which (if you were a man) you then trimmed into the shape of a woman's body, using your artistic talent.

Holding the figure in your left hand and making the sign of the pentagram with your right, you pointed to it and gave it the name of your beloved: "I name you . . .", then buried it in your garden, pouring a mixture of milk, water and your own blood over it, chanting the words,

> Blood and milk upon the grave
> Will make . . . evermore my slave.

The mandrake was left in the ground until the night of the new moon, when it was dug up with the recitation,

> Moon above so palely shining
> Bestow this night thy sacred blessing
> On my prayer and ritual plea
> To fill . . .'s heart with love for me.

The mandrake was then thoroughly dried, periodically steeped in incense, and addressed with more spells; after which, if the victim had not left the district, she would certainly succumb.

Having attracted your lover, you must then of course demonstrate your potency, and a large number of possibilities existed, from taking lizards drowned in a man's urine to sprinkling on your penis the ground dust of a horse's tooth. Rhinoceros horn (first catch your rhinoceros) was, and still is, considered an aphrodisiac in China,

The mandrake epitomizes aphrodisiac power.

rendering the penis as hard and invincible as the horn. In addition, particular oils were massaged into the body of one's partner, in order to evoke desire.

There have been, of course, perfectly innocent aphrodisiacs, the only objection to which is that they probably failed as often as they succeeded. Many of them originated in the Middle East. *The Perfumed Garden of Sheikh Nefzawi* (among the books found and translated by Sir Richard Burton) suggests a man eat the yolks of several eggs every day; accompanying them with chopped onions will add a vigour to the enthusiasm with which one could then attempt the amorous techniques taught elsewhere in the book. Failing desire could be spiced by daily eating boiled asparagus fried in fat, to which egg yolks and powdered spices had been added. Camel's milk mixed with honey "develops an astonishing vigour, and keeps the member in erection all day and night", while "he who will feed for several days on eggs cooked with myrrh, cinnamon and pepper, will find an increased vigour in his erections and in his capacity for coition."

On the whole, it is difficult to dissent from the ancient Chinese saying that "the best aphrodisiac for a man is a passionate and beautiful woman inviting desire" – whereas many of the ancient recipes, certainly if their content was known to the admired one, can only have resulted in nausea.

Take, for instance, the process recommended in one grimoire or magic book: one must go to "the stews" – or public baths – and remain in the hottest room until one sweated profusely. Then dusting one's body with white flour, one scraped the caked mixture off, put it in a bowl, added a few nail clippings and hairs (from the head and elsewhere), baked a cake adding the mixture, and invited one's intended to tea. He or she would instantly fall victim to one's charm.

There are other potions at least as unpleasant: a mixture prepared from a dove's heart, a sparrow's liver, a swallow's womb and a hare's kidney, mixed with one's own blood. Persuading the woman to eat it must have been quite as difficult a proposition as to seduce her more conventionally.

Slightly less offensive, perhaps, was another piece of grimoire advice – to watch a bitch on heat until she was mounted by a dog, and then to place a mirror so that it reflected the scene.

Wrapped in green cloth, the mirror was first placed secretly in the desired one's bedroom for some days, then removed and carried about until the beloved fell into the spell-caster's arms, which would be fairly soon. Incidentally, if you then wished to make sure she did not transfer her affections to anyone else, you took the genitals of a wolf and hairs from its cheeks, eyebrows and beard, burned them, and gave them to her in a drink – "and she shall desire no other man".

That spell is from Albertus Magnus' *Boke of the Mervayles of the World*, which includes further advice to the effect that "when a woman desireth not her husband, he should take a little of the tallow of a bucke Goat [and] anoint his privy members with it, and do the act of generation. She shall love him, and shall not do the act of generation afterwards with any other."

The link between the goat's reputation for libidinous behaviour and this remedy is clear; but the potions themselves seem excessively unlikely to work as aphrodisiacs, while clearly very likely to make unwell the unfortunate people to whom they were administered. It was suspected for instance that the illnesses suffered for two years by King Louis XIV of France were the result of love potions fed to him by his mistress, Madame de Montespan, as mentioned earlier.

Other recipes were also available for other purposes than seduction. The *Grimorium Verum* offers an infallible recipe for making a girl dance naked in front of one. First find and kill a bat, and with its blood write the word FRUTIMIERE on a clean piece of parchment. This must be placed under a doorway through which the girl will walk. On doing so, she will instantly remove all her clothes.

If, having observed this event, you wish to go further, strike up a conversation (whether waiting until she has resumed her clothes or not is unspecified), and in the

*The divine female energy is
invoked in most cultures.
The many-breasted Great
Goddess, Diana of Ephesus
(**right**), offended St Paul,
but an African earth mother
image (**far right**) is
reverenced to this day. Lilith
(**above**), demonized by
patriarchal Judaism, was
worshipped by the
Babylonians as the deity of
childbirth. The Celtic
"Sheela-na-Gig" (**top**), once
a potent symbol of feminine
power, appears as a gargoyle
outside the church of St Mary and
St David in Kilpeck, Herefordshire.*

middle of it look her straight in the eye, and declaim: "*Kaphe, kasita, non kapheta et publica filii omnibus suis.*" She will instantly fall desperately in love with you.

A magic ring is considered useful for seduction, and can be obtained by laying a table for three in your bedroom, going to bed, and reciting the following prayer:

> *Benedictum consolatio veni ad me vertat Creon, Creon, Creon,*
> *cantor laudem omnipotentis et non commentur. Stat superior carta*
> *bient laudem omviestra principiem da montem et inimicos meos o*
> *prostantis vobis et mihi que passium fiery sincisbus.*

Three visitors will then appear, of the opposite sex to yourself, and after conversing on such matters as where you may discover buried treasure, will present you with an aphrodisiac ring.

Lest it be thought that aphrodisiacs and aphrodisiac spells were only used by pagans or witches, it should be pointed out that Christians were by no means entirely averse to the use of magic in matters of love. The 137th psalm – the one which begins "By the waters of Babylon, there we sat down, yea, we wept . . ." – was used in one spell, recited over a goblet in which oil extracted from a white lily had been placed; then the name of the angel Aniel (associated with Venus and human sexuality) was pronounced, together with the name of the beloved. The angel's name was then written on a piece of cypress bark, dipped in the oil and tied to the right arm. On touching the beloved's arm with the right hand, "love will be awakened in her". Incidentally, this spell should, for utmost power, be used at dawn on the Friday after a new moon.

Some fortunate young lovers who for one reason or another were particularly successful with the ladies were said to have a "magic eye" which, once fixed on a woman, made them irresistible. This phenomenon was utterly accepted at the time of the Renaissance, when Marsiglio Ficino, in his *Commentary on Plato's Symposium*, laid it down that the heat of the heart generated spirits from the blood, which "send a ray like itself through the eyes as though through glass windows" – a ray which, darting between two people, carries out a sort of spiritual transfusion which results in love. He described the phenomenon as it occurred between two Greeks, Phaedrus the Myrrhinusian and the orator Lysias:

Lysias stares open-mouthed at the face of Phaedrus. Phaedrus sends into the eyes of Lysias the sparks of his own eyes, and with the sparks sends along a spirit. The light of Phaedrus is easily joined by the light of Lysias, and the spirit also easily joins his spirit. The vapour of this sort springing from the heart of Phaedrus immediately seeks the heart of Lysias, [and] the blood of Phaedrus is now in the heart of Lysias, a truly remarkable phenomenon. Hence each immediately cries out: Lysias to Phaedrus, "Phaedrus, my heart, dearest body!" Phaedrus, to Lysias, "Oh my spirit, my blood, Lysias." Phaedrus pursues Lysias because his heart seeks its own humour. Lysias pursues Phaedrus because the sanguine humour desires its own proper vessel . . .

This was in a sense an aspect of the "evil eye", and indeed "changing eyes" could result in an almost magical exchange of emotions – in "love at first sight", no idle phrase, and one with which we are all familiar. Though there is no complete explanation, psychology suggests some answers.

Finally, it should be remembered that while most men and women sought aphrodisiacs, some needed anaphrodisiacs to remove desire. A man who feared his wife was too attractive to other men, or perhaps had a lover, could if he wished apply to her body blood drawn from that of a tick which had been sucking a wild black bull. The woman concerned would immediately turn against the whole idea of making love. A perhaps easier way of provoking the same reaction would be to give her the urine of a he-goat to drink.

*Love at first sight (**opposite**)*
was long believed to be a
magical effect.

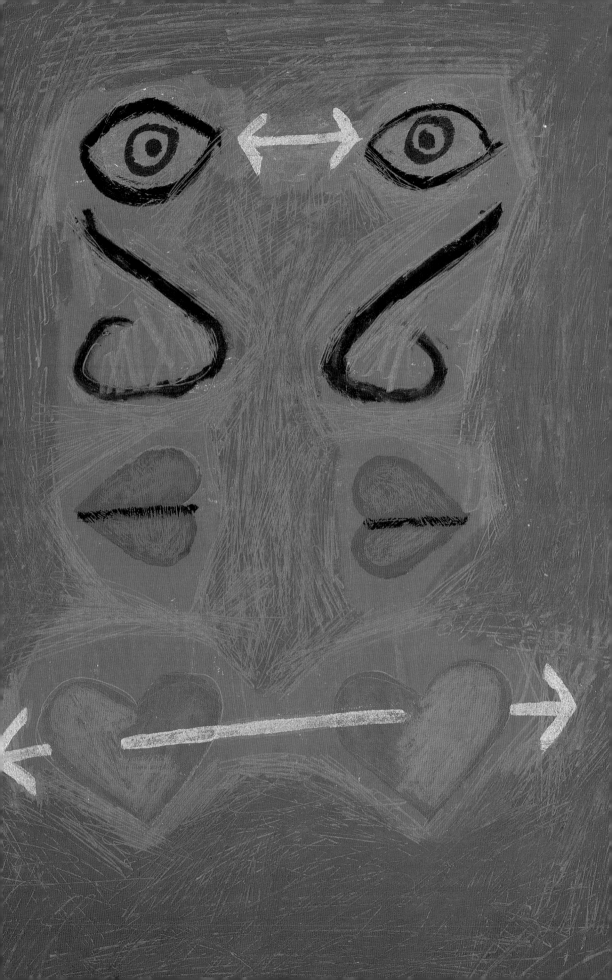

8.

Alchemy

The general view of alchemists is that they were preoccupied with turning base metal into gold. It was certainly one of their aims – but by no means the only one, for the conversion of base to "noble" metal reflected a general striving of all things towards perfection. Another aim of the alchemists was to defeat all sickness and disease, so that mankind could live an agreeably long and healthy life. And there was a third ambition: to create life itself – actually to make a human being.

Far from being irreligious magicians, alchemists were generally highly spiritual men with strong religious convictions and a belief in the power of prayer. Some authorities maintain that there were alchemists in ancient Egypt; others claim that the art originated in the third century BC in Taoist China, and came from there to the West. In the Middle Ages many alchemists believed that Moses' connection with the Golden Calf showed knowledge of the Philosopher's Stone.

In many ways, alchemy is the precursor of modern chemistry, with its apparatus and painstaking experiments. But it would be a mistake to see alchemy simply as a materialistic search after gold or some elusive elixir of life. Alchemy must also be understood on a deeper level.

Almost from the beginning of time, gold has been regarded as the most mysterious, beautiful and valuable of metals: it has been wrought into jewellery, used to cover the faces of the dead and embellish the bodies of the living, stored away by the covetous and wealthy . . . . Its rarity has always been a prime mark of its value, and it is not surprising that some men have looked for ways of counterfeiting it – even of making it, one goal of the alchemist throughout the centuries. Nor has the 20th century lost sight of the true motive of alchemy, which was not – or not only – to transform base metal into gold, but to transform base man into "the golden likeness of the Sun".

*The androgyne (**opposite**) in alchemy represents the conjunction of opposites as a first stage in the path to perfection.*

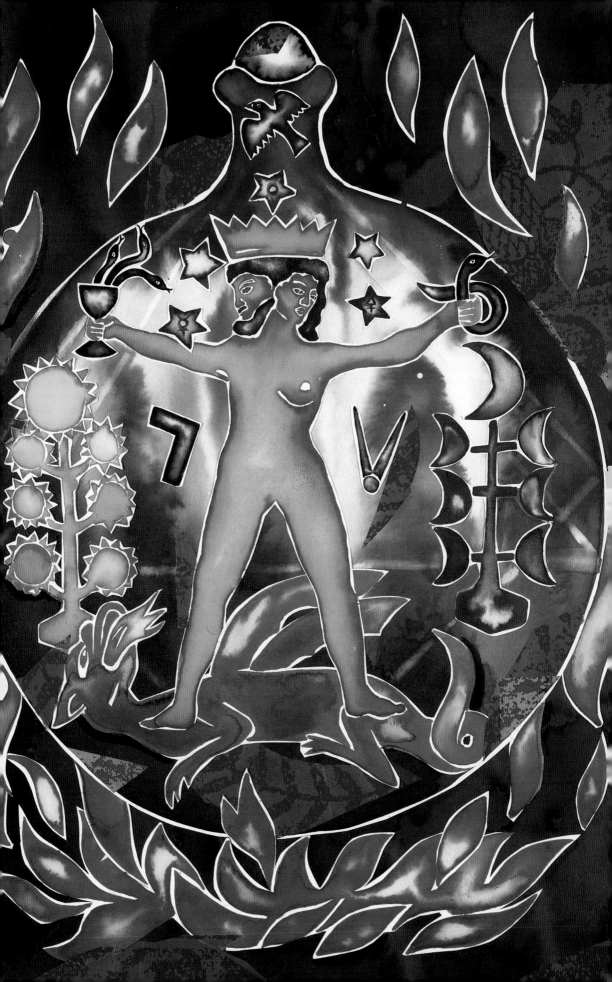

The alchemist confronts his work as he
prepares the winged "principle of
Mercury" for further development.

THE ORIGINS OF ALCHEMY

Alchemy is a very ancient concept indeed. Some alchemists claimed that Adam was the first man to undertake the "Great Work", as they called it; others that the first alchemist was the Egyptian god Thoth, who became Hermes in Greece and Mercury in Rome. The earliest known alchemical texts date from the third century BC, while the earliest complete book on the subject, *Physika*, was published by Bolos of Mendes, who claimed that his knowledge had come from the fifth century BC Greek philosopher Democritus.

Apart from those whose names we know – Aristotle and Robert Fludd, Isaac Newton and Paracelsus – a vast number of unknown men and women studied alchemy, and alchemists were interested in the art chiefly as a way to the true meaning of life, as a means of curing sickness, or for self-improvement.

In the Far East, especially China, alchemy seems originally to have involved a search for a liquid which would enable man to extend his life, perhaps even for ever. The energy of the universe, the masculine, fiery *yang* and the feminine, passive *yin*, was of course crucial: and immortality being a masculine principle, *yang* was most important, so gold and jade (*yang* materials) were much used in the battle against mortal corruption.

In Greece and Egypt the interest seems rather to have been in the transmutation of metal. Arabic translations of the alchemical works of the Greek philosophers were widespread, but known only in the Arabic world until about the twelfth century, when they began to become familiar to Western scholars. Their fascination was perhaps predominantly in finding what some people called the Elixir of Life, others the Tincture, yet others the Philosopher's Stone. This would certainly turn base metal into gold – but possessed other and perhaps more profound powers. Since it concentrated within it the spirit which linked together all the elements of the universe, alchemists believed that it was the key to all knowledge – that, in the words of John of Rupescisia in the fourteenth century, it held "the secret of the mastery of fixing the sun in the sky".

The nature of the Stone itself has always been mysterious: and here it should be said that a problem in studying alchemy is that it is surrounded by enormous secrecy – texts are written in code, mysterious symbols thick on the page and in the mind: ravens and crows, pelicans and eagles, doves and dragons, the swan, the red and white rose and the green lion. Alchemical books are notoriously opaque to anyone who has not made a prolonged study of the peculiar language used by their authors – hence the fact that what we know of alchemy today is largely based on legend, on anecdotes of remarkable successes or ludicrous failures. The most sensible attitude to take when reading this is one of reasonable doubt. But many alchemists nevertheless had excellent reputations in the fields of the medicine and science of their time, and thus there is every reason to take their writings seriously.

The Athanor, or furnace of the philosophers, hatches the Philosophic Egg that will eventually yield the Philosopher's Stone. Within the Egg, the two principles of the "Materia Prima" interact; one is solar, hot and male (sulphur), the other lunar, cold and female (mercury). As the outer fire is slowly intensified, coagulation and desiccation occurs, followed by the appearance of the Whiteness (albedo). From this emerges the White Rose (Rosa Alba), leading to the "third work", the goal of which is the creation of the Philosopher's Stone itself.

PURPOSE

The connection between alchemy and medicine is age-old: the most notable name in the canon of alchemical medicine is probably that of Paracelsus, otherwise Theophrastus Bombastus von Hohenheim, born near Zurich in 1493. Studying medicine (he was once offered the post of city physician and Professor of Medicine at Basel University), he found the attitude and ignorance of his fellow physicians intolerable – "ignorant sprouts" was the most inoffensive term he applied to them. He became convinced that it should be possible to release from various metals the celestial power they obtained through the influence of the ruling planet, and to use this in the preparation of medicine.

He advanced the remarkable and highly sympathetic theory that the body itself was an alchemist, transforming the food and drink it consumed into material which was of use to it, and rejecting the rest. He also believed that the most poisonous substance could be used in medical treatment (in a sense, he prepared the way for immunization, and certainly for homeopathy).

Nowadays it is probably true to say that the idea of "making gold" (even the symbolic gold of a curative medicine) has to a great extent given place to an interest in alchemy as a metaphor, a largely symbolic means of working

The zodiac was important to alchemy, with the sign of Aries corresponding to the Materia Prima or subject of the Great Work. Alchemical apparatus emphasizes the relation between alchemy and modern chemistry.

towards the perfectibility, or at least the enhancement of the nature, of man. The transformation, in this case, is not from base metal into gold – but from the base material of which man is made, into spiritual gold.

Philosophically, the best alchemists, though concerned with the transmutation of metals, have always looked chiefly at man: they still started with base, even disgusting, material – that of which man and woman are made – and sought to turn it into the golden flesh of immortality. They sought to make man recognize the gold within himself, and expose it. Man should be refined not in the literal furnace with which the alchemist worked with metals, but in the spiritual furnace of love.

The great modern psychiatrist C. G. Jung (1875-1961) found alchemy an extremely important precursor of analytical psychology. He became interested in the subject when asked to write a foreword to a Taoist alchemical book, *The Secret of the Golden Flower*, and as a result of studying it began to recognize ancient alchemical symbols in his dreams and the many dreams recounted to him by his patients. "The experiences of the alchemists were, in a sense, my experiences, and their world was my world," he wrote excitedly; and years later, in his old age, he published an entire book on the subject, *Psychology and Alchemy* (1944).

Jung believed that the alchemist, working in his laboratory, based his work on psychic experiences which paralleled the chemical processes he so carefully arranged;

The Weighing of the Worlds, with the sun as the fulcrum, shows the left rising and the right falling. The former represents the "light fire" of heaven, the latter the "heavy earth" of the elemental realm.

attempting to "liberate" gold from the original base material with which he worked, he was also striving to liberate himself from the dark, base material of his unconscious. If he could make gold, that infinitely beautiful and rich material, he could make himself equally beautiful and pure. Just like the modern psychologist, he was searching out reality – seeking self-knowledge.

Jung took this theory to great and often persuasive lengths, for instance seeing in the very language of alchemy more parallels with modern psychiatric practice: *Nigredo*, or blackness, was the darkness of the unrealized psyche; in *Separatio* there was a parallel between childhood complexes and adult fullness, to separate the ego from the shadow. *Melancholia* was recognizable depression; *Albedo*, or perfect white, represented the moment of self-knowledge which led on to the *Lapis Philosophorum*, when the king and queen of the alchemists symbolism became the hermaphroditic perfection of fully realized humanity.

Anyone who doubts that the alchemists can speak to us today has only to read *Psychology and Alchemy*, or the admirable summary of it published in Dr Anthony Stevens' *On Jung* (1990). It is an excellent point of meeting between our glimpse of ancient magic and a look at modern magic – of how, today, "some occult controlling principles of nature" can be recognized and used in our everyday lives.

*"Alchemists at work", by Pieter Breughel the Elder (1525-69), shows the medicinal role played by alchemists in the community. A reconstruction of an alchemical laboratory (**right**) includes apparatus familiar to this day.*

FAMOUS ALCHEMISTS

It would be silly to suppose that the alchemist Johann Friedrich Schweitzer was a credulous fool. Known as Helvetius, he was a first-rate physician, and not given to romancing. However, he tells a remarkable story which most sane people would immediately doubt: he says that on 27 December, 1666, a stranger visited his house – a man "of a mean stature, [with] a little long beardless face, slightly pocked, and very black, straight hair", and after discussing the possibility of manufacturing a cure-all medicine which would act successfully on all illnesses, took from his pocket a box containing three pieces of stone, "each about the size of a small walnut, transparent, the colour of pale brimstone". He also showed the surprised Helvetius some gold medallions which he said had been struck from this alchemical gold.

After some discussion, on a later appearance the stranger gave the physician a piece of this mysterious material; and working with it Helvetius, with the aid of his wife (alchemists almost always worked with a female assistant) succeeded in turning lead into "the best, most refined gold".

There are some independent witnesses: the philosopher Baruch Spinoza checked and accepted the story, and the contemporary head of the assay office of the province in which Helvetius lived tested the gold and found it genuine. Are we to believe the story? Or to believe – perhaps with greater ease – that it was a parable? Cherry Gilchrist in *The Elements of Alchemy* (1991) points out that the physician's description of the strange visitor and his behaviour "is a perfect portrait of Saturn personified", and

Saturn was the guiding planet of alchemists. But at any event we should resist the idea that Helvetius was deliberately telling a silly story – and his tale is by no means the only one which strikes at the least a chord in the collective unconscious.

Another alchemist to whose claims some attention should be paid was Nicholas Flamel, who recorded that "in the year of our Lord 1382, April 25, at five in the afternoon, this mercury I truly transmuted into almost as much gold, much better indeed than common gold, more soft also, and more pliable. I may speak it with truth, I have made it three times, with the help of Perrenelle my wife, who understood it as well as I, because she helped me in my operations . . ."

The writings Flamel left have a distinctly honest ring about them. He claimed that his knowledge of alchemy was almost all from *The Book of Abraham the Jew*, a manuscript he acquired in 1357, full of strange symbols and at first impossible to decipher. With the help of some cabbalistic scholars, he finally believed that he had understood the book's instructions, successfully made gold, and from the riches acquired endowed fourteen hospitals, three chapels and seven churches in Paris, and performed similar work of charity elsewhere in France. It is at least worth asking where a poor copyist of manuscripts (Flamel's occupation) acquired the money to do all this, if not by selling material that at the least closely resembled gold.

Flamel's tombstone is in the Cluny Museum in Paris; for years after his death his house and garden were ransacked for the manuscript book, or for a piece of the Philosopher's Stone – and eventually a magistrate confiscated all his belongings in order that an organized search might be made; but nothing of consequence was ever found.

In those early alchemical writings which have survived, the authors, claiming success or near-success, make it clear when they write of their triumphs that they are withholding key information in order to protect their discovery from misuse. Often they simply decline to say with what material they started their work.

This may have been a metal of some kind, may have been mud or slime or earth.

Ancient alchemists often insisted that the material must be particularly "base" – a substance so worthless, perhaps so unpleasant, that no one in their senses would think of employing it. Alchemists in the Middle Ages therefore began their experiments with some very strange substances: "Poudres diverse, ashes, dong, pisse and cley," as Chaucer's Canon Yeoman put it.

Interestingly, one of the most detailed alchemical texts to have survived comes from colonial America – from *Hercules ex Rore Rosatus*, sent to England in manuscript from Philadelphia in 1769 by William Gerard De Brahm, a German who had been an engineering officer in the army of the Emperor Charles VII, and remained in America as Surveyor General of the South. Without suggesting that his recipe would not be quite as difficult to follow in practice as that in any other alchemical text, at least it is written in English:

> *Collect for this Operation spagerically [alchemically] a grand Vessel as much as three Philosophical Weights, then prepare three Athanors, each capacious to hold three Pounds; in each of these Athanors put one pound of the Vessel, with two Pounds of the favorite Subject (Chaos). N.B. each Pound of the Vessel is equal in measure to two Pounds of Chaos.*
>
> *In each Athanor gently and with great judgement generate a particular Earth, as per instance, in the first Athanor produce a Mercurial Earth of a two-fold Nature, in the above Fable, called by the Names Sosias and Mercurius: The Earth is obtained by Sublimation, Precipitation, Circulation, Digestion and Calcenation.*
>
> *In the second Athanor is made a phlogistic [inflammable] Earth of two different Natures, named Amphitryon and Jupiter, Which are kindled by Precipitation, Calcenation, Circulation, Digestion & Filtration. And in the third Athanor is formed a vitresible [glass-producing] Earth, also of a double Nature mentioned above by the Names Alcemena and Juno, which is produced by Circulation, Digestion, Filtration and Congelation.*

Sun and moon are symbolic figures in Michael Maierus's 17th-century Atalanta Fugiens *(opposite). According to the* Emerald Table *of Hermes Trismegistus, "The Sun is [alchemy's] father, and the Moon its mother." The lion devouring the serpent, in Maierus's treatise (right), symbolizes the process of distillation. The serpent represents the raw psychic energy of the soul, while the lion stands for the sun, the legendary father of alchemy.*

The problem for those of us tempted to try the experiment is that like so many alchemists before him, De Brahm declines to tell us what "the favourite Subject (Chaos)" actually is, or where it can be found. But we are assured that after the proper procedure had been followed,

> Alcemena will bring forth her Son Hercules, which means that the Light of Nature in Disguise by help of the mercurial Earth will penetrate through the Sulphur of Nature and impregnate the Vitresible Earth, which [is] saturated in that Sal enixum [distilled salt] whose Virtue entitles it to be a Panacea, not volatile, but able to sustain the same degree of Fire with a fluid Metal, nor solid, but adapted to mix with any Vegetable Juice for the greatest Benefit of Human Nature.

Evidence strongly suggests that this panacea was actually made up, in London, by scientists commissioned by Lord Dartmouth, and administered to King George III in an attempt to cure his madness. In this objective, at least, the mixture proved ineffective.

Mercury, mentioned by De Brahm, has always been closely associated with

The seven stages of the soul bird.

1) *The soul bird perches on a skull, symbolizing the death (Nigredo) that leads to separation between soul and body.*

4) *The soul's essence is transformed into a crown and carried aloft by the soul birds.*

5) *Planted in the earth, the essence begins to grow, watched by the soul birds.*

alchemy; so is pure water – in particular, dew, which is believed to be capable of holding and expressing the virtue of plants and natural substances with which it has been in contact. It, or at least distilled water (which is the best substitute), is still used in several forms of unorthodox medicine – in crystallography, for instance, when crystals are steeped in water which is then consumed, or in the preparation of Dr Edward Bach's remedies, which are obtained by a process of distillation. Dr Bach's remedies, distilled from a wide variety of plants, enjoy a high reputation among those who have tried them, and are said to work on animals as well as on humans.

Attempts to find the Elixir or Stone almost always involved the principle of distillation: a liquid might be distilled and redistilled 100 or even 1,000 times. Eventually, a White Stone would result from the process which would turn base metal into silver; further work would result in the creation of the Great Stone itself. This would be done under very carefully controlled conditions – frequently involving astrology, for each metal was (and is) connected to a particular planet, whose position in the sky at the moment of the experiment would be crucial.

The practice of alchemy was regarded as dangerous, not only because one was working with forces the nature of which was unknown, but because it involved furnaces and often intense heat; accidents in the laboratory were not unknown, and were sometimes fatal.

2) *The soul bird gazes at its reflection in the dead earth realm, seeing the essence of its being.*

3) *Two soul birds raise the essence of the soul towards a higher spiritual realm.*

6) *Soul Tinctures begin to form: rose blossoms represent the Red (solar) Tincture, the unicorn represents the White (lunar).*

7) *Resurrection of the body, seen as a female figure, marks the return of the alchemist to full consciousness.*

Alex Barbault, a modern alchemist, presides
over flasks containing elixir of gold and
silver, said to be made from concentrated dew.

MODERN ALCHEMY

It is worth remembering that modern science owes something to the alchemist. Just as astronomy was a child of astrology, so modern chemistry is the child of alchemy. Early discoveries indeed took place in the alchemist's laboratory, where potassium was discovered by Albert le Grand in the eleventh century, sodium sulphate by

Johann Glauber (1604-68), benzoic acid by Blaise Vigenère (1523-96), tin monoxide by della Porta (1541-1615). Both Robert Boyle (1627-91), often called the father of modern chemistry, and Isaac Newton (1642-1727), considered by many the greatest scientist that ever lived, were practising alchemists.

The processes of modern chemistry of course differ from those of the alchemists: Today scientists are interested in repeatable experiments, in "proof" – and the change of emphasis was extremely confusing for those alchemists to whom spiritual adventure was at least as important as repeatable results – to the extent that some even committed suicide (or so it has been claimed) when they found their colleagues incapable of an imaginative leap which could comprehend theories outside their own experience.

However, alchemy did not die with the coming of the Age of Enlightenment. Twentieth-century alchemy begins, perhaps with the mysterious figure of Fulcanelli, the author of a book claiming that the secrets of the art are enshrined in the carvings of the central porch of the cathedral of Notre Dame in Paris. There are unlikely claims that Fulcanelli assisted some scientists working on the early stages of liberating atomic energy.

Nevertheless, modern science was by now working in areas where alchemy no longer seemed so unlikely. In 1910, Rutherford transmuted nitrogen into oxygen, and a German chemist, Franz Tausend, inspired by the news, turned his attention to alchemy and claimed in the 1920s to have changed iron oxide and quartz into gold. General Erich von Ludendorff formed a company to exploit the discovery, and in 1928 Tausend is said to have made 723 grams of gold, and share certificates were issued; but the firm failed, apparently as a result of Ludendorff diverting funds into the account of the Nazi party.

The claims of the ancient alchemists are usually impossible to check, and (because the literature is so confusing) their experiments impossible to recreate. Some certainly claimed to have found the Philosopher's Stone, and to have created gold; and the chances are that some were successful in manufacturing reasonable simulacrums. This aspect of alchemy has continued to interest some experimenters until comparatively recently. Archibald Cockren, an osteopath, claimed (in his *Alchemy Rediscovered*, 1940) that working with a particular metal – he did not, of course, reveal which – he had succeeded in finding "the Mercury of the Philosophers, the Aqua Benedicta, the Aqua Celestis, the Water of Paradise", which took the form of a gas which smelled like "the dewy earth on a June morning, with the hint of growing flowers in the air, the breath of the wind over heather and hill, and the sweet smell of the rain on the parched earth."

Later, Cockren announced that he had managed to condense the gas into a golden coloured water, which when added to salts of gold produced "oil of gold" which he believed had great curative properties (it was fashionable at the time to inject gold salts as a cure for rheumatism and arthritis). Unfortunately, he seems to have taken the matter no further, and when he was killed in the London blitz, the secrets of his work died with him.

More recently Eugene Canseliet, Roger Caro, Louis Cattiaux and Alex Barbault have worked along the same lines in France. Barbault, best known of these latter-day alchemists, is a distinguished astrologer, and started his work with what he called "the Philosopher's Peat", which was dug from some centimetres under the earth (at the proper astrological moment, and at a particular place).

Like the ancient alchemists, Barbault has never revealed the nature of this basic material; but to it dew was added (collected by trailing a sheet over the grass, at dawn, then ringing it into a tub) and a little powdered gold, the mixture being boiled for four hours at a specific temperature, and allowed to stand for four hours. This process was repeated seven times, and the result was a clear golden liquid – "vegetable gold". Barbault and his doctor friends claim to have used it to cure (among other things) multiple sclerosis, uremia and syphilis.

9.

Soothsaying

Throughout history, there have been people who claimed to have "the sight": the innate ability to predict future events. Often, this ability has been associated with heredity: the seventh son of a seventh son has always been believed to have prophetic gifts, and similar powers are also attributed to gypsies.

However, prophecy – the whole idea of foretelling the future – probably began, as so many aspects of magic began, as an element of religion. In classical Greece a prophet was the voice of the oracle of the gods, who themselves spoke in tones too frenzied to be comprehensible, so at the Delphic Oracle, for instance, the Pythia was interpreted by the Guardians of the Shrine, who translated her words just as a legion of authors have tried to translate the enigmatic verses of Nostradamus.

Looking into the future, whether successfully or unsuccessfully, is always a dangerous business, and it is no surprise that prophets often spoke in riddles, thus allowing them an escape route should their prognostications be wrong. This however had its disadvantages, for their incoherence gave ammunition to disbelievers, especially in the Hellenistic period. However, at the same time the public had a reverence for those who in ecstasy spoke "nothing of their own", but words which seemed to issue from some other dimension of time.

The Old Testament prophets were spiritual leaders and interpreters of the Word, but there is no doubt they were also seen as predictors of the future, and what would or at least might happen in it. The author of the Book of Samuel devoted himself to the service of Jehovah and to predicting future events. In Egypt at about the same time a youth at the court of a Phoenician prince was one of many men engaged in prophecy; dependable prophets were so valuable that (as reported in I *Kings* 18) Elijah went to great lengths to protect 100 from Queen Jezebel, who had massacred many of their colleagues – while maintaining 850 prophets of her own, devoted to interpreting the words of Baal and Asherah.

*The spinning wheel of chance (**opposite**) brings both good and bad fortune, even to those who can predict its movement.*

In Israel, prophets were many – at one end of the social scale the itinerant sooth-sayer and at the other the guardians of famous sanctuaries, who went into a trance in which they heard the words of spiritual beings able to communicate news of future events. Their predictions permeated every stratum of society.

What has been called the golden age of Hebrew prophecy came in about 750 BC, when the prophets Amos and Hosea were at work in northern Israel, and Isaiah, Micah and Jeremiah in Judah. There are plenty of examples of what seem to be accurate predictions made by them and their contemporaries, and ordinary people would have regarded it as outrageous to suggest that the future could not be foretold by inspired godly men and women. That suggestion was to come later, two or three centuries after Christ, when religion and magic began to be seen by some theologians as irreconcilable, and the Biblical prophets' work was interpreted as offering poetic versions of various aspects of life rather than actual predictions.

SEERS

It was in Greece – at Delphi, below Mount Parnassus – that for over 800 years the most famous of oracles was to be found. Here, at a shrine said to have been built by Apollo himself, the Pythia, usually an elderly and ugly virgin (an early, beautiful Pythia had been seduced, and her talents wasted) seems to have entered a hallucino-genic trance, aided by breathing the vapours exhaled from a deep cave and by chew-ing bay leaves. When asked questions, she gave vent to obscure utterances which were interpreted by her prophets; the fact that immense wealth was poured out in offerings at her shrine suggests either that the oracle was very frequently accurate, or at least that it was persuasive – surely its reputation would not have lasted for eight centuries and more if at least a proportion of accurate predictions had not been made? Though the most likely solution is that, like Nostradamus's predictions, the oracle's were so gnomic as to be capable of a number of interpretations sufficient to ensure that one of them was approximate to the truth.

*Many people believe that the future lies in the palm of your hand (**opposite**). In ancient times, however, the Oracle at Delphi, Greece (**above**), was seen as the seat of prophecy, situated above a cleft in the living rock.*

*A Gypsy fortune-teller
uses a crystal ball to scry
into the future.
Soothsaying may be a
hereditary talent, but
some writers believe it is
inherent in the human
psyche.*

TECHNIQUES OF PROPHECY

Soothsaying has not always been the sole prerogative of those gifted with "the sight". There have also been tried and tested techniques, which people could learn in order to become competent soothsayers.

The development of astrology (which is outside the scope of this book) encouraged the belief that it was possible to predict the future – though it did so by using an empirical system based on scientific observation; more popular forecasters relied on trance and ecstasy – though later, especially in Greece, there was great interest in other techniques. The emphasis on Fate made the idea of prediction not only possible but probable; though those who believed in free will found it more difficult to accept.

Meanwhile in Egypt prophetic dreams were in fashion, some professional dreamers making their beds on graves the more easily to contact the dead, who were the source of the predictions. Those in Rome followed another method – by examining the livers of dead animals. The *haruspices*, or interpreters, came originally from Babylon, by way of Etruria, and built up enviable practices in Rome. An ox would be ceremonially slaughtered on an altar, its liver extracted, and its shape, number of lobes, weight, and blood content would all be considered significant in answering questions about the future. Clay models of livers have been found, used to teach students. Later, sheep entrails were "read" in a similar manner, and later still animals' hearts; a college of 60 *haruspices* was established in Rome for the teaching of *hepatoscopy*, and were regarded with as much reverence as priests.

Many omens predicted whether a particular day would be lucky – some of them highly eccentric (a study of the pattern made by oil spread on the fingernails of a male virgin may not have satisfied the strictest scientific examination), and many were arbitrary (noting the foot – left or right – with which your horse first stepped over the doorway of its stable in the morning). These omens had more to do with luck than anything else. Most people were particularly superstitious in believing that human actions could provoke fortunate or unfortunate events: lists of lucky and unlucky days were regularly published, while numerology predicted particularly important years in a life – the "grand climacteric" for instance was said to be one's 63rd year (arrived at by multiplying the two important numbers seven and nine). There was a great deal of superstitious behaviour: lucky or unlucky actions could lay out a fortunate or unfortunate future.

The church took an equivocal view of all this: many churchmen believed that God vouchsafed advice to his people in the form of coded messages delivered in dreams or through particular people (who more often than not announced themselves as spiritual leaders, and were frequently imprisoned for their claims).

For most of the Roman emperors – and to an extent, later, for many of the popes – astrology soon overtook hepatoscopy and these other techniques as a means of supposedly accurate prediction. Only some sects of the Christian church disapproved of it, but not with great intensity.

FAMOUS SOOTHSAYERS

The Western tradition has included several notable examples of individuals who claimed to have the ability to predict the future. Among these were Nostradamus and Joanna Southcott.

Individual seers – soothsayers – whatever you may call them – built up their own reputations, some in small, some in large ways. Anecdotal evidence suggests that some of them made remarkably accurate predictions; but in almost every case one's reaction must be that the anecdote is amusing rather than necessarily true.

Many latter-day prophets were astrologers, but like Nostradamus and John Dee combined their astrological technique with others – they conversed with spirits, used crystals or pools of water to focus their visions, or simply "received" their predictive statements in some kind of trance. The latter must surely be the way Nostradamus worked, and though his reputation among certain people seems to be almost as high today as it was in his own time, it is based on very shaky ground.

Michael de Nostradame (1502-66), a physician born at St Rémy in France, whose work as a conventional doctor was beyond reproach (he acted with great bravery during the plague), set himself up as a prophet when he was about 35. In 1555 he published the first edition of his *Centuries*, a collection of obscure quatrains which became the most famous book of prophesies ever produced in Western Europe. Innumerable "interpretations" of these verses have been published, many of them contriving to associate them with events which have occurred up to and including the present time – including the First World War, the dropping of the atomic bomb, and the assassination of President Kennedy.

It is very easy indeed to draw such conclusions, for the verses are sufficiently vague and opaque to bear almost any interpretations, and it is difficult to escape the proposition that it is the hard work of those interpreters who have twisted his verses into shape which is responsible for any apparently accurate forecasts, rather than Nostradamus himself.

How he produced his quatrains remains an open question: not, certainly, by astrology – perhaps by some form of crystallomancy or scrying – a technique much the same that used by Dr Dee, the Elizabethan magus, into whose magic mirror Queen Elizabeth would peer, hoping to make sense of the dark patterns swirling there (the mirror

Nostradamus, a 16th-century French physician and soothsayer, proclaimed the future in obscure verses that some people see as accurate prophecies.

can still be seen in the British Museum). Dee is said to have predicted the death of Mary Tudor, the execution of Mary, Queen of Scots, and the defeat of the Spanish Armada.

There are plenty of similar but less well-known prophets in history. The Irish mage Malachy O'Morgair, in the eleventh century, was known for his habit of levitating, and left a number of prophesies as to the identity of future popes, many of which seem surprisingly accurate; Thomas the Rhymer, a Scot who lived in the thirteenth century, also predicted the kind of men who would be elected to the papacy – among them a Pope Leo XIII with the motto *lumen in caelo*: Leo's coat of arms turned out to contain a comet!

The eagerness of ordinary people to believe in prophecy is illustrated by the enthusiasm which greeted the claims of Joanna Southcott, a Devonshire woman born in about 1750, who merely by presenting herself as an oracle – she evidently had considerable dramatic talent – attracted something like 100,000 followers, and left when she died a famous box supposed to contain the secrets of the future, to be opened only in the presence of 24 bishops. Unsurprisingly, it was difficult to persuade the Archbishop of Canterbury to convene a gathering; and anyway the box when opened proved to contain nothing but rubbish (maybe, of course, the absence of the bishops was responsible for the disappointment).

There have been more modern prophets – some more eccentric than others. The Rev. Dr George King of London, for instance, claimed to have been visited in 1954 by extraterrestrial beings who took him off into space, where he witnessed a battle between the Venusians and the Martians; later, he met Jesus on the top of a Devonshire hill and predicted the end of the world, which was to occur in February 1962. Mr David Icke, a television and radio sports commentator and sometime spokesman for the British Green Party, has more recently predicted the Second Coming, among many other events of cosmic significance.

Considerable claims have been made on behalf of the American Jeanne Dixon, who is said to have successfully predicted the assassinations of President Kennedy, Mahatma Gandhi and Martin Luther King.

Almost without exception the prophets of the past – from the earliest days until perhaps the eighteenth century – believed in the possibility of predicting events. The "scientific" age has produced a consensus view that this was not possible; but more recently the suspicion has returned that we may not know everything about the nature of time – that, as the psychologist C. G. Jung stated, "the fact that we are unable to imagine a form of existence without space and time by no means proves that such an existence is in itself impossible"; and if that is the case, the prediction of events may be entirely possible. But for a contemporary view of prediction, the reader must wait until the second part of this book.

PART II
LIVING

MAGIC

10.

Witchcraft Today

Witchcraft – or Wicca, as witches prefer to call it – is probably more widespread today than for many centuries. For various reasons it has been much maligned: the fundamentalists of most religions hate and fear it, and its nature has been completely misunderstood (until comparatively recently the popular press used "witchcraft" and "Satanism" almost synonymously, and associated it particularly with sex and often with ritual torture and even child abuse).

Witches firmly claim that Wicca is a religion; and indeed it is difficult to argue against that claim if one defines religion as belief in a supernatural controlling power entitled to obedience and worship. But the power they worship is of course a different one from that recognized by, for instance, Christianity; the gods of Wicca are the ancient gods invoked by Prospero in Shakespeare's *The Tempest*:

> *Ye elves of hills, brooks, standing lakes, and groves,*
> *And ye that on the sands with printless foot*
> *Do chase the ebbing Neptune, and do fly him*
> *When he comes back: you demi-puppets that*
> *By moonshine do the green sour ringlets make,*
> *Whereof the ewe not bites . . .*

It is difficult to imagine a practising Christian – or indeed a member of any other religion – finding it also possible to be a witch, though witches are not interested in denying the truth or possible truth of any other religion; their general tolerance indeed is remarkable.

*A Wicca postulant (**opposite**) is usually "sky-clad", following a belief that nudity protects against evil.*

Wicca takes various forms in the modern world. Because its practices have always been secret – and often indeed illegal (as they were in England until the repeal in 1951 of the Fraudulent Mediums Act) – there is no formal record of them – no Wicca Book of Common Prayer, as it were. Though they keep a personal handwritten record of the knowledge passed on to them in what are called their "Book of Shadows", initiates must take an oath to "ever keep secret and never reveal the secrets of the Art except it be to a proper person, properly prepared . . ."

Secrecy is considered extremely important: some American Wiccas reinforce the power of the spoken oath with a signed document in which the initiate promises "to keep the secrets of the Craft of the Wise; never to reveal the rank or identity of any Witch . . . never to reveal the location of the covenstead, methods of working, or the manufacture or consecration of the tools," never to "misrepresent the Craft as being a parody of Christianity or any other religion [or] in any way connected with Satanism" on pain of "the power of just retribution" – which in effect means losing their good name and standing among their peers.

Interest in "modern" Wicca grew through a number of influences – especially that of Gerald Brosseau Gardner, who was said to have been taught by a witch called Dorothy Clutterbuck, who may or may not actually have existed. Gardner, an enthusiastic member of the Order of the Golden Dawn and a friend of Aleister Crowley, evolved new rites and rituals (which he recorded in his own private grimoire) and became a committed follower of the Horned God. He more than any other single person is responsible for the revival of Wicca in the modern Western world, and from his writings (in particular *Witchcraft Today*) others took their own lines. In England, for instance, there are two mainstreams of Wicca practice, Gardnerian and Alexandrian (named after Gardner and Alex Sanders, who allegedly learned the craft from his grandmother). These two streams are by no means antagonistic and their aims are much the same; but to differentiate between them, much less to consider other variations which exist in Europe and North America, is clearly impossible. We must confine ourselves to those aspects of Wicca practice which are more or less common to them all.

It is not unduly difficult to make contact with a coven. In England, the Pagan Federation will answer enquiries; there are many "New Age" magazines in Europe and North America which carry advertisements or news of covens and welcome serious enquiries. We must emphasize the word "serious"; no doubt as the result of long and sometimes unfortunate experience, witches are good at judging the intentions of people who contact them. Those who do so, either because they believe an interest in witchcraft is a pass to orgiastic sex, or because they want to learn how to cast a spell which will disable a rival, will swiftly be disillusioned. Indeed, much of the magic with which modern covens are concerned is directed at self-improvement, at the opening out of the psyche, at encouraging people to come to terms with their own personalities and develop the power within themselves – activities which swiftly bore those whose interest is more sensational.

Once the genuine interest of an enquirer has been established, the first step in most Wiccas will be to prepare him or her for initiation. There are usually three initiation ceremonies, the first presenting the initiate to the coven in the way in which a postulant is presented to a religious order. This happens when both the leaders of the coven and the postulant feel that the time is right (classically, the initiation should take place a year and a day after the first approach).

A woman postulant is initiated by a man, a man by a woman. In her fascinating book *Wicca: The Old Religion in the New Age*, the Jungian psychologist Vivianne Crowley associates this ancient tradition with Jung's theory of the anima (the female aspect of a man) and the animus (the male aspect of a woman). It is worth noting, incidentally, that the Wicca movement and the feminist movement sometimes close ranks to exclude men from certain covens; an equation between Diana, the goddess of the Old Religion, and the conception of the Christian God as female is by no

*Modern witches prepare for Wicca ceremonies. A witch from Hertfordshire, England (**top**), arranges ritual objects on an altar; the Cornish witch Cait Sidh (**above**) begins the invocation.*

*Within the magic circle (**left**) a witch enacts the rite of the "Goetic Circle" and the rite of Thoth, designed by the 19th-century magician Eliphas Lévi. The sabbatic goat (**right**) is evoked in a traditional ritual.*

means unknown. In such covens, the Horned God – a fertility god more usually equal in stature to the Goddess, Diana – yields precedence to her.

An initiate is almost always "sky-clad" (the delightful Wicca synonym for nudity) – an ancient tradition associated not only with innocence and vulnerability, but with the theory that nudity protects one against evil, and also with the belief that nudity puts one in direct contact with the cosmos. She is blindfold, and symbolically bound with cords (once more emphasizing vulnerability, but also trust in the Wicca coven and its members).

A circle is then "cast" or "built". We have already seen the importance of the circle in the history of magic, and all Wicca rites take place within one. The method and ceremony used to construct it differs from coven to coven, but it is usually symbolically drawn in the air, marking out a space (not always in fact circular) which ancient tradition saw as existing "between the worlds . . . the world of humans and the realms of the Mighty Ones", but which modern witches are more likely to see as lying between the psychological and the spiritual – a place in which the physical can meet with the immaterial.

Enchantingly, that great traditional symbol of witchcraft, the broom, is used as part of the ritual preparation of the circle – sweeping the space, sweeping unwanted thoughts and associations from the minds of members of the coven. An invocation is then chanted – covens often devise their own, or use one passed down verbally or in writing – and a dagger or *athame*, the symbol of Will, is used by a priestess to describe the circle, creating as it were a vacuum which can be filled with the energy the coven will generate, protected from outside influences. The circumference of the circle is cleansed with spring water mixed with salt and consecrated by the priestess; the priest, priestess and members of the coven are then also consecrated with the water, as is the ground itself.

Some aspects of the ritual associated with Wicca ceremonies are clearly very ancient – for instance, the fact that the north part of the circle is consecrated first: the north has always been the home of the gods in many traditions and, as Vivianne Crowley points out, is now, as the direction through which the Sun passes at night, associated with the deepest part of the unconscious mind.

The circle having been drawn, the four quarters or Watchtowers must be established by the use of invocations and the inscription of pentagrams by the *athame*. Into these Watchtowers are invited the guardian spirits or regents of the four elements – air, fire, water and earth: Eurus, Notus, Zephyrus and Boreas – symbolizing the elemental powers both of the outer and inner worlds.

Within the circle, the initiation ceremonies then take place. In the first ceremony, the Bagahi Rune, dating from at least the 13th century, is recited – a medieval text beginning:

> *Bagahi laca bachahe*
> *Lamac cahi achabahe*
> *Karrelyos . . .*

The divine force having been invoked by this chant, the broomstick (which is both a male and female symbol, and so that of sexual union) is placed to mark a "door" into the circle by which the postulant can enter to meet the point of the *athame* and a challenge to her bravery: "It were better to rush on my blade and perish than to make the attempt with fear in thy heart." Having assented, the postulant is then welcomed with a kiss, is presented to each of the Towers in turn (in order that their Lords will recognize her, and come when summoned), and members of the coven "circle three times with dance, step and chant" – usually, the witches' rune:

> *Darksome night and shining Moon*
> *East then South then West then North*
> *Harken to the Witches' Rune*
> *Here we come to call thee forth.*
>
> *Earth and Water, Air and Fire*
> *Wand and pentacle and sword*
> *Work ye unto our desire*
> *And harken ye unto our word.*
>
> *Cords and censer, scourge and knife*
> *Powers of the witches' blade*
> *Waken all ye into life*
> *And come ye as the charm is made.*
>
> *Queen of Heaven, Queen of Hell*
> *Horned Hunter of the Night*
> *Lend your power unto our spell*
> *And work our will by magic rite.*
>
> *By all the powers of land and sea*
> *By all the might of Moon and Sun*
> *As we do so mote it be*
> *Chant the spell and be it done.*
>
> *Eko, eko Arazak*
> *Eko, eko Zamilak*
> *Eko, eko Cernunnos*
> *Eko, eko Aradia.*

Both the dance and the rune are extremely important in Wicca ceremonies. At the initiation ceremony they are the prelude to the most important moment: after the postulant has been taken to the west of the circle and the initiating priest or priestess has spoken about the divine spirit within humanity and how it can be united with the divine forces, she is taken to the eastern part of the circle, and a bell is rung. The most senior high priest or priestess now kneels before the postulant, and reciting the words of the fivefold kiss, salutes the appropriate part of his or her body:

> *Blessed be thy feet that have brought thee in these ways.*
> *Blessed be thy knees that shall kneel at the sacred altar.*
> *Blessed be thy phallus/womb without which we would not be.*
> *Blessed be thy breast/s formed in beauty and strength.*
> *Blessed be thy lips that shall utter the sacred names.*

Reminded of the sacredness of the body and ready to take the vow, the postulant now has his or her feet loosely tied together ("feet neither bound nor free"), and is measured as for a shroud (such measurements were traditionally regarded as having a powerful magic, for possession of them gave one power over the person measured); the bell is rung again, and the postulant lightly scourged 40 times.

The oath then taken is chiefly one of loyalty and secrecy, and at the end of the initiation the bell rings for a last time, the blindfold is removed and the initiated postulant given a magic sword, an *athame*, a white handled knife to be used only within the circle, a wand (a phallic symbol), a pentacle, a censer of incense, a scourge (symbolic of suffering) and the cords with which he or she was bound.

The First Instruction is then given – that witches' power comes within, and that there is no part of mankind which is not divine; and the witches' law – "an it harm none, do what you will."

After considerable study over a period of time (again, at least a year and a day), a witch having learned a great deal about the basic use of magic can take a second and third initiation. The second degree, which in ritual is somewhat similar to the first, involves encountering the Horned God, the Dark Lord of Death; this is symbolic of the full realization of the existence of both good and evil – the emphasis is on "suffering to learn". She or he uses the magic instruments to raise a circle, invoke the Watchtowers, and control the powers which are evoked.

The Legend of the Goddess is then acted out: the Goddess is a manifestation of the spirit of the earth itself (or perhaps the other way about), and the legend is an ancient narrative in which birth and death, love and fear, the Horned One and the Goddess, are reconciled. Having understood and accepted this (again the emphasis is on "suffering to learn"), the initiate may be given the title of high priest or high priestess.

The third initiation entitles a witch to set up and run a coven, and involves the Great Rite, an act of ritual sex which can be performed "in true" or "in token" – that is in fact or in symbol. The "Book of Shadows" instructs that the Great Rite should be performed at every sabbat; it is now usually performed in private, between the high priest and priestess, anima and animus united.

It is usual for two witches – one man and one woman – to work together towards the third initiation and be initiated together; in many cases the couple are married or are lovers, in which case there is no difficulty about their performing the Great Rite "in true"; in other cases they prefer to perform it "in token". Some covens appear to insist that the Rite should always be performed "in true", pointing out that the sexual union is between God and Goddess rather than between man and woman, and that the people concerned should be able to "set aside the human element".

Any summary of the third initiation can only be cursory, and only the roughest impression can be given of it (in any event some aspects of it remain secret). But at one stage, for instance, the God asks the Goddess:

Will you pass now through the veil and the gates of night and day?
Will you be at one with me who am both death and life? Will you
kneel before me and worship me?

The Goddess having assented, and been reminded of the aspect of the God which represents darkness and death, she then addresses him:

I am light and thou the darkness, I am darkness and thou the light,
and there must be no separation between us. Will you love me
beyond all things and be the instrument of my desire? Will you love
the darkness that is within thee and open your arms to it? Will you
flee not from shadows and the fears, but embrace them and so make
yourself whole?

After warnings of the perilousness of the road they are taking, the female initiate kneels, surrounded by unlit candles in the shape of a hexagram (the symbol of the union of opposites), and the male initiate, having been questioned by the high priestess and answered correctly, lays down his sword (the phallic symbol of the mastery which kills love and trust) and approaches her. The Sacred Marriage, the Great Rite, then takes place, either "in token" or "in true" (with many other ceremonial gestures, symbols and incantations).

The question remains, what actually *happens* at a coven gathering? How does the magic work? Witches make the point that since magic *does* work, and that since in our present state of knowledge we apparently cannot know why, a preoccupation with the mechanics of the matter is superfluous and perhaps even damaging.

Each coven uses its own forms of ritual to raise the power by which its members will work their magic, but there are some common factors – such as choosing the time of the full moon for important Wicca meetings. The psychic energy of the full moon is legendary – but there can also be no doubt that real energy is involved; the effect of the moon on many areas of life, from the woman's cycle to the tides, from the human psyche to animal behaviour, is too obvious for further comment.

WITCHES' YEAR
Major meetings or sabbats
held at the times of a number of ancient festivals:

December *20 or 21* **Yule**, *the time of the*
winter solstice

February *1 or 2* **Imbolc** *or* **Candlemas**
favourite time for initiations

March *20 or 21* **Eostre**, *the time of the vernal*
equinox and a fertility festival

April *30* Beltane *or the* **Eve of May Day**

June *21* **Midsummer**

August *1* **Lammas**

September *20 or 21* **Harvestide**

October *31* **Samhain** *or* **Hallowe'en**

The witches' year revolves within a context of mystic colours and plants, such as oak leaves, mistletoe, deadly nightshade and elderberry. Surrounded by a snake, symbol of rebirth and renewal, the wheel of the seasons includes the new moon and snowdrops of **Imbolc**, the February festival

welcoming the Maiden; primroses to mark the vernal equinox; the fire festival of **Beltane**; the summer solstice; the August **Lammas** festival of harvested corn; and the spiral dragon lying beneath the earth, symbolizing the energies that are released at **Samhain** – Year's End.

Cornish witches near Falmouth participate in a ritual invoking the "Owlman". They are "sky-clad" for closer contact with the Cosmos, and have timed the ceremony to coincide with Samhain, also known as Halloween. This was the key point of the Celtic year, and signalled a convergence between the worlds of spirits and human beings.

At sabbats or more ordinary Wicca meetings, ritual dancing will certainly take place. The effect of rhythmic movement and sound on the human mind has been observed for many centuries, and is well known: it raises the consciousness, gives those concerned a sort of corporate personality, and can have a hypnotic effect, clearly observable in the dances of primitive tribes. At a Wicca meeting part of the usefulness of dance is to release the concentration with which witches have to act in order to cast their circle, and to release the energy which instils magical power.

Dancing always appears to have taken place in these circumstances, and in previous times was alleged to have taken a wildly salacious form. That may well have been the case, but the concentration in modern times is on rhythm and movement as a means of concentrating psychical rather than physical energy, though the two are evidently interconnected. It is the case, incidentally, that the dancers are whenever possible naked, for clothing seems to inhibit the power they wish to raise.

The dance itself is usually performed in a spiral clockwise direction – "widdershins" or anti-clockwise movement (against the apparent direction of the sun in the northern hemisphere) is traditionally considered to be diabolic (the "left-hand path"), though it is used under some circumstances. Wherever possible men and women alternate in the line of the dance, so that their energies are properly balanced. At the end of the sabbat or meeting, there is a joyous feast before the circle is broken.

Whatever we may think about the effect of dancing and chanting in raising magical powers, that it has a psychological effect can scarcely be doubted by anyone who has had any experience of group movement, whether in a dance group, an aerobic class, or in the ordinary circumstances of a dance-hall. The dionysiac frenzies released by, for instance, "jive" sessions during the 1940s or by rock 'n' roll during the 1950s are only the most vivid recent images of the energy generated by more or less ecstatic dancing. The use of similar devices (sometimes dancing, more usually chanting or singing) in fundamentalist religious meetings can also be seen, especially in North America.

The arousal of dionysiac frenzy is not a purpose of the dancing done by Wicca covens, but the raising and release of energy certainly is; and so is the binding effect that such behaviour has on a group. No one who has worked intimately with a number of other people – in an acting class, perhaps, or even in a sports team – will have any doubt about the power of the group consciousness which can evolve, not only tenaciously binding one member to another but also creating a group identity which can impress itself vividly on "outsiders".

It is the power of the group which raises the energy by which magical acts are accomplished. As to what these acts are, they appear to cover all areas of life, from working to cure someone suffering from severe illness, to helping someone unemployed to get a job. During the 1991 Gulf war some covens are said to have worked against Saddam Hussein, just as in the 1940s they met to cast spells to protect Britain from German invasion. More recently, in America, Wicca power has been used to reinforce attempts to heal the earth's ecology. There have been Earth Day festivals in Boston, Massachusetts, for instance, when Goddess Gospel singers performed on the waterfront; near Mount Horeb, Wisconsin, the Circle Sanctuary offered prayers to "heal Planet Earth".

Predominantly female American Wiccas (membership of which is calculated as being over 100,000) concentrate on the idea of a female deity – God the Mother – whose power and personality are those of the old European Great Goddess of prehistoric times. Their ideas are taken very seriously: a witch teaches in an institute at California's Roman Catholic Holy Names College, for instance, and two United Methodist pastors have proposed experimental Bible readings about the crucifixion which replace Jesus with Sophia (Wisdom) – a name for the divine personality used by feminist worshippers.

Those of us who stand outside the Wicca movement can only conjecture why its magic works, if indeed it does. Those who believe or "know" that distant healing or ESP is effective will have no difficulty in accepting the proposition that Wicca magic also works. If individual psychic power can be raised and focused to heal a sufferer, there is no reason why group psychic power should not work – and work a great deal more strongly.

Magic is, for the scientifically minded, wholly irrational; but, as we must continually remind ourselves, so in the recent past were propositions which are now everyday facts (the wireless, television, x-rays, dowsing – the examples are too numerous to list).

Some aspects of Wicca may seem more irrational than others – the invocation of the ancient gods, for instance. Some witches fervently believe in these gods and worship them in a literal sense, others revere what they stand for; but consciousness of them is in any event extremely important – and as with all magic, to the extent that it works there may be a rational basis to such invocations which will one day be understood – and this may apply to magic as a whole, including the efficaciousness of spells. Even now, many witches would claim that the power of their magic is natural rather than supernatural.

Dr Vivianne Crowley speaks for instance of left- and right-hand brain activity, pointing out that measurable brain rhythms differ when people enter that state in which they are engaged in psychical or paranormal acts such as healing, mind-reading and metal-bending. She suggests that at a Wicca meeting a higher or deeper state of consciousness is entered which approximates to the contemplative state called *samadhi* in Eastern meditative systems, and that it is from this state that witches are able to establish connection with the people they wish to help (or harm), and work their will.

The invocation of ancient gods is an imaginative part of the process of moving from an everyday state of consciousness into a higher, even "divine" plane; gods in every civilization have been the expression of forces which men have, however dimly, apprehended and wished to control or at least use. But Dr Crowley, echoing the recent theories of some scientists who see the earth as a living entity in itself, speaks of "the presences found in trees, caves and pools not as divine but as elemental forces which are also known as devas or nature spirits. It is the planet itself which is seen as divine . . ." This in turn is a comment on the reverence with which witches throughout history have treated nature. Members of Green movements in our own time will be in sympathy at least with the idea of apologizing to the spirit of a flower when one picks it.

An interest in witchcraft and the desire to practise it need not necessarily mean or lead to membership of a coven; there are self-taught witches who have learned the craft through reading traditional or contemporary texts, and there are a number of courses which attempt to lead students through the rituals which invoke and enable powers to be used.

Amateurs are, however, warned that this is difficult; second that it is hard work; and third that it is to be taken seriously. Open a door, it is sometimes said, and you do not know what may come through it; it may also be very difficult to close it again.

Whatever view you take of magic, it is absolutely clear that certain forces are released by its practice which, whether occult or psychological (and these are not mutually exclusive terms) are intense enough to do either a great deal of good or a great deal of harm to the individual who either controls or is controlled by them.

The theory and the practice of Wicca are far too complex to explore thoroughly in a brief chapter, but it is possible to see that while it is clearly no easy matter to master the rituals or to perform them (magic is again and again referred to as "hard work") there is at bottom an enviable simplicity about the idea – one which has appealed strongly to men and women throughout the ages, and has at its core the notion of all things being one. Witchcraft and what power it has can of course be misused, but what evidence there is suggests that the balance tips towards the positive. Major attacks on Wicca are generally misinformed, and in any event invariably come from those with a vested interest – either from scientists who wish to prove that the very idea of magic is silly and insupportable (as so many of them believed radio and space flight to be), or from committed Christians (not so much from members of other major religions) who regard the worship of the forces of nature as wicked.

A hooded figure stands at Wayland's Smithy, Wiltshire,
a place for ceremonies linking the living and the dead.

11.

Practical Magic

Practical magic? Can the two words be put together? Over thousands of years it was believed that they could; and many people still consider that to be the case. But today, the word magic means different things to many people. A great number of followers of various religions from all over the world believe in the power of prayer; and we should remember that prayer may be seen as an attempt to influence occult powers (and divinity represents the greatest occult power we know). It is not devoid of an element of magic, though it works through submission and supplication while magic works by command and instruction. Therefore priests and people of religious movements – whether they be nonconformist Christians, Quechua speakers of the Catholic Church in the High Andes, Ahmadiya of Islam, or Ch'ondogyo of South Korea – need not take offence if we suggest that the invocations they address to their Maker are not entirely at variance with invocations made by Dr Dee to his angelic companions, or even the muttered words with which some people will don an amulet or talisman.

*Talismans (**opposite**), once they have been magically empowered, can touch the heart even in today's sceptical climate. They may draw their strength from a magic inscription, such as Abracadabra, or from a symbolic shape, such as the ancient Egyptian ankh.*

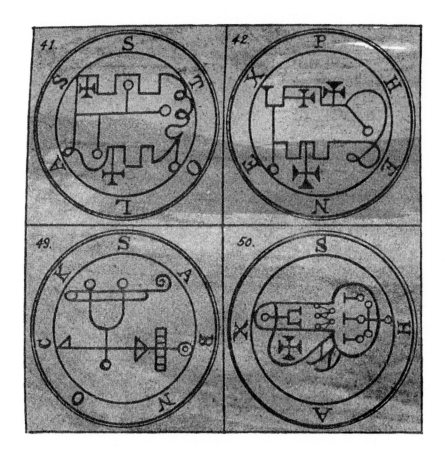

TALISMANS

Talismans have been worn since the beginning of civilization, in the confidence that they confer or contain certain powers. The Catholic church in particular continues to set store by – for instance – rosaries blessed by the Pope. Can these talismans be equated with "lucky charms"? Can a talisman, in the 20th century, have anything to do with "practical magic"? The answer (if we are as cautious as we should be), may well be a qualified yes.

Men and women wear or carry talismans in an attempt to make themselves singular in a world in which a rapidly increasing population makes it clear that individuality is at a premium. Almost everyone wears a talisman of some sort – often unconsciously. Many men and women wear a charm around their neck, often given them by a friend or lover, sometimes bought unthinkingly at some holiday resort because to wear one is the fashion, sometimes bought to mark some event – but still endowed with special power for the owner.

In times of danger, men have often worn or carried some lucky object. When we lose an object of this kind our emotions remind us of the perhaps irrational importance we place on them. When an article we have worn or carried for many years is lost or stolen, we feel as though something far more powerful than a mere piece of material has gone. We may not consciously suppose that a chain with a symbol of some kind on it can make us powerful or protect us from evil; but somewhere at the back of our mind there is a small acknowledgement of belief.

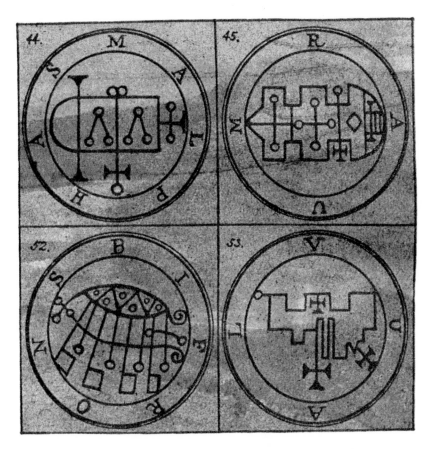

Talismans from a modern grimoire bear symbols elaborated from medieval magical practice. The psychological need for protection and reassurance conferred by such objects remains strong in the 1990s.

This is not surprising when we consider for how many millennia such a conviction was strongly held. Belief in talismans shook even some Christian saints – St Justin asked himself wryly why, if his God was creator of all, the talismans of the pagan Apollonius apparently still had such power. The power resides, of course, in belief – for here, as in every area of magic, belief is all-important. Before the present age of scientific materialism, our ancestors of long ago believed that a talisman inscribed with the name of a god conferred upon the wearer something of that god's power; later, that a talisman inscribed with the glyph of a planet and the name and insignia of the angel particularly associated with it would offer the wearer all the reassuring power of that planet.

We may believe we have "grown up" as the year 2000 approaches; but psychology reminds us that we are weak creatures, the strongest of whom is in need of reassurance of one kind or another. Perhaps there is something to be said for wearing a talisman which emphasizes, in however obscure a form, one's individuality, or the sort of person one ideally wants to be.

How is this best done? There are very few wholly individual inscriptions that can be placed on a talisman: one would be a fingerprint, another one's full horoscope or birth chart – though even that ceases to be entirely individual if another baby is born at the same minute in the next bed! However, we have one or two suggestions, based on the procedures of the grimoires.

MAKING YOUR OWN TALISMAN

In the past, this was an extraordinarily complicated business and the very complications made the process more mysterious. There is no reason to suppose that a simpler method will not have the same result. There should be a process, a ceremony, of some sort, for as with almost everything else in life something that is too easy – in this case a mass-produced symbol bought in some shop and simply hung around the neck without a second thought – will have little effect (occultists will argue in any case that an object which has knocked around in a shop, perhaps for months, will have lost much of the power it started out with – and may even have picked up some untoward potency with which you will not want to be associated).

It is as well, then, to make your own talisman. This is not as difficult as it sounds, even when the metal involved is silver or gold. If you cannot afford real gold, plain gold-plated or even gilt medallions can be found on which you can scratch the proper symbols. The general rule is that if the proper metal is not obtainable, one should use something which looks like it (the doctrine of correspondence, again). For Mercury, for instance, if silver is unobtainable, one may use tin or brass.

The kind of talisman you make depends on your own point of view; you make of it what you will, and for what purpose you will. But as to actually preparing it, there are one or two general rules – the chief one of which is that the work should be done when the Moon is waxing, and never when it is waning. If you use any astrological symbolism, it is important to work on the day associated with the planet whose symbol or glyph you are inscribing: for the Sun, Sunday, the Moon, Monday; then Tuesday, Wednesday, Thursday, Friday and Saturday for Mars, Mercury, Jupiter, Venus and Saturn respectively, in that order. The planets that have been discovered in modern times, Uranus, Neptune and Pluto, are not used; they may have Zodiac signs, but occultists feel that they have as yet little magical power.

Talismans have traditionally been purified and consecrated. Such a ceremony is not always necessary – unless you feel it to be, or believe that to follow at least some form of ancient practice will give you added confidence in their power. The process of purification is a simple one: you can wash the talisman in pure water, blessing it in the name of the principal power whose symbol it bears; you can hold it up to the four corners of the earth and invite the four elements to purify it; or you can purify it by laying it in the open air, under a piece of glass, so that moonlight falls on it.

Consecration is another matter – it is generally believed that the more effort you expend on that ceremony, the more efficacious the talisman will be. The form the ceremony takes can vary – you can invent one, or you can follow specific rules such as those laid down by such authorities as Eliphas Lévi – though these are sufficiently complicated to give some trouble. For instance, to consecrate a talisman to Venus, Lévi says you should decorate your room with green and rose-coloured cloths and copper ornaments, wear a turquoise ring and a crown of lapis lazuli and beryl, carry a fan of swan's feathers and wear a copper pendant with the name of Aniel engraved on it. If you are making a talisman of the Sun, you must stand on a lionskin carpet – an instruction which will not find favour with conservation-minded readers.

In order that the talisman collects as much of your personal energy as possible, it is best to be naked when consecrating it; the donning of clothes at the end of the ceremony will mark its close. The right day must be chosen for the ceremony (using the same rule as for making the talisman). Also the simplest means of imbuing it with energy is – first making yourself as comfortable as possible and trying to ensure that you are not interrupted – simply to hold it in your hand and concentrate on the task with which you wish it to help, or the emotion or purpose you desire for it. In a process which has been compared to charging a battery, you should hold the talisman for as long as your concentration lasts; when it begins to become difficult to maintain it, bring the ceremony to an end, and repeat it on another occasion.

If you wish to add something of your own to the occasion by a special invocation,

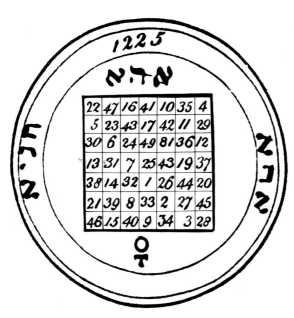

SEAL OF VENUS

the playing of music, or whatever, you are free to do so. It is best however not to involve another person: as Robin Skelton points out in the best available modern book on the subject, *Talismanic Magic*, however sympathetic a friend or lover may be, there is no means of telling how wholeheartedly they will join in such a ceremony, and scepticism can be fatal in some circumstances.

But now to the matter of what you can inscribe on your talisman. The classical astrological talismans bear recognized symbols. Some of these are astrological, others are connected with associated angels and even demons, and most importantly there is the magic square – the Zahlenquadrat or Kamea – containing numbers related to the spirit of the planet concerned.

As an example, let us look at the talisman for Venus (above). On one side, we find at the top the number 1225. This is the total of the numbers in the Kamea (below left), and is also the number of the Seraphim, the highest order of angels in the pseudo-Dionysian hierarchy and also in Jewish lore. The "intelligence" of Venus is Hagiel, associated with the cabbalistic number 49. The "spirit" or Demon of Venus is Kedemel, whose number is 175. The columns of the square, vertically, horizontally and diagonally, add up to that number, which is not only Kedemel's but is associated with the Hebrew goddess Meny, or Venus (below right).

On the other side of the talisman, we find a number of signs. At the bottom right is the glyph of the planet Venus. At the top is the planet's traditional seal – originally designed so that the lines in it, if superimposed on the Kamea, will pass through all the numbers in it. Below, is the sign of the planet's intelligence, Hagiel: superimposed on the Kamea, the lines pass through the numbers which spell out, in ancient numerology, the angel's name.

The Table of Venus in her Compass

22	47	16	41	10	35	4
5	23	43	17	42	11	29
30	6	24	49	81	36	12
13	31	7	25	43	19	37
38	14	32	1	26	44	20
21	39	8	33	2	27	45
46	15	40	9	34	3	28

In Hebrew

ר	לה	י	אלא	יו	מז	כב
כט	יא	מב	יז	מג	רג	ה
יב	לו	יה	מט	כד	ה	ל
לז	יט	מג	כה	ל	לא	יג
כ	מד	כו	א	לב	יד	לח
מה	בז	ב	לג	ח	לט	כא
כח	ג	לד	ט	מ	יהו	

The Seal of Venus

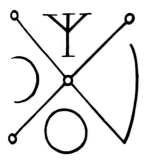

Her Intelligence

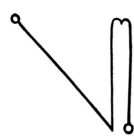

Her Spirit

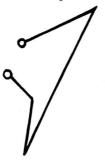

Her Wisdom

So you can make up the talisman for the planet associated with your astrological Sun sign. Remember that the Sun rules Leo, the Moon rules Cancer, Mercury rules Gemini and Virgo, Venus rules Taurus and Libra, Mars rules Aries and Scorpio, Jupiter rules Sagittarius and Pisces and Saturn rules Capricorn and Aquarius.

Or you can make a talisman for a particular purpose – that for the Sun, which should be engraved on gold, makes one amiable, successful, well known, and "elevates the fortunes, enabling one to do whatever he will". The Moon's talisman, engraved on silver, makes one pleasant and cheerful, brings honour, drives away ill-will, makes journeys safe and is productive of good health.

Saturn, whose talisman should be engraved on lead, is said to help childbirth, make one powerful, and to bring success in requests or petitions. Mercury's talisman, drawn on silver, tin or brass or written on parchment, brings good luck in general, attracts money, prevents poverty, helps "the memory, understanding and divination" and also assists in "the understanding of occult things by dreams".

Venus' talisman, on silver (or, some modern authorities say, copper), promotes friendship and ends arguments and discord, attracts the love of the opposite sex, helps women to conceive, and gives protection against antagonistic magic.

Mars' talisman, drawn on iron, strengthens the physique (it made a man "potent in war . . . terrible to his enemies"). And Jupiter's talisman, engraved on silver, brings riches and favours, love and peace, dignity and honours, and reconciliation with enemies.

If you do not wish to make use of the traditional symbols, then there is no reason why you should not invent your own, perhaps using a code difficult for anyone not in the know to read. You may like to use one of the ancient alphabets, writing your initials or part of your name in one of the ancient scripts. The best-known of these were reproduced by Francis Barrett in his famous textbook *The Magus*.

Theban Alphabet

The Theban alphabet, in Barrett's figure, is self-explanatory; to interpret the Celestial Writing (sometimes called the alphabet of the Magi), the Malachim alphabet or the alphabet called "passing the river", you need to know the Hebrew names of the letters:

A – Aleph	R – Res	V – Vau
O – Vau	G – Gimel	L – Lamed
B – Beth	S – Samekh	W – Vau
P – Pe	H – He	M – Mem
D – Daleth	T – Teth	Y – Yod
Q – Qoph	J – Yod	N – Nun
E – He	U – Vau	Z – Zain
	K – Caph	

In addition to these, Tau represents a "soft" T, pronounced at the back of the throat, and Kuff a similar "soft" K. Shin represents the sound "sh", Cheth "Ch", as in "checkers", and Zade the sound "Tz", foreign to most Western languages.

It will be noticed that some Hebrew letters are duplicated (He representing E and H, and Yod both J and Y); and some Roman letters are not represented at all – there is no equivalent of C, F, I, or X. For C, of course, one can use Cheth, or Caph; where I occurs, it is often possible to organize some substitute. It would be possible to spell the name Julia, for instance, Yod, Vau, Lamed, Yod, Aleph.

The Characters of Celestial Writing

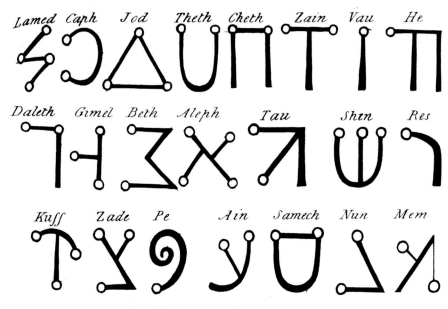

The Writing called Malachim

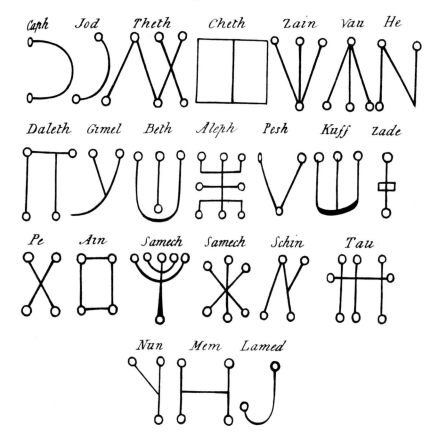

The Writing call'd Passing the River

There are various other possibilities apart from the examples illustrated: you could use Dr Dee's own private language, Enochian, which is available in various forms; or you could invent your own hieroglyphs.

Together with your name, the name of your lover, or indeed any inscription, you might like to include a number – the numerological signification of your name, or perhaps your date of birth. Roman numbers, written plain, could be used.

Finally, there are the various traditional inscriptions: the arrangements of letters in squares, for instance – the SATOR square we have already encountered; other very ancient squares include:

S A L O M A R E P O L E M E L O P E R A M O L A S	*This dates from at least 1458, but presents a difficulty in that its occult purpose is extremely unclear.*
R O L O R O B U F O L U A U L O F U B O R O L O R	*This palindrome was designed by the magician Abra-Melin in order to enable the wearer of the talisman to fly like a crow.*

The best-known inscription of all, and one of the most mysterious, is of course ABRACADABRA, which on a talisman should be written as illustrated here.

ABRACADABRA
ABRACADABR
ABRACADAB
ABRACADA
ABRACAD
ABRACA
ABRAC
ABRA
ABR
AB
A

The meaning of the original word is unclear, but Dr Erich Bischoff, who deals with it exhaustively in a book on the Cabballah, suggests that it sprang from the Chaldean words *Abbada ke dabra* or "perish like the word" – an imprecation which cured the fever. It is also considered an invocation of the deity Abraxas to restore wholeness.

Finally, it is possible of course simply to choose one of the many traditional symbols which are popular all over the world, and are found worn about the necks of people from Thailand to North America, from Japan to New South Wales. With these, however, there is the problem that their original meanings are often lost in the mists of time – they are worn, too often, merely as decorative ornaments.

A case in point is the cross, which many people choose to wear perhaps without much thought – although a number of people of course wear it from a deep religious conviction. Although primarily associated with Christianity, the cross is very much a pre-Christian symbol – examples have been found from as long ago as the late Stone Age, and non-Christian examples are numerous in India, Syria, Persia, Egypt, pre-Columbian Mexico and North America. In many cases it was connected with nature-worship, very often as the T-shaped *tau*; in Egyptian and Assyrian sculptures we often find it with a little loop or handle at the top – it is then associated with the idea of divinity.

But after the crucifixion it was not long before the significance of the cross became, at least in the West, entirely Christian, and its pagan magic association was weakened, probably for ever. Should you wish to wear a cross, there are many forms available to you, from the traditional Latin cross to the Cross of Lorraine, the heraldic, Maltese or Coptic cross, or the *tau* or St Anthony's cross.

The swastika or *fylfot* is also a kind of cross, formed by the Greek capital letter gamma placed in a fourfold pattern (it is known also as the *crux gammata*). It is found as a religious emblem in India and China, and was in existence long before the Christian era. The swastika seems to have originated in India, and was perhaps originally a symbol of fire, though there are also theories that it represents the spring sun, the four quarters of the world, or the symbol of the god Thor. Its appeal as a good luck symbol was strong until the rise of the Nazi movement in Germany in the 1930s, since when it has inevitably declined in popularity. It is now usually associated with extreme right-wing movements, both in Western Europe and the US. However, it can take many forms, and perhaps the time has come when it is possible to choose one of them, should the idea of this very ancient symbol appeal. Hindus use it to this day, painted in red on doorposts or steps.

The key is another very potent and ancient symbol – though not as ancient as the cross, for it has of course only been in use since the invention of locks. The whole point of a key is that it allows us to open doors – the doors of perception, or freedom, or knowledge. In Greece, it was considered sacred to Apollo; in Rome, to Janus. In some countries, three keys linked together are used, signifying health, wealth and love. The key is also of course the symbol of St Peter.

A symbol which seems to combine both cross and key is the Egyptian *ankh*. This is found on the earliest Christian tombs, though when the Egyptian gods are shown

bearing it, they carry it as a phallic symbol of the energy of life itself.

The Egyptians often wore or carried a model of a scarab or dung-beetle; watching this little beetle rolling its egg up in a ball of dung and placing it in the sun to hatch, the Egyptians saw its activities as a paradigm of the creation of the world, and wore the scarab talisman as a potent protection against evil which also held in it part of the energy of creation. (Elsewhere in the world, the delightful ladybird has been similarly used.)

The Egyptians sometimes also wore an *udjat* representing the eye of the mighty sun-god Ra, which when joined with the eye of Thoth, the moon-god (who is also the god of magic and learning), was a talisman which made the wearer immune to all evil.

A list of all the world's talismans would be very long indeed. It would include, among many other emblems, the mandala, the *yang/yin* of the Chinese, the international pentagram or five-pointed star (much used, as we have seen, in traditional magic), and the St Christopher medal beloved of travellers. All these are readily available; though authorities agree that if they are bought from some wholesale source, they should be "personalized" by being consecrated to the use of the individual wearer.

Talismans have been used in all ages and in all human societies, including the present. Their prevalence indicates a stubborn belief in magic and the supernatural, a rarely acknowledged allegiance to magical powers that seems to persist when more rational solutions fail.

All these talismans, whatever their traditional associations, signify in the end chiefly what they mean to you. When you inscribe or consecrate them, you give them the energy you wish them to have, and which they then keep and reflect; a personal talisman is what – and how – you make it.

The swastika pre-dates Nazism,
appearing with the Hindu elephant-god
*Ganesh (**top**), as a Roman mosaic*
*(**above**) or as a prehistoric rock carving*
*(**centre**). Other lucky talismans*
*include the Chinese Tao-ch'i (**bottom**)*
and the Egyptian ankh.

TALISMAN NECKLACE FOR A WOMAN

bestowing emotional healing and female power.
Created by Amie Hertzig.

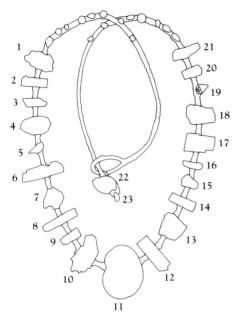

1 Peacock ore *Grounding, anchoring to earth, creativity, self-esteem*

2 Watermelon tourmalite *Healing the heart, voice vibration, balancing emotions, deflecting negativity*

3 9 Imperial topaz *Golden light, warmth,*
16 20 *manifestation, abundance*

4 Labradorite *Opening 3rd Eye, psychic vision, sealing holes in aura*

5 19 Tropical shell *Sea energy, emotions,*
22 *spiral flow of life force energy, beauty*

6 17 Aquamarine *Healing like the ocean, calming, soothing, purifying, expressing universal truths, opening heart chakra*

7 Rhodacrocite *Grounding the emotions, integrating, sexual energy*

8 Kyanite *Travelling through time, connecting to past lives*

10 Crystalized rosequartz *Highly evolved formation of the lovestone, unconditional love, opening and healing heart chakra, nurturing*

11 Chalcedony rose *The Goddess stone, the Divine Mother, Female power, womb energy, opening the heart, compassion*

12 Golden beryl *Wisdom, intellectual stimulation, joy*

13 Opal *Inspiration, fire energy, inner peace*

14 Blue tourmaline *High spiritual energy, creativity*

15 Tibetan turquoise *Grounding expression, communication, friendship*

18 Lapis lazuli *Intuition, illumination, calming the mind*

21 Crystalized fossilized wood *Spirit of the forest fairies and elves, magic of the woods*

23 Freshwater pearl *The Divine Mother, femininity, compassion, purity, beauty*

This talisman captures the essence of the Divine Mother, goddess energy. Its main purpose is emotional healing and female power. It is meant to open the wearer to her ancient goddess spirit and bring this energy onto the planet through her actions and spoken words. These ancient truths and highly evolved energies have the power to heal and nurture the planet. Notice the centrepiece appears to have the image of a Madonna on it.

The necklace is customized and designed with the collaboration of the person it is for. Hours are spent choosing from an enormous selection of gemstones, crystals, shells, charms and beads. The person selects the objects intuitively, choosing what she is drawn to rather than using the intellect or reason. During this process a spiritual, creative flow guides the chooser, as if the stones themselves are making the choice. When all the elements are selected they are laid out in a specific order to create an organic balance, which is also guided by intuition or the "higher self". String colours too are chosen with consciousness of their vibrational influences. When each necklace is woven together – a process that takes up to 20 hours – the maker goes into deep meditation. As she wraps each stone she recognizes its spirit and harnesses its energy in the binding. The power of the necklace is amplified by the focus and attention devoted to its creation. Most of the elements are natural, carrying the sacred energies of Mother Earth. After the weaving is completed, beeswax is melted into the strings, sealing it all in and purifying the stones with the fire element. Then the necklace is rubbed with lavender oil and blessed, followed by a process known as "smudging", a Native American ritual where dried sage is burned and the smoke is used to cleanse and purify. Now the necklace is ready to do its work. When the recipient puts on the necklace, it's amazing to see how the stones light up and seem alive – an affirmation that the piece is fulfilling its mission.

TALISMAN NECKLACE FOR A MAN

bestowing warrior energy with healing and balancing power.
Created by Amie Hertzig.

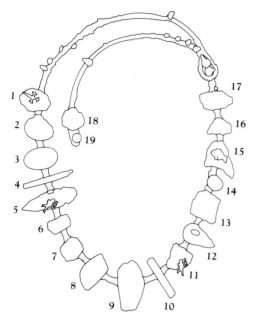

1 Turquoise Opening throat chakra, creative expression, communication, spirit

1a Sword of King Arthur Carrying the legends, linking old world and new world

2 Nigerian seashell Vibration of the ocean, bringing out emotions (the shell has personal value to the wearer and has a tiny rainbow tourmaline hidden inside)

3 Ancient Moroccan fossil carrying ancient wisdom, linking to the past

4 Clear quartz crystal Clarity, white light, amplifying energies

5 Flint arrowhead Warrior energy, connecting with Native Americantraditions, sharpness, truth, protection, a tool

5a Sea pearl (also around back of necklace) Feminine energy, the Divine Mother, Purity, compassion, devotion, beauty

5b Cherub Guardian angel, shooting arrows of love, innocence

6 Green beryl (aquamarine) Purification, healing, prosperity

7 Opal Energizing, creative inspiration

8 Labradorite Opening 3rd Eye, psychic vision, sealing holes in aura

9 Golden calcite Mental stimulation, concentraton, balancing male and female polarities. joy, lightness

9a Amethyst Spiritual guidance, raising consciousness, transformation, calming the mind

10 Black tourmaline Protection, deflecting negativity, weaving light into aura

11 Chrysocolla Strength, healing, opening heart and throat chakras

12 Arrowhead See No. 5 above; the brown colour is grounding, anchoring to earth

13 Lapis lazuli Intuition, illumination, a symbol of royalty

14 Chinese turquoise scarab Ancient Egyptian symbol of sacredness, good luck, protection, eternal life

15 Abelone Inner beauty, inspiration, security

15a Amethyst fish Sacred symbol of life, fertility, and see No. **9a** above

16 Celestite The crystal of the heavens, ethereal energy

17 Rosequartz The lovestone, unconditional love, healing and opening of the heart, nurturing, inner peace

18 Trilobite 500-million-year-old fossil of first backboned animal, the imprint of time, wisdom

19 Evil eye bead 2,000-year-old bead from Mali, Africa, protecting against evil

This necklace has a strong male warrior energy, balanced out with feminine softer strength. It inspires the wearer to go out into the world and succeed, and also reminds him always to lead with his heart and listen to his inner voice of truth and wisdom. It is for someone on a spiritual path of growing consciousness and psychic awakening. It contains a lot of healing and balancing energies, and is also extremely protective. It is meant to reflect his divine nature and the purity of his soul.

TALISMANIC BELT.
Created by Tajullah Xolali Skylark.

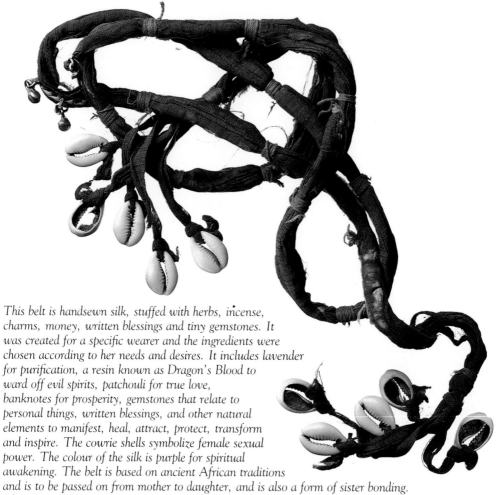

This belt is handsewn silk, stuffed with herbs, incense,
charms, money, written blessings and tiny gemstones. It
was created for a specific wearer and the ingredients were
chosen according to her needs and desires. It includes lavender
for purification, a resin known as Dragon's Blood to
ward off evil spirits, patchouli for true love,
banknotes for prosperity, gemstones that relate to
personal things, written blessings, and other natural
elements to manifest, heal, attract, protect, transform
and inspire. The cowrie shells symbolize female sexual
power. The colour of the silk is purple for spiritual
awakening. The belt is based on ancient African traditions
and is to be passed on from mother to daughter, and is also a form of sister bonding.
The creator has made it as a gift of love and has sewn it together as a focused meditation, praying
for its receiver as it was made. The belt is not an object of ornamentation, but a personal
talisman that works on a vibrational level. It should be worn around the waist at all times, even
when bathing. It is not to be taken off until its wearer feels that it has done its work. Then it's
time to remove it and create another one.

APHRODISIACS AND SEXUAL MAGIC TODAY

A medieval magician, asked for a spell to capture a reluctant maiden, told his desperate client that he could provide one which needed no rare ingredients, no magic incantation, did not even make use of specially prepared herbs. "If you want to be loved, "he told the young man, "then you must yourself first love."

That is very good advice to those who now scour the street stalls of Beijing for genuine ginseng, take a holiday in the Cameroons on the off-chance of buying some yohimbine, or turn their teeth deep red by chewing betel nuts. Good sex begins in the heart and mind; the effects of true passion are magical indeed. Don Juan, the number of whose celebrated seductions so scandalized Europe ("And in Spain, one thousand and three!" boasted his servant, who kept the record of his conquests), would have scorned the help of aphrodisiacs. He relied on a power which is available, it seems, to everyone with sufficient confidence in their powers of attraction.

There are many examples of men who were on the surface apparently unattractive, and yet who only had to crook a finger to lure someone into their bed. One of the most celebrated, in this century, was the English novelist H. G. Wells, the author of *War of the Worlds*. A squat, plain little man with a rather tubby body, he had innumerable amorous successes; and his mistresses, when asked, found it impossible to explain his attraction – the nearest one got to define it was to say, in a rather dazed voice, "His flesh smelt of honey."

What Wells had, we can guess, is complete confidence in his own power of attraction; and experience does suggest that if one fixes one's attention with sufficient single-mindedness on the man or woman in question, seduction becomes almost a matter of course. It may be objected that this is hardly magic in the strict sense of the term, and yet it is undoubtedly a power incapable of rational explanation. And it certainly has something to do with the fact that each of us stands at the centre of his or her own universe: in the final analysis, we are all we know. Someone else who seems to agree – who is ready to give us absolute attention, absolute devotion, can become deeply important to us.

However, it might be said that certain aphrodisiacs also have a magical effect. If we continue to look at the classic definition of the term – for some of them certainly are capable of producing "marvellous physical effects" by the use of some "occult controlling principle", even if, eventually, it should be possible to analyze how they work (chemical analysis of various drugs and substances has already gone some way towards this).

So neglecting the use of powdered unicorn's horn, and the repellent potions described earlier in Chapter Six, let us now look at some of the aphrodisiacs in use today. The old, well-tried aphrodisiac of atmosphere is still highly effective, and is magical at least to the extent that we do not fully understand how its effect is produced. If, as some experts maintain, there is nothing mysterious about sexual attraction – it is simply a built-in compulsion to copulate in order to preserve a species – why should the process of seduction be more successful if romantic music is playing, and a languorous perfume hangs in the air?

History has associated certain foods with sex because of their shape: the banana is an obvious example and figs are another case in point. Today, except in fun, this theory is no longer followed. But certain foods are still, partly for traditional reasons, believed to be aphrodisiac.

Indian advisers divide aphrodisiacs into three kinds – animal, vegetable and mineral. The eggs of various birds are recommended, different kinds of milk (but especially goats' milk), and the flesh of healthy and active animals. Caviare, mussels and oysters, and the sex organs of a large number of animals, are all said to have aphrodisiac properties. "Prairie oysters", which were popular in England in Victorian times, are bulls' testicles, eaten raw. They certainly contain male hormones; but perhaps only the desperate would now contemplate this dish.

Eastern doctors take particular care in preparing vegetable aphrodisiacs, the ingredients of which include ginseng (of which more later), ginger root, fennel, mushrooms, onions, liquorice, pine nuts, black pepper, raisins, honey (from particular flowers), and some drugs such as marijuana and opium. Mineral aphrodisiacs are prepared from elements of sulphur, copper, arsenic, gold, silver, amber, coral and even from rubies, sapphires and diamonds.

Certain aphrodisiacs are applied directly to the sexual organs: sandalwood oil with crushed ginger and cinnamon, for instance; diluted oil of cloves; a mixture of camphor and oil . . . but it must be remembered that the genitals are sensitive, and too strong a mixture can have anything but the desired result. It should be said, and firmly, that cantharides (a powder made from the bodies of certain insects) is extremely dangerous when applied in this way.

The aphrodisiac effect of perfumes was recognized very early in history. The earliest record of their use was in Egypt, and the Hebrews learning the art of perfumery there exported it to the western world, providing lovers with a new means of atmospheric persuasion.

Women continue to wear perfume because it makes them feel more attractive; and from time to time the rumour still circulates that particular perfumes have a magical and successful effect in attracting the opposite sex. The last major sales pitch being for musk, some 20 years ago, when innumerable musk-based aftershaves and perfumes were produced for sale to men who were persuaded that it would make them irresistible to women.

One must not overlook the natural odours of people themselves; when Napoleon was about to return to Paris after a campaign, he would write to Josephine instructing her not to wash – he yearned for the natural smell of her body. This is perhaps extending this idea a little too far, for most people; but the sexual attraction of the odour emanating from the flesh is strong. We might remember that physicians in the past used their sense of smell in diagnosis – typhoid smelt like baking bread, German measles like plucked feathers and yellow fever like a butcher's shop.

When we think of using perfume for magical purposes – that is, to attract someone else by this still somewhat mysterious means – we should remember that as in so many other areas, there is an astrological association. The perfumes or oils specially associated with Venus are said to be aphrodisiac – in particular aloe-wood oil (often mixed with musk), ambrosia oil, amyris oil (said to have been used in the rites of the temples of Venus in ancient times), artemisia oil (which restores lost virility), and cardamom oil (allegedly the sexiest of perfumes). Lovage and orris oils are simply used to attract the opposite sex.

But let us turn to those traditional aphrodisiacs which are still available, and still touted as effective. In some cases, the reason for an aphrodisiac effect is well understood; in others a kind of magic indeed seems to be involved. The one case in which an aphrodisiac recognized as such over many hundreds of years turns out indeed to be more or less what it claims, is that of the mandrake root.

This has already made an appearance in this book, together with the legends attached to it. Today, it is still taken, just as it was in Biblical times. The mandrake root (*Mandragora officinalis*, of the potato family) grows in southern Europe. Powdered, it was often used by witches to make "flying ointment", although flying is more usually ascribed to the use of *Amanita muscaria* (fly agaric) mushrooms. Its chief effect is to send one into a drowsy state in which dream fantasies frequently occur. Its alleged aphrodisiac effect is presumably also based on the fact that it encourages fantasy as well as desire.

This is true of various aphrodisiacs, the effect of which is to relax one, and as a result releases one from inhibitions and allows one to express formerly repressed sexual feelings and desires. Wild lettuce (*Lactuca virosa*) for instance, producing "lettuce opium", is simply a mild narcotic. Kava kava (*Piper methysticum*) has much the same effect – but in Fiji is often used by groups of people, for it does seem to bring about a great warmth of feeling and the sort of euphoria which is pleasant without having any untoward after-effect. So it has been traditionally used to welcome guests (Queen Elizabeth II took a draught – without any visible signs of pleasure – when she visited the island some years ago). It is however often used as an aphrodisiac, sometimes among a group of lovers, and its effect when its resins are extracted and dissolved in alcohol before being taken is said to be not unlike that of marijuana.

Betel nuts are as popular, in India, as kava kava in Fiji: they are chewed in enormous quantities by the male population. They contain arecoline, an oil which stimulates the central nervous system, and seems to have the effect of making time seem to pass more quickly than usual; if betel nuts are used for one particular purpose, it is to make Tantra sexual practices more easily performed.

Some aphrodisiacs in use in the 20th century are less innocent than these, of

APHRODISIAC TEA

Take equal quantities of cinnamon bark and green cardamom, mix with fresh ginger root, black peppercorns, cloves, nutmegs, ginseng and saffron. Infuse. Use honey to sweeten mixture.

cinnamon bark

green cardamom

fresh ginger root

black peppercorns

cloves

nutmeg

ginseng

saffron

honey

course. Iboga', for instance, (*Tabernanthe iboga*), which grows naturally in the Congo and Gabon but is now cultivated in West Africa, can cause not only nausea but paralysis and convulsions. Secret societies in the Congo traditionally use it in initiation rites, and it is taken in preparation for obtaining messages from the spirit world. In fact what it seems to do is subtly change the perception and produce striking visual images; the aphrodisiac effect is less evident, and seems to flow simply from an increased feeling of closeness to one's lover.

Unpleasant effects can stem from a use of yohimbine (*Corynanthe yohimbine*), too. Traditional peoples of West Africa have used shavings from the inside of the bark for generations in male orgiastic rituals which can go on for over a fortnight, getting more and more frenzied as more yohimbine is consumed. The yohimbine (made as one makes tea) stimulates the central nervous system and produces hallucinations, but also seems to affect the spinal ganglia, causing extremely persistent erections which can last for over two hours despite any amount of sexual activity.

Yohimbine has been used in Western countries, in recent years, at Wicca weddings, but it should be noted that it can be really dangerous if taken with alcohol or certain medically prescribed drugs, or even some cheeses, causing a great leap or sometimes a startling drop in blood pressure. However, it is an element of some medicines prescribed by doctors for loss of virility, and seems to have its effect chiefly by improving the flow of blood to the genitals.

But what of perhaps the most famous modern aphrodisiac, ginseng (*Panax Schinseng*)? Genuine ginseng is expensive, and the very best is very expensive. This comes from China, where ginseng has been taken for at least 6,000 years. As with the mandrake, the phallic shape of the root perhaps first drew it to attention as a possible aphrodisiac. A related variety was also used centuries ago by certain Indian tribes of North America (it can be found growing in the wild in many American states).

The best way to take ginseng root is to chew it. The Chinese make a sort of ginseng tea, but the root itself is also swallowed. Ginseng pills, commonly available in the West, are said to be very much less efficacious. No doubt the results are to some extent psychosomatic, but the sapogenins in the root have a measurable effect on the system. Whatever the actual effect on their love life, millions of people all over the world now take ginseng regularly, on a daily basis, on the grounds that it increases their vitality and makes them feel a great deal better than they feel without it.

The most popular drug of all, of course, remains alcohol; and the porter in Shakespeare's *Macbeth* really had the first and last word on this, as an aphrodisiac: it provokes the desire, but takes away the performance. It is true that it is a relaxant, of course, and disposes to some extent of nervousness. But like any other drug it loses its effect if taken too often; and certainly, if taken in large doses, alcohol can make a man depressed and quite possibly impotent.

Of all alcoholic drinks, the one with the strongest reputation as an aphrodisiac is absinthe, made from a plant, *Artemisia absinthium*, of the sunflower family, commonly known as wormwood. Wormwood crops up throughout history as an aphrodisiac, used particularly in Mexico, but also in Europe, when it was taken with vinegar and honey (together with marigold flowers, marjoram and thyme) on St Luke's Day, to help girls to dream of their lovers.

The reputation of absinthe as a drink (particularly fashionable and popular in France in the last century) was based on the relief it offered from depression and tension – which made it to an extent an aphrodisiac. It is now banned, and Pernod (which tastes much the same) has been substituted – though this does not seem to have the same effect, chiefly because it lacks thujone, which is indeed highly aphrodisiac both to men and women. (Thujone is minutely present in vermouth, so the aphrodisiac reputation of the dry Martini is not entirely to be dismissed, provided it is not too dry).

All this is not to say that a glass or two of wine as an accompaniment to a good dinner in pleasant surroundings may not equally have the desired effect!

A LOVE NECKLACE
Created by Amie Hertzig.

This necklace was created for a lover to empower him with his own sexual energy and life force. In the centre, a ruby is set for deep love, passion, strength and vitality. The quartz crystal point below focuses and amplifies the energies and is a tool of light. On either side are topaz stones for warmth, creating a halo of golden light. Four of the lover's own milk teeth are woven in, carrying his own vibration and filling him with spiritual power, symbolizing his initiation into manhood.

The beads are for protection, and at the clasp is a snowflake obsidian heart for balanced love. Also at the clasp is a sea pearl, to include the feminine element, compassion, devotion, purity and emotional understanding. The wearer will feel charged with passion, desire and love. With the necklace is a patchouli plant from India. It has a heavy, earthy, warm and sensual fragrance, and is generally considered to be an aphrodisiac, with a scent that awakens and inspires sexual energy.

12.

Healing & Medicine

Consciously or unconsciously, mankind has always assumed an intimate connection between mind and body, and within the past 40 years or so this has been explored not only by unconventional medicine but by psychiatrists and physicians. Magic rituals may exploit this connection in bringing about bodily changes.

It has always been recognized that the exercise of the will to recovery – the will to live – is crucial in a fight against any serious illness; while the connection between tension and anxiety, susceptibility to infection, and the onset of certain diseases (most notably cancer) is now taken seriously.

Those who believe they can affect the minds of others have naturally interested themselves in healing – for if one mind can project into another images and even messages – as has been shown to be the case in extrasensory perception experiments – there is no reason why signals should not also be sent which can encourage the process of a fight against illness, and strengthen the patient's will to live.

The belief that certain people have the power to heal has been prevalent for millennia; the Greek physician Hippocrates (c.460-c.357 BC) certainly believed that *dunamis* – the power to heal by a simple touch of the hand – was possessed by certain people. Healing power was reported in the Old Testament, too: the prophet Elisha, summoned to help a child who was in a death-like coma, lay on top of him, mouth to mouth, hands to hands, and the boy recovered. Sceptics might claim that this was an early example of mouth-to-mouth resuscitation, but it seems more probable that this was a shamanic healing ritual, and there is a hint of magic in the air, for as he recovered the boy sneezed seven times – a recurrence of the "magic" number seven.

The early Christians practised healing by the "laying on of hands", which they believed to focus the power of the Holy Spirit, until the church authorities put an end to this, fearing an association with witchcraft. The modern church often recognizes healers, however, and prayers for the recovery of the sick are recited during the

*The hand (**opposite**) contains the power to heal – a traditional belief shared by many today.*

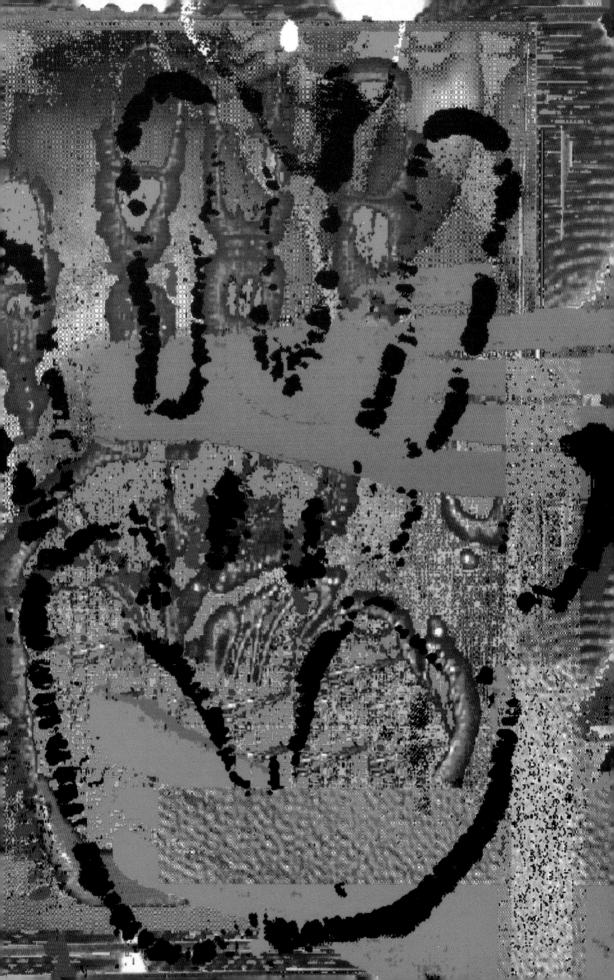

formal services of almost every branch of the church – though the actual practice of healing as part of a service is more common, at present, among members of the charismatic churches.

Outside the church, healers work in a number of ways. The most dramatic remains "the laying on of hands". Certain men and women tour from town to town, holding what are in a sense "revival" meetings – there is almost always a religious context – and inviting the sick to come to them, when they place their hands on the heads of the sufferers – or sometimes on the affected part of the body – and both pray that they should be cured. In a sense they "instruct" the body to heal itself, but they also invoke an external power.

Healers themselves have various theories as to the nature of their apparent power – the majority are intensely spiritual people who believe that they are simply channels for a divine power: they would never think of this as "magical" – though it clearly falls within our fairly wide definition. There is some evidence that cures are more effective if they can instil a similar confident spiritual attitude in their patients, though this is by no means necessary. Militant atheists may not be high on the list of those cured by faith healing, but there have been many cases of infants and even animals apparently cured in this way – and others in which a sick person's condition has dramatically improved as the result of the intervention of a healer, though the patient was unaware of his interest.

DISTANT HEALING

Indeed, it is the case that the healer need by no means necessarily be in the presence of the sick person in order to work with him or her. Distant or absent healing is very often practised, and occasionally (though preferably not) without the knowledge of the patient. The history of absent healing is not as long as the history of healing by touch; indeed it seems to have become prominent only since the turn of the century, and perhaps chiefly as the result of the work of Thomas J. Hudson, whose theory was not dissimilar to that of the Christian Scientists. Hudson did not believe that sickness was imaginary, but that it was the result of the body being in disharmony with nature, and that harmony could be restored by using what he called the "subjective mind", in which (and psychiatry has tended to confirm this) every impression received during life is successfully stored.

Hudson performed many experiments in which he attempted to place his subjective mind at the disposal of a patient, perhaps as distant as 100 miles away, and found that working together he and the patient could effect remarkable improvements in certain medical conditions. Those interested in Hudson's theories often formed groups to practise absent healing, and the practice continues today. These groups "met", sometimes physically and sometimes simply by deciding previously on a time at which they should concentrate on healing a particular patient, and join together to send a healing force to him or her. Occasionally, if they meet in a group, they will work with a sample of the patient's hair, or even a drop of blood – a process known as "radionics" when such an object is placed under a pendulum and used as an instrument of diagnosis.

The use of pendulums in healing is relatively rare: the theory is that radiations from the body can communicate the nature and degree of an illness; the degree of success depends entirely on the individual. There is some evidence that almost anyone can learn to use a pendulum to discover, for instance, underground streams; by no means everyone has the necessary instinct and skill to be able to use a pendulum to discover the nature of an illness.

Scientific investigation into the claims of healers has produced highly equivocal results. Some of the most interesting research has however gone some way to combat the claim that remissions of illness may have simply been the result of unquestioning

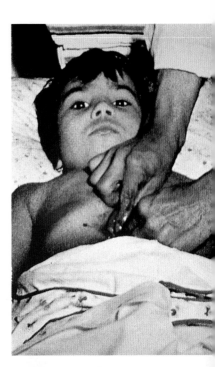

*Self-mutilation with skewers (**left**) dramatically illustrates the power of mind over body in the case of a Hindu holy man at the festival of Thaipusam, Singapore. Later, when the skewers were removed and the yogi emerged from his trance, there was no trace of a wound. Psychic surgeons in Brazil (**above right**) and Paraguay (**below right**) perform operations without anesthetic involving the apparent removal of organs from the body. Patients feel no pain and in many cases seem restored to health.*

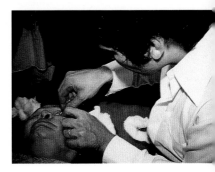

confidence on the part of the patient. One experiment revealed, for instance, that a healer was capable of affecting the growth rate of plants. Experiments held at London University in the 1980s seemed to demonstrate conclusively that cress seeds on which a psychic healer had concentrated his powers grew at a faster rate than precisely similar seeds which had not been subjected to his influence.

The connection between mind and body is still insufficiently thoroughly explored. Well-known techniques of torture used by various oppressive regimes have made use of this connection: iced water said to be boiling and poured onto the skin has produced the physical effects associated with first-degree burns. Is there any reason why such suggestion should not work in reverse, the effect of actual injuries being reduced or negated by the equally strong suggestion that the damage is imaginary? Surely not.

One aspect of healing remains to be mentioned: self-healing. Especially in the treatment of cancer – perhaps because that disease has so often resisted even the most sophisticated conventional medical treatment – autosuggestion has been used, and has often had a notable effect (though it must be said that temporary remission has been more common than permanent cure). A sort of self-hypnosis may be employed; the patient imagines a legion of "good" cells marching upon and defeating the army of "bad" cells which communicates the cancer. White blood cells have measurably increased under this "self-help" treatment.

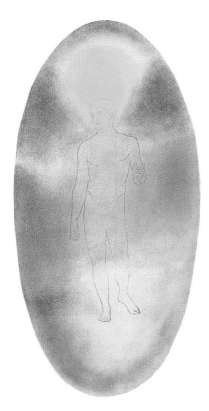

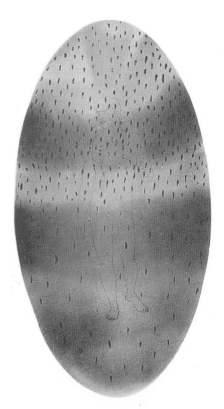

This "astral aura of an intelligent man"
was drawn by Leadbeater, the theosophist
and disciple of Mme Blavatsky.

The "astral aura of an angry man",
according to Leadbeater.

MAGICAL MEDICINE

Many elements of conventional modern medicine have elements of the mysterious about them. While the effect of drugs, for instance, is often calculated to the most minute degree, the effect of healing, suggestion or hypnosis is certainly not susceptible to the same kind of analysis.

An Austrian scientist, Rudolph Steiner (1861-1925) produced a theory, called anthroposophy, that included the idea that men and women have in addition to their physical bodies, etheric and astral bodies – the former encouraging them to grow away from the earth, and therefore its ills, and the latter encapsulating their emotions. Steiner's ideas were a development of theosophical doctrines formulated by the Russian-born occultist Madame Blavatsky (1837-91) and her circle, ultimately stemming from Hindu mystical concepts. Blavatsky's Theosophical Society took the concept of these auras very seriously.

The etheric and astral bodies, together with the physical body and the ego (the spiritual centre) were roughly equivalent to the classical four elements – earth, water, air and fire – and were interconnected, so that perfect health depended on perfect equilibrium and rhythm. On the other hand, perfect equilibrium if infinitely sustained would inhibit development; what is needed is that we become aware of the inevitable imbalance of the four anthroposophical elements, and learn to bring them under control.

Anthroposophical doctors will use a variety of treatments, including herbal medicine, homoeopathic remedies and aromatherapy, but also conventional drugs. In

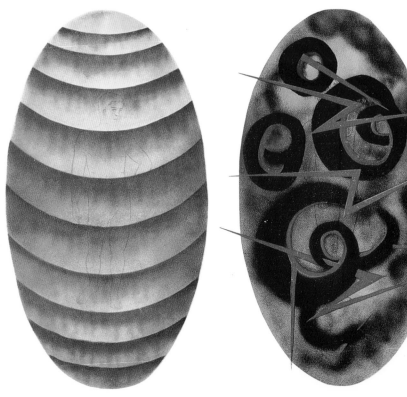

Bands on a "miser's aura" indicate someone "who has shut himself away from the world".

A jangle of lines crisscross the "aura of an irritable man".

general they will rely on various substances – some devised by Steiner's colleague Dr Ita Wegman (1867-1943), the co-founder of the movement – including gold, silver, mercury, lead, copper, iron and tin. Each metal is associated with a bodily function, and can be used to treat it when illness affects it.

AROMATHERAPY

The natural oils of plants and flowers have been used in medicine for thousands of years (the Chinese and Persians may have been among the first to do so); plant essences were often used in witchcraft. Aromatherapists rely on a great body of empirical information reprinted in textbooks often of great age. Plant essences are distilled, and an "essential oil" produced which is sometimes dissolved in alcohol. These oils are used in massage, administered in baths or as inhalations, and it is claimed that they can treat most conditions – including not only illnesses such as sinus disorders, digestive problems or migraine, but depression, stress and anxiety.

ART

Art – music, painting, writing – is one of the great mysteries of human existence, and perhaps the most obvious indication that man has a spirit as well as a body and an intelligence. Picasso claimed that art was magic, and the arts have been used, espe-

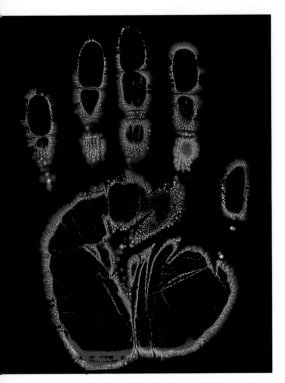

*A field of light, which many experts identify with the ancient concept of the aura, is seen around living organisms in Kirlian photographs using specially coated film (**left**). A healing contact (**right**) appears as a filament between two touching fingers. Kirlian photographs show diminished auras when the subject is sick, enhanced ones when the subject is spiritually developed.*

cially during this century, to treat certain mental and emotional states, and the positive results have been as mysterious and magical as the creative instinct itself. In England in the 1940s a Jungian psychotherapist, Irene Champernowne, pioneered the use of art therapy, collecting together a number of artists, musicians and dancers to help treat disturbed patients through practising the arts.

Sound therapy has a very ancient history. Drums have been used from prehistoric times to the present day in shamanic healing rituals from many cultures all over the world. Early religious ceremonies relied heavily on sound to build up an effect or an atmosphere, and some therapists believe that sound waves have an effect not only on the hearing apparatus but on various cells of the body – that harmony will produce a positive effect, disharmony a negative one. They will attempt to correct the ill effects of disharmony by directing harmonious vibrations at the affected parts. Chanting is also used (particularly the use of mantras – see page 83) in some forms of treatment.

Ultrasound – sounds too highly pitched to be audible to the human ear – is used by some practitioners to treat muscular sprains or other injuries and accelerate healing. There is of course no spiritual dimension to machine-generated ultrasound, but it is interesting that its use can produce effects similar to those claimed by healers using "magical" sound techniques.

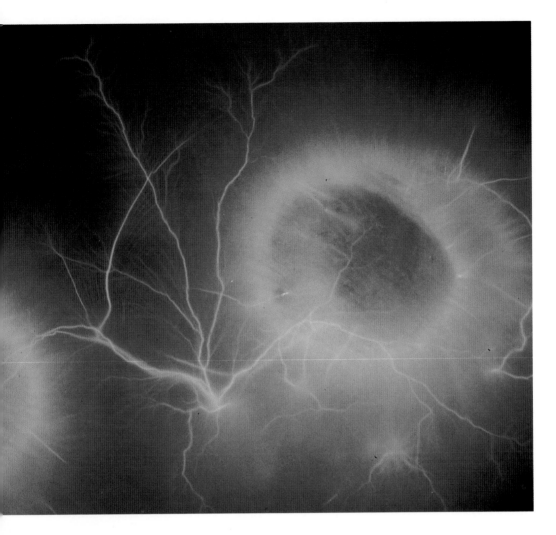

THE AURA

Whether the idea that every living thing on earth has an aura belongs to the world of magic or the world of scientific fact, remains debatable. Even some people who entirely accept the idea believe it to be impossible to prove that the aura exists. Rudolph Steiner always claimed that it was a "gross illusion" to suppose that the spiritual aura could be investigated by science. On the other hand, there seems little doubt that the Russian Semyon Kirlian began in 1939 to photograph the auras of people and plants, and produced innumerable images over the next quarter of a century. Kirlian discovered by chance that living things, plant or animal, possess energy fields or patterns that can be seen when the object is placed in a high-frequency discharge. Moreover, the size and brilliance of these patterns reflect the condition of the object: a growing plant, for instance, has a far stronger "aura" than one that has been cut. Observers have noted that the strongest light patterns from the skin of a human being do not seem to relate to major nerve endings, arteries or veins, but *do* correspond with the pressure points shown on standard Chinese acupuncture charts. This suggests a link between the aura and the Chinese concept of *ch'i* or subtle energy.

Auras can be seen clearly by most clairvoyants; but it is claimed that everyone can teach themselves to see auras. Therapists use the colours of the human aura to

*Flower remedies (**left**) have brought relief to many Westerners. Traditional herbalists of India (**right**) and China (**far right**), make little distinction between the magical and medicinal properties of plants.*

diagnose sickness of all kinds – a red tinge in the aura, for instance, can indicate malfunction of the sex glands, orange signals problems with the spleen or adrenal glands, yellow relates to the digestive system or pancreas, and so on.

COLOURS

We have seen how important colour has always been in (for instance) setting up the conditions for performing magic. Clearly colour has always had an important effect on humans, and it is not surprising that colour therapy has been used in medicine – not only in ancient times, but today, when it has been found that colours which surround a patient have a certain effect on his or her wellbeing. This occurs even when the patient is blindfold, suggesting that colour affects the body, even when not perceived.

HOMOEOPATHY

It may seem impertinent to suggest that homoeopathy can have anything to do with magic, when such a large minority regards it as a proven form of medical treatment. But looked at from the point of view of modern science, where it works it seems to do so in an entirely magical way – that is, there is absolutely no means of discovering, scientifically, how it produces its effect.

Briefly, and over-simply, homoeopathy works on a basis suggested by the Greek physician Hippocrates that "like cures like" – by treating illnesses with substances which themselves produce the symptoms suffered by the patient – but in such highly diluted forms that they can be safely administered. The more closely the remedy counterfeits the symptoms, the more successful the treatment is. Of course, the age-old principle of sympathetic magic goes far beyond Hippocrates. It is one of the most fundamental parts of magic worldwide.

The objection of conventional doctors to homoeopathy is that the medicines administered are often so diluted that it is unlikely, in some cases, that so much as a

single molecule of the original substance remains in the medicine. The positive result of a treatment could therefore strictly be described as magical! Scientific trials have sometimes seemed to show conclusively that the magic treatment does work (homoeopaths explain this by claiming that a memory – the "footprints" – of the original substance remains in the medicine, even if this cannot be scientifically checked).

It is possible to test the efficacy of the homoeopathic theory oneself, by using Dr Bach's remedies. Dr Edward Bach (1880-1936) distilled 38 medicines from various plants, which he believed could treat certain states of mind; and most health food shops and many chemists now stock them. The bottled essence must be again diluted, and only a drop or two of the diluted preparation taken – so the same practical argument arises as with homoeopathy in general. Enthusiasts argue that, for instance, the remedy prepared from gentian can cure despondency, that from holly ameliorates feelings of jealousy, hatred and envy, and that from the Star of Bethlehem can be efficacious in treating sudden shock.

13.

Numerology & Prediction

Has numerology a place in the modern world? Does it "work" in the way that some other systems do, which might be described as magical? Certainly there are practitioners who advertise in occult magazines claiming that they can be particular about the virtues and vices of being a Seven, or a Three; one can even buy computer programs which will analyze one's name and offer lucky numbers, days or colours.

The ancient tradition of numerology relates to the belief that numbers have, like minerals (and indeed, it is argued, everything else in the known world) certain resonances.

How these resonances, these "vibrations", work, no numerologist can explain; but then, the point – even the appeal – of magic in our day is chiefly that it *is* inexplicable. As far as can be gathered, the belief is that the combination of numbers found in the name (and indeed the birth-date) of a subject – the total number, the number of vowels, the number of consonants, the recurrence of certain numbers, and so on – reveals to the practised examiner aspects of the personality which other methods fail to uncover. "Each soul," says one modern practitioner (Eileen Connolly, who has worked out her own complex system of interpretation), "has its own unique vibratory structure."

The obvious question is, of course, how our forename, chosen for us at birth by our parents, can have such resonance. There are various possibilities, the chief one being perhaps that we do indeed have a very personal and sometimes very strange relationship with our given name: sometimes we dislike it so cordially that we actually voluntarily change it; we may shorten it to a nickname (or others may do this for us); and in a subtle way we seem also to "grow into" it. Psychology has shown an interest in this close identification which we have with our names; and this has sometimes spilled over into an interest in numerology – not as a pseudo-science, but in the sense

*The death of President Kennedy (**opposite**) was predicted by many dreamers worldwide.*

that it does seem that we can be pursued by the idea of a specific number and its significance to us. (The psychologist Freud found himself possessed, in this way, by a series of numbers, and was never able clearly to explain his preoccupation.)

As we said in Chapter Three, a simple table (the so-called Pythagorean System of numerology) is used by many modern numerologists to work out the basic numbers of one's names. The values given to the letters are as follows:

1	2	3	4	5	6	7	8	9
A	B	C	D	E	F	G	H	I
J	K	L	M	N	O	P	Q	R
S	T	U	V	W	X	Y	Z	

Now simply total the numbers which represent the letters of your name.

JOHN PHILIP BROWN *would total*

JOHN $(1 + 6 + 8 + 5) = 20 = (2 + 0) = 2$

PHILIP $(7 + 8 + 9 + 3 + 9 + 7) = 43 = (4 + 3) = 7$

BROWN $(2 + 9 + 6 + 5 + 5) = 27 = (2 + 7) = 9$

These numbers have their own significance. That of the family name offers a general generational influence. The number of your forename, given name, Christian name – whatever you call it – is the most important to use in numerology: and it should be used in the form in which most people use it (if Mr Brown is usually known as "Jack", then that is the name which would be used in numerology – and the most significant number for him would be 7 rather than 2). A "middle" name or names is less important, and its influence less marked.

Looking at a combination of traditional factors in numerology, we would interpret the effect of the number of the forename as follows:

1. ◆ *Above all, you will be an excellent communicator, and in one way or another will always be able to explain your arguments or emotions to others, whether on a personal level or in your business or career (and you may work well in the media). You are reasonable, but highly argumentative and adaptable and perhaps opinionated; you are perceptive, but very critical – sometimes hypercritical; you are versatile but can be very tense and uptight.*

2. ◆ *Modest and shy, you are meticulous in everything you do and diligent in completing every task you undertake. Your perfectionism can make you a less than welcome workmate, for your own high standards will make it impossible not to seem to be criticising others, however hard you try to avoid this. Criticism can become carping, and self-criticism can turn to introversion and worry. Your natural discrimination is trustworthy, and provided it is disciplined and not expressed in grumbling about others' standards, it can make you an ideal employee.*

3. ◆ *Charm and diplomacy, romance and sociability are all qualities of this number; but they can hide a certain weakness, masking indecision, changeability and gullibility – you are highly susceptible to persuasion. Decision-making is not your strong point, and your* relaxed attitude can result in your never reaching a conclusion about anything at all. You like luxury, a quiet life (even at any price?); you can be resentful of anyone who seems to be standing between you and a harmonious and untroubled existence.

4. Your true feelings are probably hidden behind an extravert exterior and an outwardly brash and forthright manner. Determined and forceful, passionate and an exciting personality, you can also be obsessive, resentful and jealous. You're not likely to give way to even the strongest arguments of those you believe to be in the wrong; and your feelings about any dispute that may arise will be supported by the most powerful and well-sustained reasoning.

5. This is the number of learning – and not just the accumulation of random facts on a number of subjects (as with ONE), but real, in-depth study. Religion and philosophy may interest you; you will possibly find the study of languages attractive. You will be optimistic, loyal and much concerned with justice – but beware of self-indulgence and conceit, and indeed of over-optimism.

6. This number is associated with the planet Venus and hence with the emotions; you will be particularly eager to find a partner and enjoy a satisfactory emotional relationship. This may lead to your committing yourself too soon, and somewhat thoughtlessly. The feminine side of your personality will be emphasized (whichever sex you are), and you may well have an interest in art or fashion. Gentleness, friendship, tact and social adaptability will probably come easily to you – but you should beware of blind optimism, and of continually wearing rose-coloured spectacles.

7. Optimism, good humour, honesty are the hallmarks of this number; the reverse of the coin displays the possibility of over-optimism, carelessness and irresponsibility. You are a free spirit, always concerned for the freedom of the individual whether on a local or worldwide basis. You can be tactless in expressing your forthright opinions, and your emotions can carry you away to such an extent that you become offhand and superficial. Sport may well interest you more than usual.

8. This is a number much concerned with ambition, supported by practical, patient, disciplined theory and work. You may be a little too conventional, and this together with an inherent pessimism and fatalism can make for an all-work-and-no-play attitude to life, which may be somewhat joyless. Your sense of humour can be a saving grace, not only for yourself but in your relationships, and your prudence should pay off in your business life.

9. Your friendliness and loyalty will mean that you need never be alone; you are original and inventive, and your independence of mind is a great asset provided you don't allow yourself to be too contrary, perverse or unpredictable. Your originality means that you are able to shed an unexpected light on – for instance – others' problems. Positive and optimistic, you may find yourself in some ways a leader. But you may also find it somewhat difficult to establish a close personal relationship.

The number associated with love is the total of all our
forenames: in the example on p. 208 this means 2 + 7 = 9.

A classical numerological system tells us that particular numbers vibrate in harmony with each other, others strike a harmonious chord, yet others are in disharmony. Some (not mentioned below) appear to have no potential either for harmony or disharmony.

1

is in **harmony** with **9**,
in **accord** with **4** and **8**,
in **discord** with **6** and **7**.

2

is in **harmony** with **8**,
in **accord** with **7** and **9**,
in **discord** with **5**.

3

is in **harmony** with **7**,
in **accord** with **5**, **6** and **9**,
in **discord** with **4** and **8**.

4

is in **harmony** with **6**,
in **accord** with **1** and **8**,
in **discord** with **3** and **5**.

5

is in **harmony** with **5**,
in **accord** with **3** and **9**,
in **discord** with **2** and **4**.

6

is in **harmony** with **4**,
in **accord** with **3** and **9**,
in **discord** with **1** and **8**.

7

is in **harmony** with **3**,
in **accord** with **2** and **6**,
in **discord** with **1** and **9**.

8

is in **harmony** with **2**,
in **accord** with **1** and **4**,
in **discord** with **3** and **6**.

9

is in **harmony** with **1**,
in **accord** with **2**, **3** and **6**,
in **discord** with **7**.

Numbers which are in harmony indicate a strong natural attraction; numbers that are in accord with each other are likely to get on well together; numbers in discord will find that their relationship will need some hard work. The most favourable numbers are those which are the same.

THE NUMBERS IN LOVE

1. *You like variety in love as in everything else, which may make for some difficulty in a long-term relationship. Your sexuality may be somewhat subdued.*

2. *You will want the security of a firm emotional commitment, but may criticize a partner more than is safe or proper. You will need a partner who is intelligent as well as warm and passionate.*

3. *Strongly attracted to the idea of a permanent relationship, you may tend to be over-quick to choose a partner who on better acquaintance may suit you less well than you thought.*

4. *In general highly sexed, you will fall deeply in love when you fall, and will need instinct reciprocity; affairs will be of the roller-coaster variety – and in love it will be all or nothing.*

5. *You may not take your love affairs too seriously, passionate though they will be (you are the least jealous of lovers); your energy must be matched by that of your partner, and your versatility may lead you astray.*

6. *Flattery is the easiest weapon to use when trying to seduce you: you're so eager for a partner that you'll believe anything they say. Beware! You need an air of romance, and will do your best to provide it.*

7. *Your passionate nature will be happily expressed, but maybe just a trifle offhand – it can be an end in itself. You are casual and rather against formality and forward planning; the idea of seduction may well occur between the main course and the sweet trolley!*

8. *A commitment, once made, will be deeply meant; but you need to be sure of your ground – the suspicion of rejection can be a terrible blow to your pride. Learn to be generous in your expression of your emotions.*

9. *You may seem somewhat distant to hopeful lovers – but once you fall, there will be no doubt about it; you may not find it easy to display your emotions overtly, and should try to keep at least one foot on the ground – Cloud Nine can be an attraction.*

It may be argued that all these attributes are so vague that they could be properly associated with anybody. There is of course something in this – just as there are elements of introversion in every extravert, elements of the feminine in every man – and those are only two categories. But if you feel that, even judging by the above much over-simplified texts, you are quite remarkably "three-ish", then the question to be posed is, Why? Why should there be a "magic" connection between names and their number symbols? There is a wide range of possible explanations, perhaps none of them more persuasive than the other. If it is genuinely the case that numerology "works" in a way that apparently defies reason, even at the most basic level, then it is impossible to deny it the title of magic.

PREDICTION

An enormous amount of magical energy has been directed in all ages towards attempting to look into the future. It is of course a natural human concern – partly because the future is so mysterious and we are so curious about it, and because it would be very convenient to be able to plan for it; and perhaps predominantly because we seek reassurance – that our luck will change, our lover return, our career prosper. While in principle we may agree with Aeschylus – "You'll know the future when it comes; until then, forget it!" – few people can resist the idea that we may be able to stride across the time barrier for just a brief glimpse of what is to come.

The possibility depends, of course, on the nature of time; and many modern thinkers have suggested that time is not necessarily serial – that we are mistaken in thinking of it as a piece of string in which a knot represents the present – we can see and have experienced everything on one side of the knot ("before"), but everything on the other side ("after") is outside both sight and the possibility of knowledge.

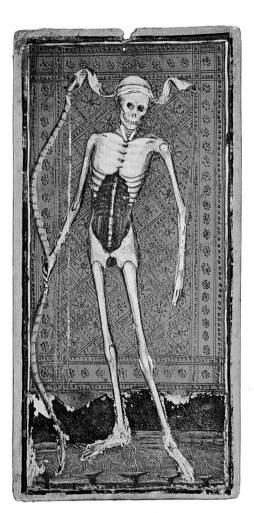

The "Death" card of the Bembo Tarot pack does not necessarily presage a physical demise.

We have been so conditioned to think in that way, however, that it is extraordinarily difficult for us to conceive of any other view. Of course breakfast comes "before" lunch, Monday "before" Tuesday. Yet it is quite possible that breakfast and lunch in some way coincide – that the "Battle of Britain" and the "Battle of Agincourt" were, are, or will be fought simultaneously . . .

The earliest peoples believed that the future could be seen in dreams; and in historical times an enormous number of techniques have been devised by those who made it their business, as professionals, to divulge the secrets of the future to the less fortunate to whom it was a closed book. Some of these have appeared, from time to time, in this book – the oracles, sortilege, crystalgazing. But what methods are being used in the twentieth century?

Most means of attempting to see into the future are still in use. Many people still place a great deal of faith in that earliest method of all, dream interpretation. Indeed, it is extremely difficult to argue with some of the examples of apparent prediction through dreams – especially the prediction of particularly traumatic events, which in a sense seem to stain the atmosphere so indelibly that the taint can be apprehended not only years later as an atmosphere or an actual ghostly event, but as a premonition or a dream before the event in fact occurs.

One of the most celebrated examples of this is of the woman in Aylesbury, Buckinghamshire, England, who dreamed of a village drowned in black mud. Two days later on 21 October, 1965, an avalanche of coal slid down the side of a Welsh mountain burying part of the village of Aberfan and killing 128 children in the village school. One is reliably reported to have told her mother, on the morning of the event, that she didn't want to go to school because she had dreamed that it had vanished under "something black".

It is only fair to invite suspicion of some dream predictions. A number of people claimed, for instance, to have dreamed (before the event) of the assassination of President Kennedy. But remembering that everyone on earth dreams five or six dreams every night, and that presidents are remarkably susceptible to assassination, it would perhaps be surprising had someone *not* dreamed of the event.

Perhaps the same cannot be said of President Lincoln's dream of his own assassination, or – certainly – of the remarkable dream of Samuel Clemens ("Mark Twain"). Twain dreamt he saw the body of his younger brother lying in a metal coffin standing on two chairs, a bouquet of white flowers upon it with a single red one at its centre. This turned out to be the scene that met his eyes over a week later after a fatal accident on the riverboat on which his brother Henry Clemens happened to be working.

Some methods of prediction originally had rags and tatters of magic attached to them, which have been lost over the centuries. The Tarot, for instance, a system of prediction relying on playing cards bearing a set of mysterious symbols, has always attracted those interested in the occult.

Many modern Tarot practitioners would claim that the most that can be done with Tarot symbols is to use them as the means of inspiring a clairvoyant "weather forecast" of possible psychological conditions which may affect the person who has requested a "reading". Similarly, the runes are now used in this way.

Modern astrologers, despite popular conviction to the contrary, do not claim to be able to predict events; and in any case, since that science or art depends on an empirical system (a centuries-old collection of references to particular planetary relationships and what they signify) it can scarcely be claimed to be magical.

The I Ching, an immeasurably ancient Chinese system, is similarly devoid of direct magical content – unless, of course, it is supposed that psychology is a system of magic. On the other hand, the Trigrams (and sometimes the Hexagrams) of the I Ching are used as magical talismans, suggesting that they have importance in the magical world, at least for those who use these systems.

This, if we followed it, would lead us into an interesting but probably sterile discussion of whether magical effects do not always occur within the minds of those who believe in them, rather than in the world of measurable things and events. Many authorities would agree that the means of tapping the magical "hidden powers" within us is almost always based in psychology.

The Tarot and the I Ching share a kind of predictive technique which sets us, as it were, at an angle to the universe: they do not tell us specifically what will happen – but they enable us to take two paces to the left and to look at the possible development of events from an original and different angle to the one we would normally take. They can therefore be of enormous assistance in this way.

The I Ching and other predictive systems are often used to give "readings" about the future, yet this is not the use that the divisers of those admirable philosoph-

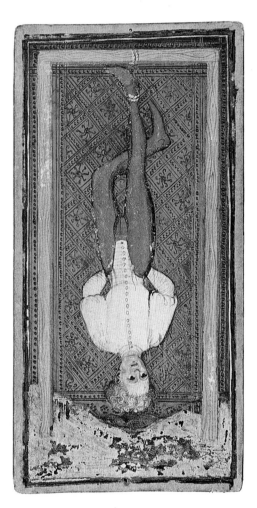

The Tarot "Hanged Man" presents a topsy-turvy vision of the future.

ical systems necessarily intended. However, there is no need to disparage clairvoyants who use them in that way. What they are doing is using the cards or the I Ching patterns just as other clairvoyants use a crystal, a pool of water or ink, tea-leaves, or whatever. People with a clairvoyant talent need something on which to concentrate their minds while the "message" comes through.

Every reader must make up his or her mind on the subject of clairvoyance. Innumerable claims have been made for the accuracy of predictions made by the best-known clairvoyants, such people as the late Maurice Woodruff, or the ubiquitous American Jeanne Dixon, who seems to have claimed to have predicted every notable event which took place during her lifetime.

Clairvoyants are on the whole born rather than made; they seem to be capable of living – at least temporarily – in a different world from us; or perhaps of experiencing another dimension in which they see our world more clearly, their faculties sharper than ours. "Seeing the future" is only part of their ability, of course; they may also see one's aura and are often healers.

It may be that we all have the facility to become clairvoyants, if we care to develop it – there are various examples of "ordinary" people suddenly becoming clairvoyant, often after an accident or illness of some kind. So there is no reason not to experiment, either by recording dreams or simply by setting the mind in "neutral", using a meditation technique, and seeing what one can "see". But if you are seriously interested, the rule must obviously be to make a carefully accurate and dated record of predictions, in order to judge to what extent they prove accurate.

The technique most people would probably mention first, where prediction is concerned, is astrology. The view that astrology predicts future events is seriously mistaken; one of the earliest astrological sayings is, "The stars incline, they do not foretell." Nor are astrologers necessarily clairvoyant – sometimes they are, but if so they should certainly restrain their clairvoyant talent while working with astrological charts, which give up their information empirically.

Astrologers work by considering the angular relationships between the planets; they predict (though many of them do not care for that word) a possible climate – rather like a meteorologist – in which certain future events are possible, or at best probable. So while it is not possible to say to a client, "You will crash your car next Wednesday at 3 p.m.", it is entirely permissible for an astrologer to warn him that on that day he may be prone to careless driving, and should beware of accidents.

There seems to be very considerable evidence that astrological prediction on a general level does work. The most dramatic recent evidence for this comes from the British astrologer Dennis Elwell, who early in 1987 wrote to a number of marine firms pointing out that astrological circumstances in early March matched those predominating when the SS *Titanic* sank, and suggesting that they warn the masters of their vessels to be particularly careful. At the same time he sent a copy of the letter to his bank to be date-stamped and filed.

As one might have expected, the various shipping firms, when they bothered to respond, merely replied that they were entirely satisfied with their safety precautions. On 6 March the car ferry *Herald of Free Enterprise* capsized off Zeebrugge and 188 people were drowned.

On a more personal level, astrologers' clients generally express themselves as happy with the kind of "predictions" supplied; those statisticians and scientists who have attempted to examine them have been less sanguine, but it may be that it is impossible to test them satisfactorily.

*Ancient and modern predictive techniques include the casting of astrological horoscopes (**opposite, top**); the consultation of the Chinese I Ching or Book of Changes by means of yarrow sticks (**centre**); and the analysis of the lines on the palm of the hand (**below**).*

Afterword

Most of us, even the least sympathetic or susceptible to
the idea of magic or the occult in general, have had at
some time or another a sense that the world may not
only consist of what we can see and touch; even that
there seems to be some other world running parallel with
our own, in which the rules by which we live may no
longer apply, and of which from time to time we receive
a misty glimpse – a premonition which proves accurate,
a "memory" of something that never happened.

Even the most scientific minds can be shaken: perhaps
Britain's leading astronomer was aghast, after a lifetime
of scientific work, to discover that when he took a
dowser's rod in his hands, he could find water beneath
the earth – a skill which he had always taken to be a
scientific impossibility. Another, while denying with the
utmost scorn that there can be anything in astrology, is a
distant healer, and proposes that at some time in the
future an as yet unknown means of space travel may
enable man to reach the most distant points of the
universe – something which by all present scientific
criteria is impossible.

But this is simple stuff: for the most part it merely
makes us pause, and wonder. The question of time,
whether it is possible to look into the future, is after all
interesting rather than dangerous. There are deeper
abysses, which we have occasionally glimpsed in this
book. Most witches may have been at worst harmful, at
best healers and comforters, intent on becoming at one
with nature. But grinning and grimacing about the edge
of the circle is the ghost of Aleister Crowley; and it is
impossible to deny that the dark side of occult power
appeals to the psyche of some of those who have
experimented with the idea of magic – of embracing and
using the negative powers of the universe.

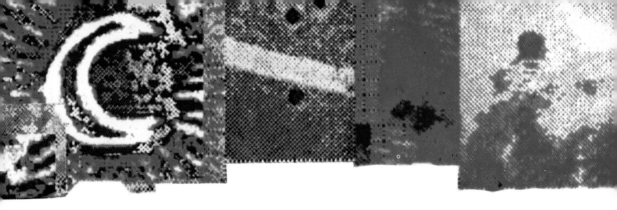

The problem is, we believe, much less prevalent than the popular press would have us believe. Only a fool would claim that the idea of witchcraft has never been used for obscene or criminal purposes. Where this is the case, criminal prosecution should of course follow – whether the participants merely insult and injure the susceptibilities of ordinary decent people (by cavorting in graveyards or desecrating churches) or physically assault animals or even humans. It should be pointed out, too, that many religions have had their evil elements, bigots or power-seekers who have perverted noble ideals to their own ends.

Both ancient and modern writers on the subject have always gone out of their way to warn readers that "tampering with unknown forces" is dangerous; and though this might be allowed to go without saying, we should add a final word. If magical forces indeed exist – and some of the matters we have spoken of in these pages are at the very least puzzling to the completely rational mind – then there is no reason to suppose that they only work positively. Clearly, they should be approached with proper respect. It is the application of magic that gives it its "colour".

Every serious person who has engaged in occult research – whatever his or her conclusion about the reality of magical cause and effect – has underlined the fact that extreme care should be taken; for whether or not unknown powers are at work, what is certainly involved is the human mind, the balance of which is all too easily disturbed. So by all means, if you wish, investigate in more detail some of the areas of ancient and modern magic with which we have dealt; but do so with care and even reverence. The old gods may not be altogether dead.

Glossary

Alchemy The art of transmuting base metals into gold. Alchemists also searched for the elixir of life, which could purify and turn the dross of ordinary humanity into the gold of immortality.

Amulet A device or object which, when worn, offers protection against evil (see "talisman").

Athame A white-handled ceremonial dagger used in witchcraft ceremonies, only within the magic circle.

Caballah An ancient Jewish mystic system of philosophy centred on the Old Testament. Popular between the 12th and 16th centuries, it was much concerned with numerology.

Ch'i The vital spirit of the Taoist system, infusing all things, and imparting life, movement and energy.

Coven An assembly of witches.

Devil's Mark Certain marks on the body – moles or birthmarks – believed to be indications of a witch.

Divination The practice of prediction through occult or supernatural means.

Dowsing Searching for underground water or minerals by means of hazel sticks or metal rods (known anciently as Mosaical rods).

Enochian A language said to have been taught by the angel Gabriel to the Elizabethan scholar Dr John Dee, through his assistant Edward Kelley.

Exorcism The expulsion, or attempted expulsion, of evil spirits from a person or a place believed to be haunted.

Extrasensory perception (ESP) The ability to perceive without using normal sensory processes, e.g. by telepathy.

Gematria The substitution of numbers for letters, much used by medieval students of the Caballah.

Gnosticism A movement of the late Hellenistic and early Christian eras, characterized by a belief in *gnosis*, esoteric spiritual knowledge, leading to liberation of the soul.

Grimoire A textbook of sorcery and magic, often said to have been compiled by supernatural means.

Haruspicate Divine or predict the future by examination of animals' entrails.

Hermetic lore Mystical and magical works, deriving from the teachings ascribed to Hermes Trismegistus, who taught the idea of correspondence or interconnection between all beings and objects.

I Ching The ancient Chinese Book of Changes, offering advice based on texts accompanying each of 64 hexagrams, selected by casting yarrow sticks or coins.

Incubus A demon believed to have intercourse with sleeping women.

Left-hand path The practices followed by those pursuing the black or ill-intentioned side of magic.

Magic circle A circle, drawn on the ground or otherwise set out, within which a magician or witch would be protected from any evil forces deployed by the spirits invoked.

Magus, mage, A magician or sorcerer from ancient times.

Mantra In Hinduism and Buddhism, sacred words having an occult affinity with particular deities or forces. Literally, an instrument of thought.

Medium A person used by spirits as a means of communication with the living.

Necromancy Spirit conjuration or, in general, black magic. Literally, the power of summoning the dead.

Oracle In ancient Greek religion, the priestess or priest who acted as a medium for divine messages. The word is also used for the prophecy or message itself, and for the shrine where the practice occured.

Possession The apparent domination of a human or animal by a spirit, often evil.

Numerology Study of the occult significance of numbers.

Pentacle A five-pointed star or pentagram, used as a symbol in magic, especially in the construction of a magic circle.

Philosopher's Stone In alchemy, the substance that can convert base metals to gold.

Poppet An image or doll made by a witch to represent someone s/he may wish to affect. Sticking pins into the poppet, or sometimes burning it, is believed to cause pain or even death.

Rosicrucians Members of an esoteric society, dating from the early 17th century but claiming an ancient Egyptian origin, whose secret doctrine included cabbalistic, Hermetic and alchemical elements.

Scrying Divination by visual means, especially crystal-gazing.

Shaman A man or woman who, in traditional societies, is credited with the power of contacting the spirit world.

Sigil A sign or device endowed with magical power, often inscribed with occult letters or signs.

Sky-clad The witches' term for naked, or bare to the sky.

Sorcery The art of magic, especially black magic or magic used for selfish personal gain.

Succubus A female demon believed to have intercourse with sleeping men (see "incubus").

Spell A word, formula or incantation, spoken or written, that is empowered to have a magical effect.

Talisman An object which, when carried or worn, is supposed to have the power to protect the bearer from occult forces, to bring good luck, or to give success. Amulets are "passive", whereas talismans, made at the right time and material, and inscribed with appropriate markings, have their own natural power.

Tantra The Hindu or Buddhist body of doctrine relating to mystical and magical practices, including the use of sexuality for mystical purposes.

Tarot Playing cards used mainly for divination and fortune-telling.

Voodoo A magical system, now chiefly practised in Haiti but derived from West Africa, which involves witchcraft and contact with spirits by means of trance. Related systems include Candomblé (Brazil), and Obeah (West Indies).

Wicca Old English word for witch, used by 20th century witches to refer to the cult of witchcraft as practised today.

Bibliography

The following is a very selective list of books the authors found especially interesting and useful.

Ashcroft-Nowicki, Dolores, *The Tree of Ecstasy: An Advanced Manual of Sexual Magic*, London, 1991.

Bischoff, Erich, *The Kabbalah: An Introduction to Jewish Mysticism and Secret Doctrine*, York Beach, 1985.

Blofeld, John, *I Ching: The Book of Changes*, London, 1989.

Brennan, J.H., *Experimental Magic*, London, 1984.

Butler, E.M., *Ritual Magic*, Cambridge, 1949.

Cavendish, Richard, ed., *Man, Myth and Magic*, London, 1974.

Cockren, Archibald, *Alchemy Rediscovered*, London, 1940.

Connolly, Eileen, *The Connolly Book of Numbers*, California, 1988.

Crowe, W.B., *A History of Magic, Witchcraft and Occultism*, London, 1968.

Crowley, Aleister, *Magick*, London, 1973.

Crowley, Aleister, *Magick in Theory and Practice*, New York, 1968.

Crowley, Vivianne, *Wicca: The Old Religion in the New Age*, London, 1989.

Deacon, Richard, *John Dee*, London, 1968.

Douglas, Nik, and Penny Slinger, *Sexual Secrets: The Alchemy of Ecstasy*, Vermont, 1979.

Flint, Valerie J., *The Rise of Magic in Early Medieval Europe*, Oxford, 1991.

Garrison, Omar V., *Tantra: The Yoga of Sex*, New York, 1964.

Gilchrist, Cherry, *Alchemy*, London, 1991.

Green, Marian, *Ritual Magic*, London, 1990.

Halevi, Z'ev ben Shimon, *Tree of Life: An Introduction to the Cabala*, London, 1973

Hudson, T.J., *The Law of Psychic Phenomena*, London, 1902.

Idris Shah, Sayed, *The Secret Lore of Magic: Books of the Sorcerers*, London, 1978.

James, T.G.H., *Ancient Egypt*, London, 1979.

Jones, Prudence, and Caitlin Matthews, eds., *Voices from the Circle*, Wellingborough, 1989.

King, Francis, *Rites of Modern Occult Magic*, New York, 1971.

Knight, Gareth, *A History of White Magic*, London, 1979.

Legeza, Laszlo, *Tao Magic*, London, 1975.

Leland, C.G., *Aradia, the Gospel of the Witches*, London, 1974.

Leventhal, Herbert, *In the Shadow of the Enlightenment*, New York, 1976.

Lévi, Eliphas, *Transcendental Magic*, London, 1968.

Long, Max Freedom, *Recovering Ancient Magic*, London, 1936.

Mathers, S.L. MacGregor, *Astral Projection, Magic and Alchemy*, London, 1972.

Miller, Richard Alan, *The Magical and Ritual Use of Aphrodisiacs*, New York, 1986.

Opie, Iona and Moira Tatem, *A Dictionary of Superstitions*, Oxford, 1989.

Pennick, Nigel, *Practical Magic in the Northern Tradition*, Wellingborough, 1989.

Parker, Derek and Julia, *Dreaming*, London, 1985.

Playfair, Guy Lyon, *If This be Magic*, London, 1985.

Regardie, Israel, *The Golden Dawn*, Chicago, 1937.

Regardie, Israel, *How to Make and Use Talismans*, Wellingborough, 1972.

Roney-Dougal, Serena, *Where Science and Magic Meet*, London, 1978.

Russell, Jeffrey B., *A History of Witchcraft*, London, 1980.

Ryall, Rhiannon, *West Country Wicca: A Journal of the Old Religion*, Washington, 1989.

Skelton, Robin, *Talismanic Magic*, York Beach, 1985.

Smart, Ninian, *The World's Religions*, London, 1989.

Tansley, David V., *Subtle Body*, London, 1977.

Thomas, Keith, *Religion and the Decline of Magic*, London, 1971.

Thorndike, Lynn, *The History of Magic and Experimental Science*, New York, 1971.

Waldo-Schwartz, Paul, *Art and the Occult*, London, 1977.

Watson, Donald, *A Dictionary of Mind and Spirit*, London, 1991.

Weinstein, Marion, *Earth Magic*, New York, 1979.

Weinstein, Marion, *Positive Magic*, Washington, 1980.

Acknowledgments

Special thanks for their invaluable assistance are due to Aimie Hertzeg, Tajullah Xolali Skylark, Fred Gettings and Glen Childs.

Illustrations

Sarah Ball 6-9

Michaela Blunden 31 38 43 139 142 143

Rydal Bowtell 49 60 66 153 154 168-9O

Osnat Lippa Cover, 11 159 161 175 197 207 216-7

Meilo So 2 13 19 69 71 74

Special photography

James Johnson 186 188 190 193 195

Picture Acknowledgments
Abbreviations: l left, r right, c centre, t top, b bottom
The Bridgeman Art Library/Musée Cluny, Paris 123 The British Museum, 63 Mary Evans Picture Library, 26 28 29l 44 45 52 81 100 109 157. Mary Evans/Explorer, 79 140 146. Mary Evans/Guy Lyon Playfair, 199tr. Mary Evans/Harry Price Collection, Univ of London, 29r. Fortean Picture Library, 44 59 76 104 111 148-9 163b. Fortean/Klaus Aarsleff, 150. Fortean/Dr Elmar R. Gruber, 92 199br. Fortean/Anthony Shiels, 170. Giraudon, 130-1. Giraudon/Musee du Louvre, 117. The Hulton Picture Library, 72 105 119 120 141 147 156. The Hutchison Library, 46 135r 214b. Hutchison/Sarah Errington, 93 94l. Hutchison/Carlos Freire, 77. Hutchison/Melanie Frend, 204-5 205. Hutchison/Maurice Harvey, 96 128b. Hutchison/John Hatt, 94r. Hutchison/Michael MacIntyre, 77tr. Hutchison/Edward Parker, 93 94c. Images/Colour Library/Charles Walker Collection, 14-15 16 20 21 22 25 32 33 35 36 38 42 50 53 54 56 80 83 86-7 88 92 95 96-7 101 102 103 105 110 114 115 117 125 128 135l 135c 145 153 164 176 177 185 199l 204l 214t 214c. Royal Commission for Historical Monuments, 135tl. Scala/Museo di S Marco, Florence, 41. Science Photo Library/ Michael Burgess, 203. Science Photo Library/G. Hadjo, 202. Syndication International, 62 99 108 144-5 163t 200 201 212 213.

Index

Page numbers in *italic* refer to
the illustrations and captions